Strengthening Deep Neural Networks

Making AI Less Susceptible to Adversarial Trickery

Katy Warr

Beijing · Boston · Farnham · Sebastopol · Tokyo

Strengthening Deep Neural Networks

by Katy Warr

Copyright © 2019 Katy Warr. All rights reserved.

Printed in the United States of America.

Published by O'Reilly Media, Inc., 1005 Gravenstein Highway North, Sebastopol, CA 95472.

O'Reilly books may be purchased for educational, business, or sales promotional use. Online editions are also available for most titles (*http://oreilly.com*). For more information, contact our corporate/institutional sales department: 800-998-9938 or *corporate@oreilly.com*.

Acquisitions Editor: Jonathan Hassell
Development Editor: Michele Cronin
Production Editor: Deborah Baker
Copy Editor: Sonia Saruba
Proofreader: Rachel Head

Indexer: WordCo Indexing Services
Interior Designer: David Futato
Cover Designer: Karen Montgomery
Illustrator: Rebecca Demarest

July 2019:   First Edition

Revision History for the First Edition
2019-07-02:   First Release

See *http://oreilly.com/catalog/errata.csp?isbn=9781492044956* for release details.

978-1-492-04495-6

[GP]

Table of Contents

Preface

Artificial intelligence (AI) is prevalent in our lives. Every day, machines make sense of complex data: surveillance systems perform facial recognition, digital assistants comprehend spoken language, and autonomous vehicles and robots are able to navigate the messy and unconstrained physical world. AI not only competes with human capabilities in areas such as image, audio, and text processing, but often exceeds human accuracy and speed.

While we celebrate advancements in AI, deep neural networks (DNNs)—the algorithms intrinsic to much of AI—have recently been proven to be at risk from attack through seemingly benign inputs. It is possible to fool DNNs by making subtle alterations to input data that often either remain undetected or are overlooked if presented to a human. For example, alterations to images that are so small as to remain unnoticed by humans can cause DNNs to misinterpret the image content. As many AI systems take their input from external sources—voice recognition devices or social media upload, for example—this ability to be tricked by adversarial input opens a new, often intriguing, security threat. This book is about this threat, what it tells us about DNNs, and how we can subsequently make AI more resilient to attack.

By considering real-world scenarios where AI is exploited in our daily lives to process image, audio, and video data, this book considers the motivations, feasibility, and risks posed by adversarial input. It provides both intuitive and mathematical explanations for the topic and explores how intelligent systems can be made more robust against adversarial input.

Understanding how to fool AI also provides us with insights into the often opaque deep learning algorithms, and discrepancies between how these algorithms and the human brain process sensory input. This book considers these differences and how artificial learning may move closer to its biological equivalent in the future.

Who Should Read This Book

The target audiences of this book are:

- *Data scientists* developing DNNs. You will gain greater understanding of how to create DNNs that are more robust against adversarial input.

- *Solution and security architects* incorporating deep learning into operational pipelines that take image, audio, or video data from untrusted sources. After reading this book, you will understand the risks of adversarial input to your organization's information assurance and potential risk mitigation strategies.

- *Anyone interested in the differences between artificial and biological perception.* If you fall into this category, this book will provide you with an introduction to deep learning and explanations as to why algorithms that appear to accurately mimic human perception can get it very wrong. You'll also get an insight into where and how AI is being used in our society and how artificial learning may become better at mimicking biological intelligence in the future.

This book is written to be accessible to people from all knowledge backgrounds, while retaining the detail that some readers may be interested in. The content spans AI, human perception of audio and image, and information assurance. It is deliberately cross-disciplinary to capture different perspectives of this fascinating and fast-developing field.

To read this book, you don't need prior knowledge of DNNs. All you need to know is in an introductory chapter on DNNs (Chapter 3). Likewise, if you are a data scientist familiar with deep learning methods, you may wish to skip that chapter.

The explanations are presented to be accessible to both mathematicians and non-mathematicians. Optional mathematics is included for those who are interested in seeing the formulae that underpin some of the ideas behind deep learning and adversarial input. Just in case you have forgotten your high school mathematics and require a refresher, key notations are included in the appendix.

The code samples are also optional and provided for those software engineers or data scientists who like to put theoretical knowledge into practice. The code is written in Python, using Jupyter notebooks. Code snippets that are important to the narrative are included in the book, but all the code is located in an associated GitHub repository (*https://github.com/katywarr/strengthening-dnns*). Full details on how to run the code are also included in the repository.

This is not a book about security surrounding the broader topic of machine learning; its focus is specifically DNN technologies for image and audio processing, and the mechanisms by which they may be fooled without misleading humans.

How This Book Is Organized

This book is split into four parts:

Part I, An Introduction to Fooling AI
> This group of chapters provides an introduction to adversarial input and attack motivations and explains the fundamental concepts of deep learning for processing image and audio data:
>
> - Chapter 1 begins by introducing adversarial AI and the broader topic of deep learning.
>
> - Chapter 2 considers potential motivations behind the generation of adversarial image, audio, and video.
>
> - Chapter 3 provides a short introduction to DNNs. Readers with an understanding of deep learning concepts may choose to skip this chapter.
>
> - Chapter 4 then provides a high-level overview of DNNs used in image, audio, and video processing to provide a foundation for understanding the concepts in the remainder of this book.

Part II, Generating Adversarial Input
> Following the introductory chapters of Part I, these chapters explain adversarial input and how it is created in detail:
>
> - Chapter 5 provides a conceptual explanation of the ideas that underpin adversarial input.
>
> - Chapter 6 then goes into greater depth, explaining computational methods for generating adversarial input.

Part III, Understanding the Real-World Threat
> Building on the methods introduced in Part II, this part considers how an adversary might launch an attack in the real world, and the challenges that they might face:
>
> - Chapter 7 considers real attacks and the challenges that an adversary faces when using the methods defined in Part II against real-world systems.
>
> - Chapter 8 explores the specific threat of adversarial objects or adversarial sounds that are developed and created in the physical world.

Part IV, Defense
> Building on Part III, this part moves the discussion to building resilience against adversarial input:

- Chapter 9 considers how the robustness of neural networks can be evaluated, both empirically and theoretically.

- Chapter 10 explores the most recent thinking in the area of how to strengthen DNN algorithms against adversarial input. It then takes a more holistic view and considers defensive measures that can be introduced to the broader processing chain of which the neural network technology is a part.

- Finally, Chapter 11 looks at future directions and how DNNs are likely to evolve in forthcoming years.

Conventions Used in This Book

The following typographical conventions are used in this book:

Italic
> Indicates new terms, URLs, email addresses, filenames, and file extensions.

`Constant width`
> Used for program listings, as well as within paragraphs to refer to program elements such as variable or function names, databases, data types, environment variables, statements, and keywords.

`Constant width bold`
> Shows commands or other text that should be typed literally by the user.

`Constant width italic`
> Shows text that should be replaced with user-supplied values or by values determined by context.

This element signifies a tip or suggestion.

This element signifies a general note.

This element indicates a warning or caution.

Using Code Examples

Supplemental material (code examples, exercises, etc.) is available for download at *https://github.com/katywarr/strengthening-dnns*.

This book is here to help you get your job done. In general, if example code is offered with this book, you may use it in your programs and documentation. You do not need to contact us for permission unless you're reproducing a significant portion of the code. For example, writing a program that uses several chunks of code from this book does not require permission. Selling or distributing a CD-ROM of examples from O'Reilly books does require permission. Answering a question by citing this book and quoting example code does not require permission. Incorporating a significant amount of example code from this book into your product's documentation does require permission.

We appreciate, but do not require, attribution. An attribution usually includes the title, author, publisher, and ISBN. For example: "*Strengthening Deep Neural Networks* by Katy Warr (O'Reilly). Copyright 2019 Katy Warr, 978-1-492-04495-6."

If you feel your use of code examples falls outside fair use or the permission given above, feel free to contact us at *permissions@oreilly.com*.

The Mathematics in This Book

This book is intended for both mathematicians and nonmathematicians. If you are unfamiliar with (or have forgotten) mathematical notations, Appendix A contains a summary of the main mathematical symbols used in this book.

O'Reilly Online Learning

 For almost 40 years, *O'Reilly Media* has provided technology and business training, knowledge, and insight to help companies succeed.

Our unique network of experts and innovators share their knowledge and expertise through books, articles, conferences, and our online learning platform. O'Reilly's online learning platform gives you on-demand access to live training courses, in-depth learning paths, interactive coding environments, and a vast collection of text and video from O'Reilly and 200+ other publishers. For more information, please visit *http://oreilly.com*.

How to Contact Us

Please address comments and questions concerning this book to the publisher:

> O'Reilly Media, Inc.
> 1005 Gravenstein Highway North
> Sebastopol, CA 95472
> 800-998-9938 (in the United States or Canada)
> 707-829-0515 (international or local)
> 707-829-0104 (fax)

We have a web page for this book, where we list errata, examples, and any additional information. You can access this page at *https://oreil.ly/Strengthening_DNNs*.

To comment or ask technical questions about this book, send email to *bookquestions@oreilly.com*.

For more information about our books, courses, conferences, and news, see our website at *http://www.oreilly.com*.

Find us on Facebook: *http://facebook.com/oreilly*

Follow us on Twitter: *http://twitter.com/oreillymedia*

Watch us on YouTube: *http://www.youtube.com/oreillymedia*

Acknowledgments

I am very grateful to the O'Reilly team for giving me the opportunity to write this book and providing excellent support throughout. Thank you especially to my editor, Michele Cronin, for her help and encouragement, and to the production team of Deborah Baker, Rebecca Demarest, and Sonia Saruba. Thanks also to Nick Adams from the tools team for working out some of the more tricky LaTeX math formatting.

Thank you to my reviewers: Nikhil Buduma, Pin-Yu Chen, Dominic Monn, and Yacin Nadji. Your comments were all extremely helpful. Thank you also Dominic for checking over the code and providing useful suggestions for improvement.

Several of my work colleagues at Roke Manor Research provided insightful feedback that provoked interesting discussions on deep learning, cybersecurity, and mathematics. Thank you to Alex Collins, Robert Hancock, Darren Richardson, and Mark West.

Much of this book is based on recent research and I am grateful to all the researchers who kindly granted me permission to use images from their work.

Thank you to my children for being so supportive: Eleanor for her continual encouragement, and Dylan for patiently explaining some of the math presented in the research papers (and for accepting that "maths" might be spelled with a letter missing in this US publication).

Finally, thank you to my husband George for the many cups of tea and for reviewing the early drafts when the words were in completely the wrong order. Sorry I didn't include your jokes.

## PART I

An Introduction to Fooling AI

This section provides an introduction to deep neural networks (DNNs), exploring how these can, and why they might be, tricked by adversarial input.

To begin, Chapter 1 takes a look at the concept of adversarial input and a little history. We'll peek at some of the fascinating research that has provided insights into DNNs and how they can be fooled. Chapter 2 then goes on to explore the potential impact of adversarial input, examining real-world motivations for fooling the AI that is the foundation of systems such as social media sites, voice control audio, and autonomous vehicles.

The final chapters in this section give an introduction to DNNs for image, audio, and video, for those of you who are unfamiliar with this area or would like a refresher. They will provide the necessary foundation for understanding the concepts in the remainder of the book. Chapter 3 explains the basic principles of machine and deep learning. Chapter 4 explains typical ways in which these principles are extended and applied to understand image, audio, and video. Both of these chapters finish with code examples that will be revisited later in the book when we examine how adversarial input is created and defended against.

At the end of this section, you will have an understanding of adversarial examples, the motivations for creating them, and the systems at risk of attack. Part II will then examine how adversarial input is created to trick image and audio DNNs.

## CHAPTER 1

Introduction

This book is concerned with deep neural networks (DNNs), the deep learning algorithms that underpin many aspects of artificial intelligence (AI). AI covers the broad discipline of creating intelligent machines that mimic human intelligence capabilities such as the processing and interpretation of images, audio, and language; learning from and interacting with unpredictable physical and digital environments; and reasoning about abstract ideas and concepts. While AI also exploits other methods such as the broader field of machine learning (ML) and traditionally programmed algorithms, the ability of deep learning to imitate human capabilities places DNNs central to this discipline. DNNs can mimic, and often exceed, human capability in many tasks, such as image processing, speech recognition, and text comprehension. However, this book is not about how accurate or fast DNNs are; it's about how they can be fooled and what can be done to strengthen them against such trickery.

This introduction will begin with a brief explanation of DNNs, including some history and when it first became apparent that they might not always return the answer that we expect. This introductory chapter then goes on to explain what comprises adversarial input and its potential implications in a society where AI is becoming increasingly prevalent.

A Shallow Introduction to Deep Learning

A DNN is a type of machine learning algorithm. In contrast to traditional software programs, these algorithms do not expose the rules that govern their behavior in explicitly programmed steps, but learn their behavior from example (training) data. The learned algorithm is often referred to as a *model* because it provides a model of the characteristics of the training data used to generate it.

DNNs are a subset of a broader set of algorithms termed *artificial neural networks* (ANNs). The ideas behind ANNs date back to the 1940s and 1950s, when researchers first speculated that human intelligence and learning could be artificially simulated through algorithms (loosely) based on neuroscience. Because of this background, ANNs are sometimes explained at a high level in terms of neurobiological constructs, such as neurons and the axons and synapses that connect them.

The architecture (or structure) of an ANN is typically layered, ingesting data into a first layer of artificial "neurons" that cause connecting artificial "synapses" to fire and trigger the next layer, and so on until the final neuron layer produces a result. Figure 1-1 is an extreme simplification of the highly advanced artificial neural processing performed by Deep Thought in *The Hitchhiker's Guide to the Galaxy*, by Douglas Adams (1979). It takes in data and returns the meaning of life.[1]

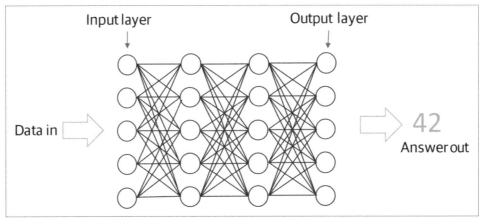

Figure 1-1. A simplified depiction of a possible DNN implementation of Deep Thought, the computer tasked with establishing the meaning of life

A DNN learns its behavior—essentially the circumstances under and extent to which the synapses and neurons should fire—by examples. Examples are presented in the form of training data, and the network's behavior is adjusted until it behaves in the way that is required. The training step to create a DNN is classified as "deep" learning because, in contrast to the simple ANNs, DNN models comprise multiple layers of neurons between the layer that receives the input and the layer that produces output. They are used when the data or problem is too complex for simple ANNs or more traditional ML approaches.

---

1 Determining the kind of input data that this DNN would need to perform the required task is left as an exercise for the reader.

Like any other ML algorithm, a DNN model simply represents a *mathematical function*. This is a really important point to grasp. Depicting it in terms of connected neurons makes the concepts easier to understand, but you won't see references to neurons or synapses in the software implementing a neural network.

The mathematics underpinning DNNs is particularly powerful, enabling a model to approximate *any* mathematical function. So, given enough data and compute power, a trained DNN can learn how to map any set of (complex) input data to a required output. This makes deep learning particularly effective in understanding data that is unstructured or where the key features are difficult to discern. DNN models have proved effective, for example, with image processing, translating between languages, understanding speech, forecasting weather, or predicting financial market trends. Perhaps even more remarkably, DNNs can also be trained to *generate* data (such as realistic images or text) in a way that appears to mimic human creativity. Advances in DNNs have opened astonishing opportunities for complex computational tasks, and these networks are becoming prevalent in many areas of our society.

A Very Brief History of Deep Learning

At the start of this century, deep learning and neural networks were a niche field restricted to specialist researchers. DNNs were primarily theoretical and difficult to implement. The key problem in the practical realization of DNN technologies is that training a DNN model (essentially teaching the algorithm so that it works correctly) requires vast amounts of training data and a computationally expensive training process. In addition, the training data often needs to be *labeled*; that is, the correct answer for each training example must be available and associated with it. For example, every image in an image training dataset would require some associated data to say what it contains, and possibly where that content is located within the image.

Some Different Ways to Train an ML Model

There are various methods for training an ML model (for more on these methods, and how they apply to an example of machine learning, see Chapter 3):

Supervised learning
> Training an ML model using a fully labeled dataset. The model is taught based on examples—inputs alongside their expected answers.

Unsupervised learning
> Using nonlabeled datasets to train ML models to spot patterns in the data. The algorithm is not presented with an "answer" during training, but it can still establish patterns in the data.

Semi-supervised learning
> Learning that exploits training data that is partially labeled.

Training a DNN to perform a complex task, such as vision recognition, typically requires tens of thousands or even millions of training examples, each of which is correctly labeled. Machine learning enthusiasts realized early on that assembling a sufficiently large amount of labeled data would be a mammoth undertaking. At the turn of the century, however, the growth of the internet suddenly made acquiring this training data possible. Internet giants such as Google and Facebook began to exploit the vast oceans of data available to them to train models for a whole raft of business uses, such as language translation. Meanwhile, researchers initiated crowdsourced projects to label training datasets by hand. A groundbreaking example is ImageNet (see ImageNet), a project that was a core enabler to the development of DNN technology for computer vision.

ImageNet

ImageNet (*http://www.image-net.org*) is a database of links to images created for advancing the field of machine vision. It contains links to over 14 million images, each assigned to one or more categories depending on image content. The database is organized in a hierarchical structure to enable varying levels of generalization (for example, "dog" or, more specifically, the type of dog, such as "labrador"). The ImageNet project exploited crowdsourcing to hand-annotate each image with the appropriate labels.

Since 2010, this project has run its annual ImageNet Large Scale Visual Recognition Challenge (ILSVRC) to advance research in the domain of visual object recognition software.

Hardware technology was advancing too. In particular, graphics processing units (GPUs) that had been developed for computer graphics and image processing (particularly for gaming) enabled complex matrix processing at speed—something required for training DNNs. From around 2010, the development of DNNs was possible. Soon they were reaching accuracies and speeds in areas of AI such as visual comprehension and speech translation on a par with, or even surpassing, human capability.

AI "Optical Illusions": A Surprising Revelation

While the accuracies and progress of DNNs were being celebrated, in 2013, researchers Szegedy et al. published a paper, "Intriguing Properties of Neural Networks,"[2] that was presented at the International Conference on Learning Representations (ICLR) the following year. This paper exposed the fact that deep learning algorithms could be "fooled" into emitting incorrect results.

The particular algorithms under scrutiny were DNNs for image classification. These take an image as input and classify it in terms of its most likely prevalent content—for example, the image might be classified as a "table" if a table were the primary item in the picture. While these neural networks were widely regarded as state of the art in terms of image classification, they made surprising mistakes when presented with images that had been intentionally sprinkled with small pixel changes that were imperceptible to humans. To a person, the image looked unchanged, but these minor modifications caused the neural networks to make significant errors in classification.

Figure 1-2 shows three examples of misclassified images that were presented in the paper. In the lefthand column are the originals that were correctly classified by the DNN algorithm. The images in the center column depict the "adversarial perturbations" created specifically for the original images on the left. These perturbations were then reduced by multiplying each pixel change by a fraction. When the reduced (less visible) perturbation was added to the original image, the image on the right was generated. All the images in the righthand column were misclassified by the same algorithm as an ostrich (specifically "ostrich, Struthio camelus"), despite appearing to human eyes to be the same as the originals.

This was intriguing, not only to those working in AI, but also to those with no detailed background in intelligent machines. The fact that DNNs could potentially be so easily fooled captured the interest of the popular press. In some articles the concept was described as "optical illusions" for AI.

Perhaps we assumed that because neural networks were inspired by neuroscience and appeared to mimic aspects of human intelligence so effectively, they "thought" like humans. As deep neural network concepts were initially inspired by a simplification of synapses and neurons within the brain, it would not be unreasonable to assume that DNNs interpreted images in a way that was similar to the brain's visual cortex—but this is not the case. They clearly do not extract the abstract features that humans use to classify images, but use different rules altogether. From the perspective of those working on neural network technologies, understanding how these algorithms can be fooled has provided insight into the algorithms themselves.

---

2 Christian Szegedy et al., "Intriguing Properties of Neural Networks," ICLR (2014), *http://bit.ly/2X2nu9c*.

Figure 1-2. Subtle perturbations result in image misclassification—the original images are on the left, and the perturbed images on the right were all misclassified as "ostrich" (image from Szegedy et al. 2014)

Since the initial Szegedy et al. paper, this vulnerability to trickery has been proven for other modalities such as speech and text, indicating that it is not restricted to DNNs that process image data, but is a phenomenon applicable to DNN technologies more broadly. In a world becoming increasingly reliant on DNNs, this was big news.

What Is "Adversarial Input"?

In the domain of image processing, the concept of adversarial input has been likened to creating optical illusions to which only AI is susceptible. An adversarial image might be generated by sprinkling seemingly unimportant pixels across an image of a cat that causes the AI to classify the image as a dog, without introducing any noticeable features that a person would discern as dog-like. Adversarial input could also be some marks on a road sign that we would interpret as graffiti, but which could cause an autonomous vehicle to misinterpret the sign. Examples also extend to audio, such as the inclusion of inaudible adversarial commands within speech that fundamentally change its interpretation by an automatic speech recognition system. All these scenarios are underpinned by DNN models.

The term *adversarial example* was first used by Szegedy et al. to describe examples such as those illustrated in Figure 1-2. This term can be defined as an input created with the *intent* to cause a model to return an incorrect result, regardless of whether the input actually succeeds in fooling the network or not. More commonly, the term's usage is restricted to inputs that achieve the aim of confusing a network. In this book, the terms *adversarial input* and *adversarial example* are used interchangeably to mean input that *successfully* fools a network into producing predictions that humans would consider incorrect. In the context of this book, therefore, nonadversarial input is data that fails to fool the network, even if it was developed with adversarial intent.

Malware as Adversarial Input

There is also increasing interest in the application of neural networks to malware detection, as the complexity inherent in software and the ever-evolving nature of malware make it impossible to articulate the features in software that might indicate a threat.

The term *adversarial input* is sometimes used to define malware when the anti-malware software is implemented by machine learning. This is a logical definition since malware is input to cause the machine learned model to return an incorrect result of "benign."

This book focuses on DNN models that process digital renderings of visual and auditory information; data that our biological brains process so easily. Image and audio data is *continuous*, comprising pixels or audio frequencies with a continuous spread of values. By contrast, other complex data, such as text, is *discrete* and not composed of quantifiable values. In the discrete domain it may be more challenging to create an adversarial example that will remain undetected because it is difficult to quantify a "small" change. For example, a small change to a word in some text may be overlooked as a misspelling, or be obvious if it results in a completely different meaning.

In the case of AI systems that are designed to process image or audio, an "incorrect" result does not *necessarily* mean that it differs from what a human might perceive. It is possible that an adversarial example will fool biological (human) intelligence too. This raises the question: do we want AI to interpret the world in the same way as we do? In the majority of cases, we won't want it to mimic human thinking to the extent that it also includes the failings of human perception. Most of the adversarial examples discussed in this book will be ones that would not fool our human brains—our biological neural networks. These examples introduce interesting threat models and also emphasize the difference between artificial and human intelligence.

Although any ML algorithm is potentially at risk of adversarial input, DNNs may have greater susceptibility as they excel at tasks where it is difficult to establish what features in the data are worth learning—therefore, we may have little or no understanding of what aspects of the data are important to a DNN algorithm. If we don't understand the aspects of the data that the algorithm uses in its decision making, what hope do we have of establishing good tests to assure the algorithm's robustness? Adversarial inputs exploit the fact that deep learning models typically deal with millions of possible input variants based on only a very small proportion of learned examples.[3] The learned models must be flexible enough to deal with complexity, but also generalize sufficiently for previously unseen data. As a result, the DNN's behavior for most possible inputs remains untested and can often be unexpected.

The attack presented by Szegedy et al. is a perturbation attack. However, there are other methods of fooling DNNs. The following sections introduce some of the different categories of approaches and the key terminology used in the area of adversarial input.

Adversarial Perturbation

The examples presented in Figure 1-2 illustrate adversarial images generated by making carefully calculated changes to the original images, altering each pixel by a tiny amount. This is known as a *perturbation attack*. An alternative approach might be to alter a few carefully selected pixels more significantly. The number of pixels changed and the change per pixel might vary, but the overall effect remains sufficiently small as to not be noticeable to (or to be overlooked by) a human. The perturbation might appear random, but it's not; each pixel has been carefully tweaked to produce the required result. Later in this book we'll look at how such perturbations are calculated to produce adversarial input.

Adversarial perturbation is not unique to images. Similar techniques could be applied to audio, for example (see Figure 1-3). The principles here remain the same—small changes in the audio to confuse the DNN processing. However, whereas an adversarial image exploits the *spatial* dimension to introduce perturbation (to pixels), adversarial audio exploits perturbations to audio frequencies that are distributed across *time*. For example, subtle changes in voice frequency over the duration of a speech

---

3 A training set will typically contain thousands of examples, but it is still a small proportion of the possible inputs.

segment that are not noticeable to a human can cause speech-to-text models to misinterpret a spoken sentence.[4]

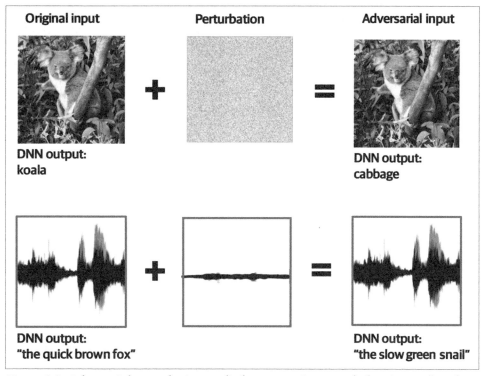

Figure 1-3. Adversarial perturbation applied across an image to fool an image classifier and across audio to fool a speech-to-text system

Unnatural Adversarial Input

In 2015, Nguyen et al. published a paper titled "Deep Neural Networks Are Easily Fooled: High Confidence Predictions for Unrecognizable Images."[5] Their research demonstrated that when the realism of the actual content is not important, adversarial images can be generated to produce confident misclassifications from DNNs despite the fact that they do not resemble anything that would be seen in the natural world. Some of the examples presented in this paper are shown in Figure 1-4.

---

4 As demonstrated in Nicholas Carlini and David Wagner, "Audio Adversarial Examples: Targeted Attacks on Speech-to-Text," IEEE Deep Learning and Security Workshop (2018), *http://bit.ly/2IFXT1W*.

5 A. Nguyen et al., "Deep Neural Networks Are Easily Fooled: High Confidence Predictions for Unrecognizable Images," Computer Vision and Pattern Recognition (2015), *http://bit.ly/2ZKc1wW*.

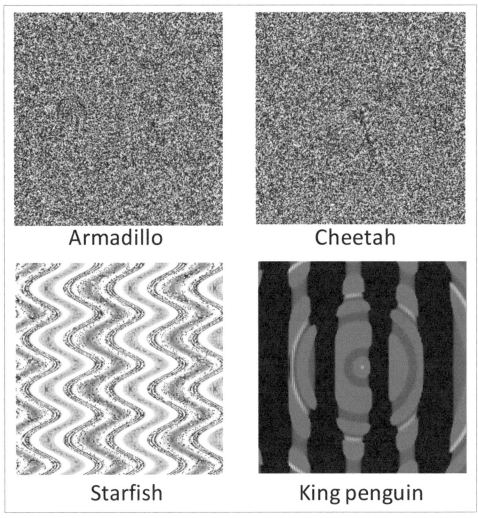

Figure 1-4. Digitally generated adversarial examples that are unrecognizable by humans with associated classifications from state-of-the-art DNNs (image from Nguyen et al. 2015)

These images are a real indication of the fact that DNNs can learn to interpret image data based on features that we as humans would not use. Clearly, these images are not going to fool anyone; however, they should not be dismissed. Examples such as these could be used by an adversary to force a system into making false-positive conclusions where the images cause a denial of service by flooding a system with data.

Adversarial Patches

Rather than distributing change across the input to create the adversarial example, an alternative approach is to focus on one area and essentially "distract" the DNN from aspects of the data that it should be focusing on.

Adversarial patches are carefully created "stickers" that are added to the data. These patches have the effect of distracting the DNN from the relevant aspects of the input and cause it to produce the wrong answer. An example of a digitally generated adversarial patch generated by Google researchers is shown in Figure 1-5. The sticker has been mathematically optimized to ensure that, from the DNN's perspective, it is a more salient feature than an object that exists in the real world and therefore ensures a confident misclassification.

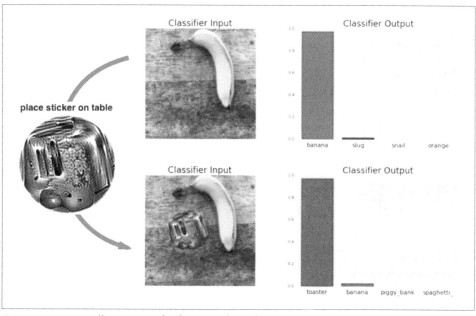

Figure 1-5. Digitally generated adversarial patch causing confident misclassification of a banana as a toaster (from Brown et al. 2017[6])

The adversarial change is obvious to a human observer, but this might not matter, especially if it is sufficiently subtle so as to not affect the interpretation of that image by a human. For example, it might be placed at the outskirts of the image and potentially disguised as a logo. We would also not be fooled into believing that the scene

---

6 Tom B. Brown et al., "Adversarial Patch" (2017), *http://bit.ly/2IDPonT*.

contained a toaster rather than a banana because the patch has been specifically designed to be salient to the DNN, rather than salient to a human.

Let's consider the same principle for audio. An audio patch might equate to a sound clip, short enough or perhaps quiet enough to be ignored by a human listener. In the same way that the adversarial image patch must be optimally sized and located spatially, the audio patch requires appropriate temporal location and intensity. The principle of adversarial patches for image and audio is illustrated in Figure 1-6.

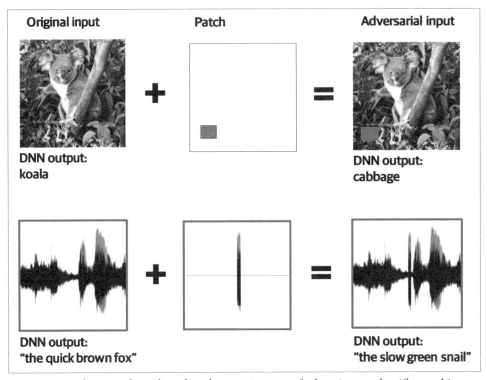

Figure 1-6. Adversarial patches placed on an image to fool an image classifier and inserted in audio to fool a speech-to-text system

An interesting feature of adversarial patches is that they may be more easily reused than adversarial perturbations. For example, a digitally generated adversarial sticker could be effective over multiple images, allowing it to be shared online or copied and stuck in multiple environments.

Adversarial Examples in the Physical World

The adversarial example illustrated in Figure 1-2 was generated by digital manipulation; in this case by changing pixel-level information across the images. However, this assumes the attacker has access to the digital format of the data being passed to the model—for example, if the adversary uploaded a digital image (such as a JPEG) to an internet site where it would then be processed.

In many settings, the adversary may only have access to the physical world[7] in order to influence the information entering the sensors (microphone or camera, for example) from which the digital data is generated. An adversary might exploit digitally generated adversarial patches in the form of 2D printouts or even 3D objects within a scene. Sharif et al. successfully demonstrate this idea in "Accessorize to a Crime: Real and Stealthy Attacks on State-of-the-Art Face Recognition"[8] by using adversarial glasses that enable the wearers to confuse face detection by facial recognition software. Figure 1-7 shows an example of such glasses.

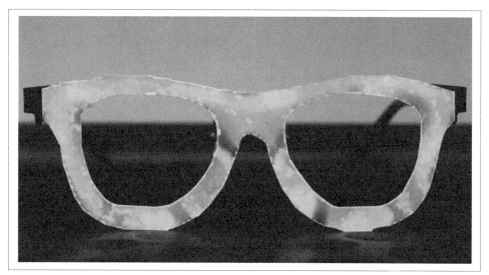

Figure 1-7. Adversarial glasses have been developed to fool facial recognition systems (image from Sharif et al. 2016)

Perturbation attacks are obviously far more difficult to achieve when the adversary has no ability to affect the digital representation of the data. An often-cited scenario of a physical-world adversarial attack is an environmental change made to confuse an autonomous vehicle in which decisions as to steering, response, speed, and so on are based on processing image data captured on camera. The vehicle's behavior might therefore be susceptible to changes to road markings, patterns on other vehicles, or

---

7 Throughout this book, the term *physical world* is used to refer to the aspects of the world that exist outside the digital computer domain.

8 Mahmood Sharif et al., "Accessorize to a Crime: Real and Stealthy Attacks on State-of-the-Art Face Recognition," Proceedings of the 2016 ACM SIGSAC Conference on Computer and Communications Security (2016), *http://bit.ly/2x1Nebf*.

road signs. Eykholt et al. have proven it possible to generate adversarial attacks in the real world based on the principles of perturbation.[9]

Figure 1-8 shows a perturbation attack using a simple traffic stop sign. The attack causes the DNN to misinterpret the sign and therefore has the potential to fool an autonomous vehicle.

Figure 1-8. Physical perturbation applied to a stop sign could fool an autonomous vehicle reliant on image data (image from Eykholt et al. 2018)

An interesting aspect of these physical-world examples is that, unlike the digital perturbation attacks previously described, they are often clearly detectable by human beings. The aim of the adversary is often to make the environmental change something that we would not notice as unusual. For example, in Figure 1-8, we can see the perturbation on the stop sign, but we might not recognize it as suspicious; it's designed to mimic graffiti and therefore appear benign to an onlooker.

It's also feasible to generate adversarial sound using broadly similar approaches. Adversarial speech can be created and disguised in other speech, sounds, or even in silence, presenting a threat to voice controlled systems (such as voice controlled digital assistants).[10]

The Broader Field of "Adversarial Machine Learning"

This book is about adversarial examples for image and audio neural network processing. However, this forms part of a broader group of attacks that fall under the more general term *adversarial machine learning* or *adversarial ML*. Adversarial ML incor-

---

9 Kevin Eykholt et al., "Robust Physical-World Attacks on Deep Learning Visual Classification," Computer Vision and Pattern Recognition (2018), *http://bit.ly/2FmJPbz*.

10 See for example Carlini and Wagner, "Audio Adversarial Examples."

porates all potential attacks on machine learned algorithms (DNNs and other more traditional ML algorithms) and all types of data.[11]

Adversarial examples are sometimes (correctly) referred to as *evasion attacks*, where an evasion attack is the modification of input to avoid detection by an ML algorithm. However, adversarial input may be used for purposes other than evasion. Many of the attacks discussed in this book are evasion attacks, but some are not. For example, a system could be flooded with adversarial examples causing it to generate many false positives, potentially leading to a denial of service.

Possible other attacks that you might come across within the field of adversarial ML are:

Poisoning attacks

A poisoning attack is when malicious data is deliberately introduced into the training dataset, resulting in the algorithm being mislearned. Systems that continually learn based on data acquired from untrusted sources are susceptible to this type of attack. This book is not about poisoning attacks.

ML model reverse engineering

If an adversary were to acquire a copy of an ML algorithm, it might be possible to reverse engineer the algorithm to extract potentially confidential or sensitive information pertaining to the characteristics of the training data. This book does not address attacks of this type

Implications of Adversarial Input

DNN models are prevalent throughout our society, and we rely on them for many aspects of our daily lives. What's more, many AI systems that contain these models work with data over which they have no control, often taking inputs from online digital sources and the physical world. For example:

- Facial recognition systems for access or surveillance
- Online web filters to detect upload of offensive or illegal imagery
- Autonomous vehicles that function in unconstrained physical environments
- Telephone voice-based fraud detection
- Digital assistants that act upon voice commands

If DNNs can be so easily fooled by adversarial examples, does this present a cyber-threat to AI solutions that ingest data from untrusted sources? How much risk does

---

11 On first hearing the term *adversarial machine learning*, it might be misleading as it could also be interpreted to mean machine learning used by an adversary to attack a system.

adversarial input really pose to the security and integrity of systems in our day-to-day lives? Finally, what mitigation strategies might the developers of these systems use to ensure that this attack vector cannot be exploited?

To address these questions, we need to understand the motivations and capabilities of adversaries. We need to understand why DNNs fall for adversarial input and what can be done to make the DNNs less susceptible to this trickery. We also need to understand the broader processing chains of which DNNs are a part and how this processing might make systems more (or less) robust to attack. There is currently no known mechanism to make DNNs entirely resilient to adversarial input, but understanding both the perspective of the attacker and that of the defending organization will enable the development of better protective measures.

Adversarial input is also interesting from another perspective: the differences between the ways in which humans and DNNs process information highlights the discrepancies between biological and artificial neural networks. While it is true that DNNs were initially inspired by neuroscience and that the word *neural* appears within the DNN nomenclature, the discipline of developing effective deep learning has become primarily the domain of mathematicians and data scientists. A DNN is essentially a complex mathematical function that takes data as its input and generates a result. The training of a DNN model is simply an exercise in mathematical optimization: how to iteratively change aspects of the complex function to best improve its accuracy. The mere existence of adversarial inputs suggests that any notion that an approximation of human thinking is embodied in DNNs is fundamentally flawed.

Finally, we must not forget that the risk of introducing disruptive, fraudulent, or harmful behavior into a computer system exists if *any* of the algorithms in the system are flawed when presented with untested input. Ensuring that a computer system is robust against adversarial input should be an intrinsic part of the broader assurance of any computer system that contains machine learned algorithms.

## CHAPTER 2

Attack Motivations

DNN technology is now part of our lives. For example, digital assistants (such as Amazon Alexa, Apple's Siri, Google Home, and Microsoft's Cortana) use deep learning models to extract meaning from speech audio. Many algorithms that enable and curate online interactions (such as web searching) exploit DNNs to understand the data being managed. Increasingly, deep learning models are being used in safety-critical applications, such as autonomous vehicles.

Many AI technologies take data directly from the physical world (from cameras, for example) or from digital representations of that data intended for human consumption (such as images uploaded to social media sites). This is potentially problematic, as when any computer system processes data from an untrusted source it may open a vulnerability. Motivations for creating adversarial input to exploit these vulnerabilities are diverse, but we can divide them into the following broad categories:

Evasion

Hiding content from automated digital analysis. For example, see "Circumventing Web Filters" on page 18, "Camouflage from Surveillance" on page 20, or "Personal Privacy Online" on page 21.

Influence

Affecting automated decisions for personal, commercial, or organizational gain. See for example "Online Reputation and Brand Management" on page 19.

Confusion

Creating chaos to discredit or disrupt an organization. See for example "Autonomous Vehicle Confusion" on page 21 or "Voice Controlled Devices" on page 23.

This chapter presents some possible motivations for creating adversarial examples. The list is by no means exhaustive, but should provide some indication of the nature and variety of the types of threat.

Circumventing Web Filters

Organizations are under increasing pressure to govern web content sourced from outside to protect against content that might be deemed offensive or inappropriate. This applies particularly to companies such as social media providers and online marketplaces with business models that depend on external data. There may also be legal obligations in place to monitor offensive material and prevent it from being propagated further.

Such organizations face an increasingly difficult challenge. There just aren't enough people to constantly monitor, and if necessary take action on, all the data being uploaded at the speeds required. Social media sites boast billions of data uploads per day. The data in those posts is not structured data that is easy to filter; it is image, audio, and text information where the categorization of "offensive"/"not offensive" or "legal"/"illegal" can be quite subtle. It is not possible for humans to monitor and filter all this content as it is uploaded.

The obvious solution is, therefore, to use intelligent machines to monitor, filter, or at least triage the data, as depicted in Figure 2-1. DNNs will be increasingly core to these solutions—they can be trained to categorize sentiment and offense in language, they can classify image content, and they are even able to categorize activities within video content. For example, a DNN could be trained to recognize when an image contains indications of drug use, enabling triage of this category of image for further verification by a human.

For an individual or group wishing to upload content that does not adhere to a target website's policies, there's the motivation to circumvent the filtering or monitoring put in place, while ensuring that the uploaded content still conveys the information intended for human beings. From the perspective of the organization monitoring its web content, more and more accurate algorithms are required to judge what is "offensive," "inappropriate," or "illegal," while also catching adversarial input. From the adversary's perspective, the adversarial web content will need to improve at a pace with the monitoring system in order to continue to evade detection by the AI and convey the same semantic meaning when seen, read, or heard by a human.

An adversary might also take another stance. If unable to fool the web upload filter, why not just spam it with lots of data that will cause confusion and additional cost to the defending organization? The decision of whether a data upload is deemed "offensive" by the AI is unlikely to be purely binary, but more likely a statistical measure of likelihood with some threshold. An organization might use human moderation to consider images or data around this threshold, so generating large amounts of benign data that is classified by the AI as "maybe" will impact the organization's operational capabilities and may reduce confidence in the accuracy of its AI results. If it's difficult for a human to establish exactly *why* the data is being triaged as possibly breaking policy (because it appears benign), the influx of data will take up more of an organization's time and human resources—essentially a denial-of-service (DoS) attack.

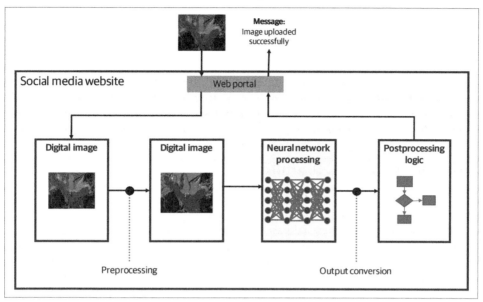

Figure 2-1. Images uploaded to a social media site might undergo processing and checking by AI before being added to the site.

Online Reputation and Brand Management

Search engines are complex algorithms that decide not only which results to return when you type "cat skateboard," but also the order in which they are presented in the results. From a commercial perspective, it's obviously good to be a top result. Companies are therefore highly motivated to understand and game the search engine algorithms to ensure that their adverts appear on the first page of a Google or Bing search and are placed prominently when served on web pages. This is known as *search engine optimization* (SEO) and has been standard industry practice for many years. SEO is often core to company internet marketing strategies.

Automated web crawlers can be used to sift through and index pages for search results based on characteristics such as page HTML metadata, inbound links to the page, and content. These web crawlers are automated systems underpinned by AI without human oversight. As it's very easy to manipulate header information, search engines rely more often on content. Indexing based on content also enables search on less obvious search terms that have perhaps not been included in the metadata.

It's the characteristics based on content that are particularly interesting in the context of adversarial examples. Updating a website's image content may affect its position in the search engine results, so, from the perspective of a company wanting to increase its visibility to a target audience, why not exploit adversarial perturbation or patches to alter or strengthen image categorization without adversely affecting its human interpretation?

Alternatively, on the more sinister end of the spectrum, there might be motivation to discredit an organization or individual by generating adversarial images, causing the target to be misassociated with something that could be damaging. For example, adversarial images of a chocolate bar that is misclassified by the search engine as "poison" might appear among search results for poison images. Even a subliminal association may be sufficient to affect people's perception of the brand.

Camouflage from Surveillance

Surveillance cameras acquire their data from the physical world, opening a very different perspective on adversarial input than considered in the previous examples. The digital content is being generated based on sensor (camera) data and is not subject to manipulation by individuals outside the organization.[1]

The digital rendering of the security footage (the video or image stills) is still often monitored by humans, but this is increasingly infeasible due to the quantities of information and time involved. Most surveillance footage is unlikely to be actively monitored in real time, but may be analyzed later in "slower time"; for example, in the event of some reported criminal activity. Organizations are increasingly turning to automated techniques to monitor or triage surveillance data through AI technologies; for example, to automatically detect and alert to specific faces or vehicles in surveillance footage.

It doesn't take much imagination to envisage scenarios where an adversary would wish to outwit such a system. The adversary's aim might be to create a kind of "invisibility cloak" that fools AI but would not draw undue human attention. The goal might be simply to prevent the AI from generating an alert that would result in human scrutiny being applied to the image or video. For example, an adversary might aim to avoid facial detection in real time by an airport security system. Similarly, there may be greater opportunity to carry out nefarious deeds if a real-time threat-detection system does not recognize suspicious activity. In non-real time, security cameras might have captured information pertaining to a crime, such as a face or number plate or another feature that might be used for searching based on witness evidence after the event. Concealing this information from the AI might reduce the chance of criminal detection.

---

1 This is obviously not true if there has been a more fundamental security breach allowing outsiders access to the organization's internal content.

Of course, the motivations may not be criminal; privacy in our increasingly monitored world might be an incentive to camouflage the relevant salient aspects of a face from AI. The individual may be motivated to achieve this through innocuous clothing or makeup, for example, in order to claim *plausible deniability* that this was a deliberate attempt to fool the surveillance system and to assert that the surveillance system was simply in error.[2]

There's another interesting scenario here: what if physical changes to the real world could be introduced that, although seeming benign and looking innocent to humans, could cause surveillance systems to register a false alarm? This might enable an adversary to distract an organization into directing its resources to a false location while the actual deed was committed elsewhere.

Personal Privacy Online

Many social media platforms extract information from the images that we upload to improve the user experience. For example, Facebook routinely extracts and identifies faces in images to improve image labeling, searching, and notifications.

Once again, a desire for privacy could motivate an individual to alter images so that faces are not easily detected by the AI the platform uses. Alterations such as adversarial patches applied to the edge of an image might "camouflage" faces from the AI.

Autonomous Vehicle Confusion

A commonly cited use of AI is in autonomous vehicles, consideration of which moves us into the realm of safety-critical systems. These vehicles operate in the messy, unconstrained, and changing physical world. Susceptibility to adversarial input could result in potentially disastrous consequences.

Autonomous vehicles are not restricted to our roads. Autonomy is increasingly prevalent in maritime situations, in the air, and underwater. Autonomous vehicles are also used in constrained, closed environments, such as in factories, to perform basic or perhaps dangerous tasks. Even these constrained environments could be at risk from camera-sourced adversarial input from within the organization (insider threat) or from individuals who have gained access to the area in which the system is operating. However, we must remember that autonomous vehicles are unlikely to rely solely on sensor data to understand the physical environment; most autonomous systems will acquire information from multiple sources. Data sources include:

---

2 See Sharif et al., "Accessorize to a Crime."

Off-board data

Most autonomous vehicles will rely on data acquired from one or more off-board central sources.[3] Off-board data includes relatively static information (maps and speed limits), centrally collected dynamic data (such as traffic information), and vehicle-specific information (such as GPS location). All these types of data sources are already used in GPS navigation applications such Waze, Google Maps, and HERE WeGo.

Other off-board data is available in other domains. For example, in shipping, *Automatic Identification System* (AIS) data is used extensively for automatic tracking of the location of maritime vessels. Ships regularly transmit their identity and location through this system in real time, enabling maritime authorities to track vessel movements.

Onboard sensor data

Autonomous vehicle decisions may also be based on onboard sensors such as cameras, proximity sensors, accelerometers, and gyro sensors (to detect positional rotation). This data is critical in providing information on changes to the immediate vicinity, such as real-time alerts and unexpected events.

There may be occasions where an autonomous vehicle must rely on sensor data only in order to make its decisions. Road positioning is an example that might be derived entirely from sensor data, as shown in Figure 2-2. Such scenarios can pose a significant safety risk as the information generated is potentially untrusted.

In practice, autonomous vehicles will base decisions on information established based on multiple data sources and will always err on the side of caution. A vehicle is unlikely to be fooled by a stop sign that has been adversarially altered to say "go" if it also has access to central data pertaining to the road's regulations (speed limits, junctions, and stop and give-way requirements). It is more likely that adversaries will exploit this caution—for example, distributing multiple benign printed stickers on the road that are misinterpreted as hazardous objects could cause road network disruption.

---

3 There may be constrained environments, such as within a factory or within the home, where the autonomous vehicle is entirely dependent on onboard sensor data to function.

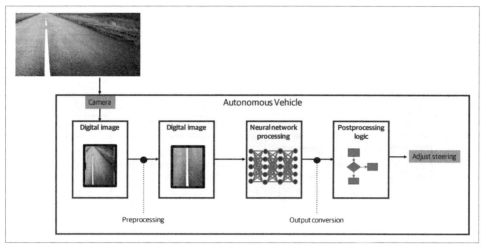

Figure 2-2. Camera data might be used by an autonomous vehicle to ensure correct road positioning

Voice Controlled Devices

Voice control audio provides a natural, hands-free way to control many aspects of our lives. Tasks ranging from media control, home automation, and internet search to shopping can all be accomplished now through voice control. Voice controlled devices such as smartphones, tablets, and audio assistants are being welcomed into our homes. The speech processing central to these devices is performed through advanced DNN technologies and is highly accurate. Figure 2-3 depicts a simple processing chain for a voice controlled device.

Audio is streamed into the home through radio, television, and online content. Unbeknown to the listener, this audio might also incorporate adversarial content, perhaps to notify listening audio assistants to increase the volume of a song as it plays. While this might be no more than irritating, adversarial audio might also be used to discredit the audio assistant by causing it to misbehave. An assistant exhibiting unpredictable behavior will be irritating and potentially perceived as creepy. Once a device is untrusted in the home environment, it is unlikely to regain trust easily. Other potential hidden commands could be more malevolent; for example, sending an unwarranted SMS or social media post, changing the settings on the device, navigating to a malicious URL, or changing home security settings.

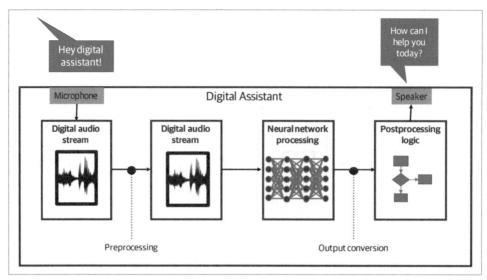

Figure 2-3. A digital assistant uses AI to process speech audio and respond appropriately

Voice controlled assistants mandate some additional security steps to perform higher-security functions to avoid accidental or deliberate misuse. The assistant might ask. "Are you *sure* you wish to purchase a copy of *Strengthening Deep Neural Networks*?" and await confirmation prior to purchasing. It's possible, but highly unlikely, that you would say "yes" at the correct time if you had not instigated that purchase. However, if it's possible to get an adversarial *command* into the voice assistant, then it is also possible to introduce the adversarial *response*, so long as no one is within earshot to hear the confirmation request.

Here's an interesting twist. Perhaps adversarial examples are not always malevolent—they might be used for entertainment purposes to deliberately exploit audio as an additional method to transfer commands. There's potential to exploit adversarial examples for commercial gain, rather than for just doing bad stuff.

Imagine settling down with popcorn in front of your television to watch *The Shining*. However, this is no ordinary version of the film; you paid extra for the one with "integrated home automation experience." This enhanced multimedia version of the film contains adversarial audio—secret messages intended for your voice controlled home automation system to "enhance" the viewing experience. Perhaps, at an appropriate moment, to slam the door, turn out the lights, or maybe turn off the heating (it gets pretty cold in that hotel)…

On that slightly disturbing note, let's move on to the next chapter and an introduction to DNNs.

## CHAPTER 3

Deep Neural Network (DNN) Fundamentals

In this chapter, we'll explore the core concepts behind DNN models, the category of machine learned models usually used for image and audio processing. Comprehending these basic ideas now will help you understand adversarial examples in greater depth later in the book. Following this basic introduction, Chapter 4 will then explore models for understanding complex images, audio, and video. The two chapters will provide sufficient background for the discussions on adversarial examples that follow but are not intended to provide a comprehensive introduction to deep learning.

If you are familiar with the principles of deep learning and neural networks, feel free to skip this chapter and Chapter 4. Conversely, if you are inclined to learn more than is required for this book, there are numerous excellent resources available to gain a better understanding of machine learning and neural networks. Links to a selection of online resources are included in this book's GitHub repository (*http://bit.ly/ 2x5Kg5I*).

At the end of this chapter, there are some snippets of Python code. As with all the code in this book, reading it is optional (you can understand adversarial examples without the code). If you are interested in the code, I encourage you to also download and experiment with some of the Jupyter notebooks provided in the associated Git-Hub repository.

Machine Learning

DNNs belong to the broader category of *machine learning* (ML); the capability for a machine to learn how to extract patterns from data, without requiring the rules behind the data patterns to be explicitly coded. The resulting learned algorithm is known as a *model*.

The model is a mathematical algorithm whose parameters have been refined to optimize its behavior. The algorithm "learns" by being repeatedly presented with training data, where each piece of training data is an example of what it needs to learn. Each training example enables the model to be incrementally improved by adjusting its parameters. When the algorithm is suitably refined, it has been trained. Typically, the model's accuracy is then tested against a test dataset that differs from the training data. The hope is that the model will perform the specific task well on data other than that in the initial training set, so it will work when presented with data that it's never seen before.

Using traditional (nonneural network) machine learning you can create models that perform fairly clever tasks. For example, based on training data representing many different plant characteristics (height, leaf shape, blossom color, etc.) and corresponding taxonomic genera, it may be possible to train an ML model to infer the genus of any plant based on a list of supplied characteristics. The plant genus may depend on a complex combination of characteristics, but given sufficient training examples and the correct ML approach, the resulting trained model should be able to classify plants without a software engineer needing to explicitly code (or even understand) the relationships between the various characteristics and plant genera.

As you'll recall from Chapter 1, there are a number of broad strategies for training ML models:

Supervised learning
> The flora classification example falls into the category of supervised learning because the model is trained using characteristics along with a label representing the correct answer (in this case, the genus).

Unsupervised learning
> In unsupervised learning, no labels are provided during the training step. The model has not been presented with clear answers—it is trained to find patterns in the data, to detect anomalies, or to find associations. A model trained using plant data without the associated labels may be able to learn plant groupings based on combinations of characteristics that often occur together. The trained model could then establish which group a new plant falls into (based on its characteristics), or perhaps whether the new plant doesn't naturally fall into any of the groupings learned by the model (i.e., identify an anomaly).

Semi-supervised learning
> Semi-supervised learning is (as you might expect) a halfway house between supervised and unsupervised learning, for when training data is available but not all of it is labeled. Typically, the model uses unlabeled data to establish patterns, then labeled data is used to improve its accuracy.

Reinforcement learning

In reinforcement learning, the ML model returns some kind of feedback to establish how good it is. The model is refined to optimize for a particular goal (such as learning how to win at a video game) by repeatedly attempting the goal, receiving some kind of feedback (a score indicating how well it has done), and adjusting its approach.

Most of the discussions in this book will relate to models learned through supervised learning, as this is where the majority of research into adversarial input has focused so far. However, the concepts of adversarial examples also apply to models learned through unsupervised, semi-supervised, and reinforcement methods.

A Conceptual Introduction to Deep Learning

Although traditional machine learning techniques are powerful, these models are unable to deal with very complex data where the relevant information—the salient features—required for the task is unclear. Plant characteristics are represented by structured data, such as a binary value to indicate whether the plant has blossoms, or an integer to indicate the number of petals on each flower. The importance of each feature in establishing the plant genus may not be clear, but the features themselves are clearly articulated.

Many tasks use data types that are unstructured or have features that are difficult to discern. In the world of AI, focus is often on unstructured raw data extracted from the real world, such as image and audio. A digital image typically comprises thousands of pixel values, each individual pixel having little relevance on its own; the meaning of the image is based on complex spatial relationships between pixels. Similarly, audio is represented by a series of values over time, where each value is meaningless individually. The order of and spacing between the values determine how the sound should be interpreted.

Visual and audio data is something that we humans and other animals are particularly good at processing with our biological "neural network" brains. The visual and audio processing areas of our brains extract the relevant information from the raw data we receive through our eyes and ears. It's so easy for us humans to process audio and visual data that it can be difficult to understand why this is challenging for a machine.

Take a simple example of recognizing a cat. For a machine, establishing object boundaries, catering for occlusion and shading, and recognizing the features that constitute a "cat" is incredibly difficult. However, for humans this is a trivial problem. We can recognize a cat from minimal information—a tail, a paw, or perhaps just a movement. We can even recognize breeds of cat that we have never seen before as "cats."

Audio is no different. Humans recognize sounds and also comprehend speech effortlessly. We filter and ignore background noise and focus on relevant detail. We understand speech based on complex orders of different sounds and context. Yet for a computer this is a nontrivial task, as the digital representation of a sound file is complex and messy, with simultaneous noises from multiple origins.

As humans, we manage visual and audio processing without difficulty. We are unlikely to even be able to explain what features and patterns make up a cat or what sound combinations make up a particular sentence. Somehow our brains manage to learn those features and patterns, and we apply this learned algorithm in our everyday lives as if it were trivial. However, it's infeasible to explicitly write code to adequately cater for all the different possible scenarios in the physical world, and traditional ML algorithms are insufficiently flexible to learn the features required to handle this complexity.

Traditional machine learning techniques may not be up to the task of audio and image processing, but deep learning is. Deep models excel in a multitude of complex computational tasks, especially when the data is unstructured (such as image, audio, or text) or where features are difficult to discern (such as predictive modeling[1] where there are many variables).

Chapter 1 introduced the concept of an artificial neural network (ANN) visually in terms of "neurons" (very roughly akin to biological neurons) and connections between these neurons which could be considered (again, very roughly) similar to the axons and synapses in the brain. This provides a nice way of thinking about artificial neural networks; they are essentially interconnected neurons, typically arranged in layers[2] as depicted in Figure 3-1. This illustrates the most basic sort, known as a *multilayer perceptron*. In this case every node in one layer is connected to every other node in the adjacent layer, so it's classified as a *fully interconnected* or *dense* neural network.

The first layer (on the left) that takes the input is called the *input layer*. The output of the algorithm is seen in the righthand *output layer*. The layers between are called *hidden layers* because they represent partial computations performed by the network that are not visible externally. The hidden layers are where all the magic happens as the computation propagates through the network, and it is the existence of one or more hidden layers that makes an ANN a "deep" neural network.

---

1 The forecasting of outcomes based on past data.

2 As any self-respecting data scientist will be keen to point out, ANNs are not necessarily arranged in layers, but let's keep it simple and not get distracted by all the possible ANN structures at this stage.

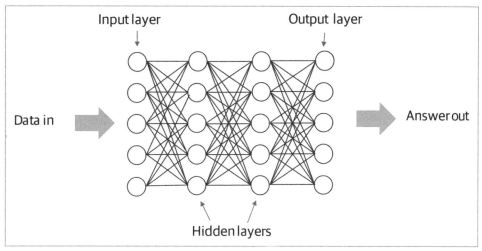

Figure 3-1. A multilayer perceptron

Figure 3-2 illustrates this idea. Data is input to the DNN through the first layer (on the left), causing the neurons in that layer to be *activated* to differing degrees. This just means that the neurons are allocated a number, an *activation* or an *intensity*. A high activation means the neuron has a higher numeric value assigned, and a low activation indicates a lower value is assigned.

Neurons firing in one layer cause the connections to relay this information to the next layer, so the activation of one layer is determined by the activation of the previous layer. Neurons respond differently to input; some neurons fire (activate) at a greater or lower intensity than others, given the same input. Also, some connections are "stronger," meaning that they carry more weight than others, so they play a more significant role in determining the effect of the behavior downstream. Eventually a result pops out at each of the nodes in the righthand layer (the output layer). This is known as a *feed-forward* network as the data flows in one direction. The information is always "fed" forward through the network and there's no looping back to previous nodes. More formally, a feed-forward network is a type of directed acyclic graph.

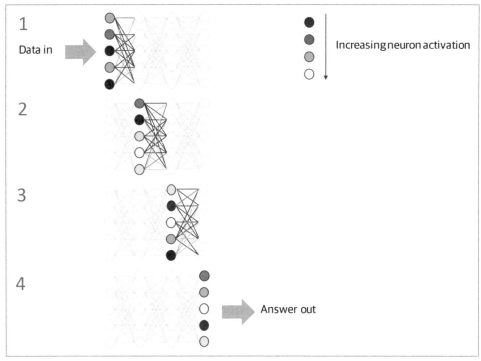

Figure 3-2. Incremental calculation steps in a multilayer perceptron

There's obviously lots of great stuff happening as the data passes through the hidden layers of the network and is transformed, perhaps from an image to a classification, or from speech to representative text. We might assume (rightly) that the hidden layers are gradually extracting the relevant information from the input (be it a bit of a cat's ear or the phoneme sound for an "a," or whatever). Higher- and higher-level features are extracted, then potentially combined, until the relevant answer is generated at the output layer.

DNN Models as Mathematical Functions

Up to this point we have considered DNNs as artificial approximations of biological processes (the brain) purely in a conceptual (visual) way by considering the neurons and their interconnections. However, ML models (including DNNs) are actually mathematical functions. The mathematics of the functions may be complicated, but an ML model is just a piece of math.

So, simply put, ML models are mathematical functions which take some input and return some output. We can therefore write them like this:

$$\mathbf{y} = f(\mathbf{x})$$

The act of training the model is working out what the function f should be.

To introduce the mathematics behind DNNs, let's use an example dataset—Fashion-MNIST. This dataset is available online (*http://bit.ly/2WQqbKZ*) for the purposes of experimenting and benchmarking ML models.

The Universality of Artificial Neural Networks

A key differentiator of a DNN model compared with a traditional ML techniques is that DNNs are able to represent *universal* functions. That is, there is a neural network that can represent an accurate approximation for every function,[3] no matter how complicated that function is. For a DNN to adhere to the universality principle, it requires just a single hidden layer.

Fashion-MNIST comprises 70,000 grayscale images of 28 x 28 pixels resolution. Each image depicts an item of clothing that can be separated into one of 10 classifications: "T-shirt/top," "Trouser," "Pullover," "Dress," "Coat," "Sandal," "Shirt," "Sneaker," "Bag," or "Ankle boot." Examples of images from this dataset, along with their corresponding labels, are shown in Figure 3-3.

The Fashion-MNIST dataset is a particularly nice one to demonstrate image classification using a DNN model because it does not include the complexity usually associated with images. First, the images are low resolution and in monochrome. This reduces the complexity of the DNN required to perform the classification, making it easier to train without specialist hardware. Second, as you can see in Figure 3-3, each image only depicts a single item, sized and placed centrally. In Chapter 4 we'll see that dealing with spatial positioning within an image requires a more complex DNN architecture.

---

3 Strictly speaking, this is true for continuous functions only where a small change in the input will not cause a sudden large step change in the output. However, as discontinuous functions can often be approximated by continuous ones, this is not usually a restriction.

Figure 3-3. The Fashion-MNIST dataset contains simply depicted fashion items and their associated labels.

We can use this dataset to experiment with simple neural network image classification: given an input image, produce a clothing classification. Figure 3-4 illustrates (conceptually) what we would like from a trained DNN given an image of trousers as input.

The DNN model is *f*. A well-trained image classification DNN model *f* presented with an image of some trousers (depicted by *x*) would return a value of *y* that means "this is a pair of trousers."

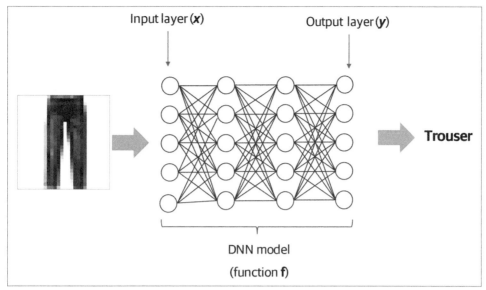

Input layer (*x*)

Output layer (*y*)

Trouser

DNN model

(function **f**)

Figure 3-4. At the simplest level, an image classification model for Fashion-MNIST will take an image and return a classification.

You don't need to be a mathematician to realize that there will be a lot of clever stuff happening in the DNN model that converts an image to one of 10 clothing categories. We'll begin by considering the inputs and outputs to the model, then consider the internals. Finally, we'll look at how the model is trained to make accurate predictions.

DNN Inputs and Outputs

Each neuron in the input layer is assigned a value representing an aspect of the input data. So, for a Fashion-MNIST input, each neuron in the input layer represents one pixel value of the input image. The model will require 784 neurons in its input layer, because each image has 28 x 28 pixels (Figure 3-4, with its 5 input neurons, is clearly an extreme oversimplification). Each neuron in this layer is allocated a value between 0 and 255 depicting the intensity of the pixel that it represents.[4]

The output layer is another list of values (numbers) representing whatever output the DNN has been trained to generate. Typically, this output is a list of *predictions*, each associated with a single classification. The Fashion-MNIST dataset has 10 categories of clothing, so there are 10 neurons in the output layer and 10 numeric outputs, each one representing the relative confidence that the image belongs to a specific clothing

---

4 In practice, it's beneficial to scale these values so that they all lie between 0 and 1.

category. The first neuron value represents the prediction that the image is a "T-shirt/top," the second represents the prediction that the image is a "Trouser," and so on.

As this is a classification task, the most activated (highest value) neuron in the output layer is going to represent the DNN's answer. In Figure 3-4, the neuron corresponding to "Trouser" would have the highest activation if the model was classifying successfully.

The list of inputs (pixel values) and the list of outputs (clothing classification confidences) are represented mathematically as *vectors*. The previous formula can therefore be better expressed as a function that takes a vector input x and returns a vector output y:

$$
\begin{pmatrix} y_1 \\ y_2 \\ \vdots \\ y_{n-1} \\ y_n \end{pmatrix} = f \begin{pmatrix} x_1 \\ x_2 \\ \vdots \\ x_{i-1} \\ x_i \end{pmatrix}
$$

where i is the number of neurons in the input layer (784 in the Fashion-MNIST case) and n is the number of neurons in the output layer (10 in the Fashion-MNIST case).

So, we have the concept of a mathematical function representing the DNN. This function takes one vector (the input) and returns another (the output). But what exactly is that function?

DNN Internals and Feed-Forward Processing

Like the input and output layers, each of the hidden layers in a DNN is represented as a vector. Every layer in the network can be represented as a simple vector with one value per neuron. The values of the vector describing the input layer determine the values of the first hidden layer vector, which determines the values of the subsequent hidden layer vector, and so on until an output vector is generated to represent the predictions.

So, how do the vector values of one layer influence the vector values of the next? To appreciate how a DNN model actually calculates its answer, we'll zoom into a specific node in the network, shaded in blue in Figure 3-5, and consider how its activation value is calculated.

The value of a specific neuron will be defined by the activations of the previous layer of neurons, each depicted by the letter a with a subscript indicating the neuron.

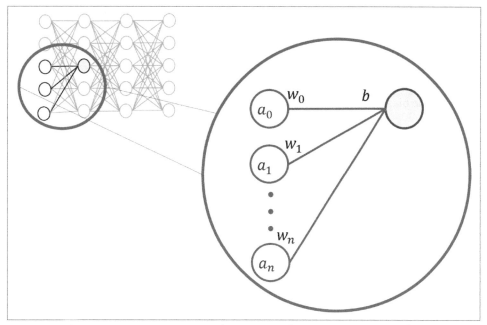

Figure 3-5. Zooming in on a neuron within a network to see its activation function

There are two types of adjustable parameters in a simple feed-forward neural network:

Weights

An individual weight value is associated with each connection in the network. This determines the strength of the connection, or the amount that the activation of the connected-from neuron influences the connected-to neuron. In Figure 3-5 the weights are depicted by the letter *w* with a subscript to indicate which connection they are associated with.

Biases

An individual bias value is associated with every neuron in the network. This determines whether the neuron tends to be active or not. In Figure 3-5 the bias is depicted by the letter *b*.

The activation of a particular neuron (after the input layer) will be determined by contributions from the neuron's upstream connections, plus an adjustment by the neuron's bias. The contribution of an individual connection is the product of the connected-from neuron's activation and the weight of the connection itself. Therefore, the contribution of the first connection in Figure 3-5 is the product of the weight of the connection and the bias associated with the connected-to neuron:

$$w_0 \cdot a_0$$

Now, simply sum them all up to get the combined input from all the contributing connections:

$$w_0 \cdot a_0 + w_1 \cdot a_1 + \ldots + w_{n-1} \cdot a_{n-1} + w_n \cdot a_n$$

And add the bias associated with the connected-to neuron:

$$w_0 \cdot a_0 + w_1 \cdot a_1 + \ldots + w_{n-1} \cdot a_{n-1} + w_n \cdot a_n + b$$

To make the DNN behave as required, the result from this calculation is then fed into an *activation function*. We'll define this as A. This gives the formula for calculating the activation of any particular neuron in the network (other than those in the input layer whose activations are determined directly by the input data):

$$A\left(w_0 \cdot a_0 + w_1 \cdot a_1 + \ldots + w_{n-1} \cdot a_{n-1} + w_n \cdot a_n + b\right)$$

There are a number of possible activation functions that can be used during neural processing. The particular function for each neuron of the network is explicitly defined when the network is architected and depends upon the type of neural network and the network layer.

For example, an activation function that has proven to work very well for the hidden layers of DNNs is the *Rectified Linear Unit* (ReLU). The hidden neural network layers are most effective at learning when small upstream contributions do not cause the neuron to fire and larger ones do. This is like the synapses in the brain that fire at a particular threshold. ReLU mimics this idea. It's simple—if the input to the ReLU function:

$$\left(w_0 \cdot a_0 + w_1 \cdot a_1 + \ldots + w_{n-1} \cdot a_{n-1} + w_n \cdot a_n + b\right)$$

exceeds a static threshold (usually zero), the function returns that value; if not, it returns zero. This is depicted in Figure 3-6.

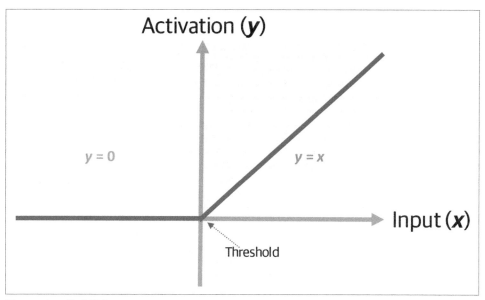

Figure 3-6. ReLU function

When the DNN is performing a classification task, it is useful for the final layer to output a set of prediction probabilities that all sum to 1. Therefore, for the Fashion-MNIST classification, we require a final layer in the network that takes the scores output from the network—called the *logits*—and scales them so that they represent probabilities and therefore add to exactly 1. Neurons in this layer will use a different activation function called *softmax* to perform this scaling step.

Applying all this to create a Fashion-MNIST classification model, Figure 3-4 can be redrawn with more accuracy. The number of hidden layers and number of neurons in each hidden layer is somewhat arbitrary, but there are some rules of thumb to get a good result. Typically, one hidden layer will suffice with somewhere between the number of neurons in the input and output layers. Let's assume there are two hidden layers, each with 56 neurons. The resulting network architecture is shown in Figure 3-7.

The next part of the puzzle is to understand how all the weights and bias values are adjusted to give a good result.

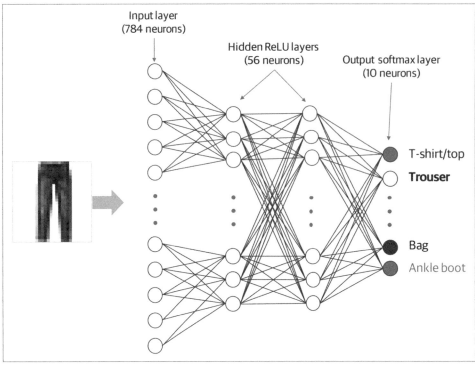

Figure 3-7. DNN architecture for image classification using Fashion-MNIST data

How a DNN Learns

So far, we have established that a DNN model is a mathematical function, f. In "DNN Inputs and Outputs" on page 33 we wrote this as a function that takes a vector representing the input data and returns an output vector. We can write this simply as:

$$\mathbf{y} = f(\mathbf{x})$$

where the bold form of $\mathbf{x}$ and $\mathbf{y}$ indicates that they represent vectors.

The function f comprises many parameters depicting each of the weights and biases in the network. These must be adjusted correctly for it to give the expected output given any input. So let's rewrite the preceding expression, this time specifying a function that takes both an input image and a set of parameters that represent all the weights and biases. The character Θ (theta) is the notation used to represent all the values of the weights and biases in the network:

$$\mathbf{y} = f(\mathbf{x}; \Theta)$$

Training the network involves adjusting these weights and biases (Θ) so that each time a training input is presented to the network it returns a value as close as possible to the training label's correct (target) label classification. Don't underestimate the task of optimizing all these parameters—the DNN function has one bias parameter for each hidden neuron and a weight assigned to each connection. So, for each layer that gives us:

$$numberOfParametersPerLayer = (numberOfNodesInPreviousLayer \\ * numberOfNodesInLayer) + numberOfNodesInLayer$$

For example, for the Fashion-MNIST classifier model shown in Figure 3-7 there are 47,722 different parameters to adjust—and this is a relatively simple neural network! It's unsurprising, then, that training a DNN requires considerable amounts of training data examples and is computationally expensive.

To begin training, the weights and biases within the network are initialized randomly. Consequently, the network will perform dreadfully; it needs to *learn*. During this learning phase, the weights and biases are iteratively adjusted to ensure that the DNN works optimally across all the training data in the hope that, given new examples, it will return the correct answer.

Here's how it learns. The network is repeatedly presented with example inputs from the training dataset and scored as to how badly it does relative to the expected labels associated with the training inputs. This score is referred to as the *cost* (or *loss*) of the network and is established by a *cost function* or *loss function*, a special function that quantifies how badly the network is performing its task. If the cost is big, then the network is giving poor results. If the cost is small, the network is performing well.

The cost function will take a number of parameters: the DNN function itself (f) with all its weights and biases (that is, all its parameters as represented by Θ), and the training examples. The training example labels will be needed too because these define what a "good" answer is—the ground truth.

For a single training example, the cost function can therefore be expressed as follows:

$$C(f(\mathbf{x}; \Theta), \mathbf{l})$$

where:

> C represents the cost function for the DNN f with the parameters Θ, given the training example $\mathbf{x}$ and its associated target predictions $\mathbf{l}$.

So what does this function C actually do? Well, there are multiple ways that we could measure how well the model has performed for a single training example. A simple method is to simply subtract the expected labels from the actual values produced by the DNN for that training example. The difference is squared to ensure that larger discrepancies between the target labels and predicted probabilities generate a dispro-portionately big loss value. This causes big differences between the target and predicted values to be penalized more than small ones.

Here's the equation that we use to measure the cost for a specific training example:

$$\left(\begin{pmatrix} y_0 \\ y_1 \\ \vdots \\ y_{n-1} \\ y_n \end{pmatrix} - \begin{pmatrix} l_0 \\ l_1 \\ \vdots \\ l_{n-1} \\ l_n \end{pmatrix} \right)^2$$

where:

l_i has the value 1 when i represents the correct target classification, and the value 0 otherwise.

Put another way, the cost for one training example is:

$$C(f(\mathbf{x}; \Theta), \mathbf{l}) = (f(\mathbf{x}; \Theta) - \mathbf{l})^2$$

For example, say we present the Fashion-MNIST image classifier with an image of a pair of trousers during training, and it returns the following vector:

$$\begin{pmatrix} 0.232 \\ 0.119 \\ \vdots \\ 0.151 \\ 0.005 \end{pmatrix}$$

The target label associated with the image is "Trouser," corresponding to the second value in the vector. Ideally, this prediction should be close to 1 rather than its current value of 0.119. If the network was performing perfectly, it would have returned the vector of predictions:

$$\begin{pmatrix} 0 \\ 1 \\ : \\ 0 \\ 0 \end{pmatrix}$$

The calculated cost for this example is the square of the difference between the target vector and the predictions for the label:

$$\left(\begin{pmatrix} 0.032 \\ 0.119 \\ : \\ 0.151 \\ 0.005 \end{pmatrix} - \begin{pmatrix} 0 \\ 1 \\ : \\ 0 \\ 0 \end{pmatrix} \right)^2 = 0.001 + 0.776 + .. + 0.023 + 0.000$$

In this case, you can see that the cost is high for the trouser classification. Therefore, some parameters in the network need to be tuned to fix this.

To really assess how good the network is, however, we need to consider the cost over *all* the training examples. One measure of this overall performance is to take the average cost. This calculation provides us with the loss function. In the case described, we're taking the mean of the squares of all the errors. This loss function is known as *mean squared error* (MSE).

Other loss functions use different algorithms to calculate loss during training. For classification models, it's usual to use a *categorical cross entropy* loss function. This function is better at penalizing errors that the network returns with higher confidence. We'll use a variation of this in the code example at the end of this chapter.

To improve the network, we want to adjust its weights and biases to reduce the average cost to its minimum possible value. In other words, the parameters represented by Θ require adjusting until the equation is the best it can be for all the possible training examples. At this point, the network will be optimally adjusted. This is achieved through a technique called *gradient descent*.

To understand gradient descent, imagine that there is just one adjustable parameter Θ_i in the network, rather than thousands. This enables a pictorial representation, as shown in Figure 3-8. The x-axis corresponds to the adjustable parameter. Given any value of x, the average cost of the network can be calculated using our chosen loss function (such as MSE). Of course, the x-axis is vastly simplified—it should really be thousands of axes, one for each parameter—but the illustration holds to represent the concept.

Any point on the curve represents the cost for a particular combination of weights and biases for the network. At the start of the training phase, when the parameters are initialized randomly, the cost will be high. We need to find the parameters that will bring the cost down to its minimum value.

Gradient descent uses mathematical methods to calculate the gradient of the cost function at the current stage of training (that is, for the current parameter settings, Θ). This gradient can then be used to calculate whether we need to increase or decrease each weight and bias in the network to improve it. Through repetitive application of this technique, the network parameters are optimized to produce a good result. Gradient descent is akin to rolling down the slope of the function in Figure 3-8. There is a risk that you will roll to a nonoptimum place, marked on the graph as "good parameter optimization." Here you would get "stuck" because you would need to roll uphill first to reach the "superb parameter optimization" location. This point is referred to as a "local minimum." Techniques can be employed during gradient descent to reduce this risk.[5]

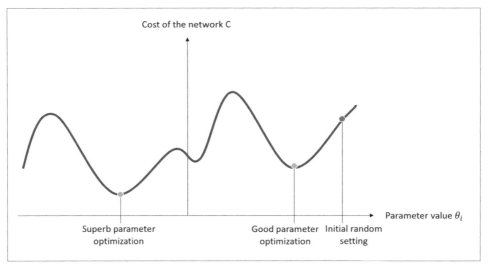

Figure 3-8. Using gradient descent, parameters of the network are tuned to minimize the cost (loss) during training.

The method of deciding which weights and biases are updated and by how much during the deep neural network training phase is known as *backpropagation* because the loss calculated for the output layer is "pushed back" through the network to cause the

---

5 In deep learning, there's an additional interesting complication whereby the number of potential changeable parameters results in *saddle points* in the cost graph. These are points that appear to be a minimum for one parameter, but a maximum for another. To picture this visually, think of a point at the center of a horse's saddle where one direction takes you up and another takes you downward.

relevant adjustments in the weight and bias parameters. The math for backpropagation is complicated and not necessary for understanding adversarial examples.[6] However, if you are curious and would like to understand this and the feed-forward aspects of neural network processing (as introduced in "DNN Internals and Feed-Forward Processing" on page 34) in greater detail, some links to useful resources are included in this book's GitHub repository (*http://bit.ly/2x5Kg5I*).

The notion of gradient descent is an important and recurring one throughout machine learning. It's a technique usually employed for optimizing models during training. However, we will see in Chapter 5 that the technique can also be applied to optimize the generation of adversarial examples.

Creating a Simple Image Classifier

Creating and training a deep learning model from scratch is a difficult task requiring understanding of the mathematics behind feed-forward processing and backpropagation. Nowadays, however, there are multiple libraries available to automatically build and train models, making it extremely simple to create a DNN without needing to code the underpinning algorithms.

Jupyter Notebook for Simple Image Classifier

The code included in this book is available for download from the book's GitHub repository (*http://bit.ly/2ISaGgG*).

To access and run the code and to set up dependencies and install the Jupyter notebook, see the instructions (*http://bit.ly/2ZxWnEI*) in the GitHub repository.

The code snippets in this section can be found in the Jupyter notebook chapter03/fashionMNIST_classifier.ipynb (*http://bit.ly/31JsseI*).

This section shows the primary code steps required to create a classification model for the Fashion-MNIST image data in Python. It's a network that demonstrates how easy it is to create a deep model using open software libraries. We'll use the TensorFlow deep learning library with the Keras API to build and train the model. This code is based on one of the online tutorials provided as an introduction to Keras.[7]

---

6 Backpropagation uses the chain rule, a mathematical technique that enables $f(\mathbf{x})$ to be optimized based on the contribution of the functions in each layer of the DNN.

7 You can see the original tutorial (*http://bit.ly/2KXQnAW*) on the TensorFlow site. The Keras tutorials (*http://bit.ly/2WOw1MZ*) are excellent resources for an early introduction to the Keras programming model.

Fully connected means that every node in each layer is connected to every node in the subsequent layer. It is also *feed-forward*, meaning that the computation travels from the input layer sequentially through all the hidden layers, and out of the output layer.

First, import the required libraries, TensorFlow, and its version of the Keras library:

```
import tensorflow as tf
from tensorflow import keras
```

The Fashion-MNIST data is provided with Keras. There are two datasets provided, one for training the model and one for evaluating it. Both datasets comprise a list of images with their corresponding labels. The labels are provided with the test data to evaluate how good the model is by testing it with each test image and checking whether the result matches the expected label.

It's also handy to provide a list of classification names corresponding to the 10 possible clothing classifications. This will enable us to print the name of the classification rather than just its number (e.g., "T-shirt/top" rather than "0") later on:

```
fashion_mnist = keras.datasets.fashion_mnist

(train_images,train_labels),(test_images,test_labels) = fashion_mnist.load_data()

class_names = ['T-shirt/top', 'Trouser', 'Pullover', 'Dress', 'Coat',
               'Sandal', 'Shirt', 'Sneaker', 'Bag', 'Ankle boot']
```

Let's take a look at the image at index 9, shown in Figure 3-9:

```
import matplotlib.pyplot as plt
plt.gca().grid(False)
plt.imshow(test_images[9], cmap=plt.cm.binary)
```

Each image in the dataset comprises an array of pixels, each with a value depicting its intensity: 0 to 255. We need to normalize the values for the input layer of the DNN so that each lies between 0 and 1:

```
train_images = train_images/255.0
test_images = test_images/255.00
```

The Keras programming interface provides a simple way to create a model layer by layer with the appropriate neuron activation functions (in this case ReLU or softmax). The following code illustrates how to create a model architecture like that shown in Figure 3-7. The compile step also includes variables to define the way that the model learns and how it judges its accuracy:

```
model = keras.Sequential([keras.layers.Flatten(input_shape=(28,28)),
                          keras.layers.Dense(56, activation='relu'),
                          keras.layers.Dense(56, activation='relu'),
                          keras.layers.Dense(10, activation='softmax')
                          ])
model.compile(optimizer=tf.keras.optimizers.Adam(), ❶
```

```
loss='sparse_categorical_crossentropy', ❷
metrics=['accuracy']) ❸
```

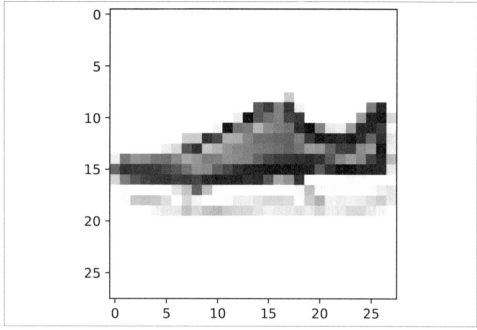

Figure 3-9. Code output

❶ The `optimizer` parameter determines how the network will be optimized during training. The `Adam` optimizer is a good choice in this case to speed up the training as it uses an intelligent algorithm to perform gradient descent.

❷ Here's where the previously described loss function is defined. The loss function `sparse_categorical_crossentropy` is a variation on `categorical_crossen tropy`, used when the target labels are passed as a single list of values rather than a zeroed array with the relevant value set to 1. This representation is possible if exactly one class is true at a time. For example, a label representing "Pullover" is represented as 2 in the training label data as it's the third label in a list starting at 0, rather than [0, 0, 1, 0, 0, 0, 0, 0, 0, 0].

❸ The `metrics` parameter determines how the model will be judged during training.

We can take a look at the generated model to ensure it is what we expected:

```
model.summary()
```

This generates the following output:

Layer (type)	Output Shape	Param #
flatten_2 (Flatten)	(None, 784)	0
dense_4 (Dense)	(None, 56)	43960
dense_5 (Dense)	(None, 56)	3192
dense_6 (Dense)	(None, 10)	570

```
Total params: 47,722
Trainable params: 47,722
Non-trainable params: 0
```

Looks good. The total number of parameters also matches the value calculated in "How a DNN Learns" on page 38.

Using the principles described in this same section, a single line of code is required to train the model. The function here is called `fit` because it is fitting the model to the requirements of the training data. The `epochs` parameter defines the number of training iterations—that is, the number of times that the model will be refined based on its calculated loss across all the training examples. Let's set that to 6:

```
model.fit(train_images, train_labels, epochs=6)
```

Which generates the following output:

```
Epoch 1/6
60000/60000 [==============================] - 4s 66us/sample - loss: 0.5179 - acc: 0.8166
Epoch 2/6
60000/60000 [==============================] - 4s 58us/sample - loss: 0.3830 - acc: 0.8616
Epoch 3/6
60000/60000 [==============================] - 3s 58us/sample - loss: 0.3452 - acc: 0.8739
Epoch 4/6
60000/60000 [==============================] - 4s 59us/sample - loss: 0.3258 - acc: 0.8798
Epoch 5/6
60000/60000 [==============================] - 4s 59us/sample - loss: 0.3087 - acc: 0.8863
Epoch 6/6
60000/60000 [==============================] - 4s 59us/sample - loss: 0.2933 - acc: 0.8913
Out[8]:
<tensorflow.python.keras.callbacks.History at 0x22f2b3b06d8>
```

As you can see, Keras displays the model's loss and accuracy during each stage of the training phase with respect to the training data. The accuracy of the model is the percentage of training data samples that it is correctly classifying. The loss decreases in each epoch as the model's accuracy increases. This is gradient descent in action! The model's weights and biases are being adjusted to minimize the loss, as previously illustrated in Figure 3-8.

Keras provides the following method for checking the accuracy of the generated model after it's been trained. We want to be sure that the model works well on data other than that provided during training, so the test dataset (test images with their expected labels) is used for this evaluation:

```
test_loss, test_acc = model.evaluate(test_images, test_labels)
print('Model accuracy based on test data:', test_acc)
```

Which generates this output:

```
10000/10000 [==================] - 0s 35us/sample - loss: 0.3623 - acc: 0.8704
Model accuracy based on test data: 0.8704
```

The model accuracy is slightly lower on the test data than the training data, illustrating that the model has been tailored a little too much for the test data. This is called *overfitting* because the model fits the training data too accurately and has not generalized enough for other data. Still, it's fairly good, returning nearly 90% correct answers for the test dataset.

Let's look at the predictions that the model generates for a particular image in the test dataset. We will take the image at index 6. First, here's the code to plot the image and its label (Figure 3-10) to show what we are expecting:

```
image_num = 6
print("Expected label: ", class_names[test_labels[image_num]])

import matplotlib.pyplot as plt
imgplot = plt.imshow(test_images[image_num], cmap=plt.cm.binary)
```

```
Expected label:  Coat
```

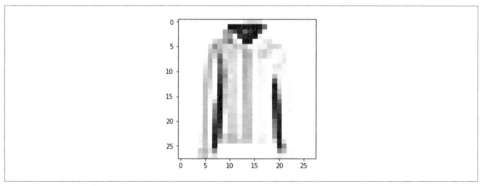

Figure 3-10. Code output

Keras uses the function `predict` to generate predictions for a set of inputs. The following code generates a set of model predictions for each of the test data images and prints the predictions for our selected image:

```
predictions = model.predict(test_images)
print("Predictions for image:", predictions[image_num])
```

This generates the following output:

```
Predictions for image: [2.0931453e-04 2.5958019e-05 5.3381161e-03
  9.3024952e-05 9.8870182e-01 3.4905071e-08 5.4028798e-03 2.1192791e-10
    2.2762216e-04 1.2793139e-06]
```

The output is the vector produced in the final layer of the model for the selected image. The softmax layer ensures that all the values add up to 1. Just to prove this, let's add them up:

```
total_probability = 0
for i in range(10):
    total_probability += predictions[image_num][i]
print(total_probability)
```

This produces the following output:

```
1.0000000503423947
```

Here's the code that takes the highest prediction and returns the associated clothing classification as a string:

```
import numpy as np
index_of_highest_prediction = np.argmax(predictions[image_num])

print("Classification: ", class_names[index_of_highest_prediction])
print("Confidence:     ", predictions[image_num][index_of_highest_prediction])
```

This generates the following output:

```
Classification:  Coat
Confidence:      0.9887018
```

The image has been correctly classified as a "Coat" and we can see that the model was confident in this prediction.

Finally, let's save the model so we can use it again later:

```
model.save("../models/fashionMNIST.h5") ❶
```

❶ The model is converted to HDF5 (*https://www.hdfgroup.org/*) format and stored in the *models* directory.

We will return to this classifier throughout the book to explore adversarial examples.

## CHAPTER 4

DNN Processing for Image, Audio, and Video

In Chapter 3, we created a neural network able to classify simple images of items of clothing to illustrate the principles of neural network technology. However, the simplicity of the Fashion-MNIST data meant that it was not a scenario with much realism. DNNs are able to solve far more complex problems through a wide range of architectures other than simple feed-forward, fully connected networks.

There are many different ways of designing a DNN, using different layering structures, different types of layers, and different ways of connecting the nodes. The network will depend upon the task, and these different flavors of DNN may also be combined with each other or other algorithms, enabling them to perform even more complex tasks.

This chapter, therefore, considers how DNN technology can be applied to more realistic image, audio, and video processing. We'll build on the basics from Chapter 3 to understand the concepts behind the neural networks commonly used in these fields and how these technologies are combined with more traditional processing to get the best results.

This discussion will focus on two key network types: *convolutional neural networks* (CNNs) and *recurrent neural networks* (RNNs). These demonstrate common patterns in the context of image and audio processing and also are referenced in discussions later in the book. CNNs and RNNs are not the only DNNs relevant to image, audio, and video processing, but they are the networks in most common use. The descriptions given here are introductory only. If you are interested in learning more about a particular network type, consult the resources (*http://bit.ly/2x5Kg5I*) available in this book's GitHub repository.

To understand how DNNs can be used to process image and audio, and to appreciate how the data may be manipulated to create adversarial examples, we must begin with the computational representation of the data. Each section in this chapter, therefore, begins by considering the digital encoding of the data for the particular data type (image, audio, and video). In later chapters, it will become clear how the digital encoding of the data and specifically the *precision* of that encoding will directly affect the ability to create adversarial input. Alterations to the data precision during data compression or transformation steps might (inadvertently or deliberately) remove adversarial content.

By the time you reach the end of the chapter you'll have acquired sufficient knowledge of how image, audio, and video are digitally represented, as well as familiarity with common neural network design patterns, to understand the discussions on adversarial examples in the chapters that follow.

Image

At the most basic level, human visual processing enables us to perceive light, a portion of the electromagnetic spectrum with wavelengths in the range of 200 to 700 nanometers. Alternatively, light can be described in terms of frequency, where the frequency of the wave is the inverse of the wavelength. Frequency is measured by number of cycles per second in Hertz (Hz), and light has a frequency range of roughly 430 to 750 terahertz (THz). Lower frequencies correspond to infrared electromagnetic radiation, and higher frequencies correspond to ultraviolet.

Three types of color receptors ("cones") in our eyes are sensitive to different wavelengths of light. One type of cone is sensitive to longer wavelengths within the visible spectrum (red light), the second to the medium wavelengths (green light), and the third to the shorter wavelengths (blue light). These receptors send signals to the brain when light of the appropriate color wavelength reaches them; so, a cone that is sensitive to light from the blue end of the spectrum will send a signal to the brain when blue light enters the eye, with the magnitude of the signal corresponding to the amount of blue light. Our visual cortex then combines these signals to create the actual color that we perceive.

Digital Representation of Images

Digital images are made of pixels, where each pixel is a discrete value representing the analog light waveform at that point. The Fashion-MNIST images are, obviously, a pretty poor representation of real life. For starters, an image in the Fashion-MNIST database is represented by its monochrome pixel intensities, each pixel having a value between 0 and 255. A pixel value of 0 represents black (minimum intensity), and a pixel value of 255 represents white (maximum intensity). Each value takes exactly 1 byte of storage (because 8 bits can represent 256 possible values).

One approach in showing color images is to represent 256 colors using the same amount of storage. This requires a "color palette"—essentially a mapping to assign each of the 256 values to its allocated color. While this is quite expressive, it still doesn't provide sufficient variety and range of colors to adequately capture realistic images. Therefore, for photographs, each pixel is typically represented by *three* values —one for red, one for green, and one for blue. These red-green-blue or *RGB* values typically are allowed 1 byte of storage each, so each has a value between 0 and 255. To calculate the color of an individual pixel, the RGB values for that pixel are combined. This representation is very flexible; RGB values between 0 and 255 allow a palette of 16,777,216 possible colors. Yes, you guessed it, this notion of creating colors from three separate red, green, and blue inputs was inspired by the cones color receptors in the human eye.

The Fashion-MNIST images are not only monochrome but also extremely low resolution—28 x 28 pixels, a mere 784 pixels per image. Even a relatively low-resolution 0.3 megapixel photograph has approximately 640 x 480 pixels. Cameras nowadays take photographs with far greater pixel accuracy (2 megapixels and above).

The precision of an image is measured by the depth of its color (the number of bits used to indicate the value of each pixel) and the number of pixels. These two attributes are respectively referred to as the *color resolution* and *spatial resolution*, as shown in Figure 4-1. Reducing spatial resolution results in less smooth lines. Reducing color resolution results in more blocky textures.

The overall image precision selected will depend upon how it was captured (the camera's settings), its usage (for example, size of print required), and storage constraints. There are several common image formats used for image processing, but JPEGs (standardized by the Joint Photographic Experts Group) are good for both capturing realism in photos requiring color depth (using RGB blending) and for high pixel resolution.

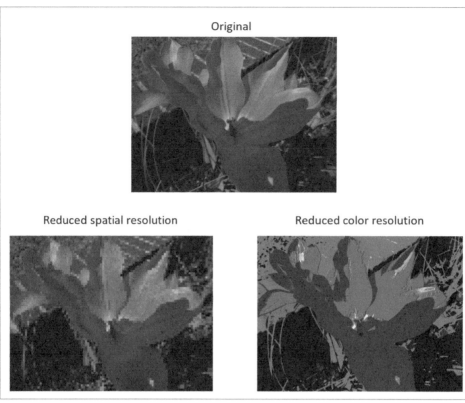

Figure 4-1. The effect of reduced spatial and color resolution on an image

DNNs for Image Processing

The most basic task of image processing is to classify an image based on its primary content, as we did in Chapter 3 for the Fashion-MNIST dataset. Most image processing will be more complex than this, however. For example:

Scene classification

Classification of a scene (such as "beach scene" or "street scene"), rather than classification based on the most prevalent object.

Object detection and localization

Such as detection of faces within an image and establishing where they are in the image.

Semantic segmentation

Fine-grained depiction of regions in the image, corresponding to different classifications. An example is illustrated in Figure 4-2.

Facial recognition

DNNs can be used for facial recognition systems. With sufficient training data, the problem of facial recognition can become simply a classification task, where the number of classifications equals the number of individuals in the dataset. A facial recognition system might be combined with a detection algorithm to extract faces from a scene and recognize them.

Figure 4-2. An example of image segmentation[1]

Solutions for some of these tasks using traditional (nonneural network) vision processing techniques have existed for many years. For example, using more traditional image processing techniques, faces can be detected within an image, extracted, and resized, and the data transformed and normalized. Algorithms can then extract the *fiducial points* of the face—that is, the important values for positioning the face and for facial recognition, such as the corners of the mouth or edges of the eyes. The fiducial measurements can then be exploited to recognize the individual, typically through statistical (including machine learned) approaches. DNNs, however, have enabled a step-change in vision processing capability and accuracy and are replacing, or being used in conjunction with, traditional approaches across image processing.

Introducing CNNs

An underlying challenge with vision processing is understanding the image contents regardless of spatial positioning and size. We avoided this problem in Chapter 3 because each clothing item in the Fashion-MNIST dataset is of roughly the same size, oriented correctly, and placed centrally within the image.

---

1 This image was generated using SegNet (*http://bit.ly/2ZyoOSQ*).

In real life such consistent sizing and positioning within an image is highly unlikely. If a DNN's predicted probability of a "cat" within an image depends upon the existence of certain "whiskery" aspects of the picture, there is no way of guaranteeing where those whiskery aspects will be located or what size they will be. It will depend upon the size, orientation, and position of the cat. What's needed is some clever way of extracting patterns from within an image, *wherever* they are located. When we have extracted patterns, we can use these to perform higher-level image processing.

Extracting *spatial* patterns within data is exactly what a convolutional neural network is able to do. This means that CNNs are usually the neural networks of choice for image processing tasks.

A CNN is a network that contains one or more *convolutional layers*—these are layers that use an algorithm to extract features from the image, regardless of their location. A convolutional layer "convolves" one or more *filters* across every part of the image. In other words, it performs some filtering on a tiny part of the image, then performs the same filtering on an adjacent, overlapping part, and so on until it has covered the complete image. The convolution means moving the filter across the image in small overlapping steps, as shown in Figure 4-3.

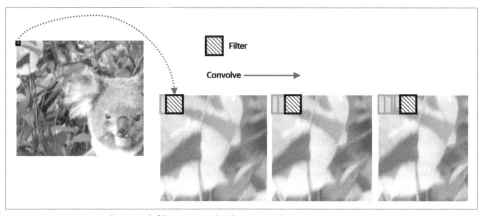

Figure 4-3. A convolutional filter is applied iteratively across an image

As the filter is applied to a small part of the image, it generates a numeric score that indicates how accurately the image part represents the feature filter.

To give you a better idea of how this works, a trivial 3 x 3 filter representing a vertical dark line against a light background is shown in Figure 4-4; it is just a simple matrix of numbers. Examples of its application to two different 3 x 3 pixel segments of a monochrome image are shown. Elementwise multiplication is performed between the feature filter and the image segment (this is simply a case of multiplying the value in each matrix with the corresponding one in the other to create a new matrix). The average (mean) of the values in the resulting matrix is then calculated.

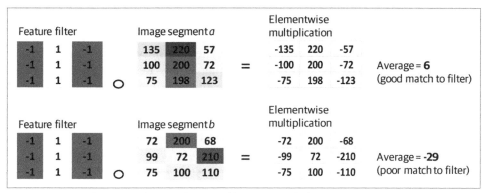

Figure 4-4. Application of a simple 3 x 3 filter to two different image segments

As you can see, the value calculated for image segment *a* is a relatively high 6, indicating that the image segment represents a little bit of vertical line. The filter output for image segment *b* is –29, correctly indicating that this part of the image is not representative of a vertical line.

All the values resulting from convolving the filter over the image are placed in an array that will be output from the convolutional layer. This is called a *feature map*.

In practice, the filters are more complex than those in Figure 4-4, and the values are optimized during training. As with the weights and bias parameters learned in Chapter 3, the filters are typically set randomly and learned. So the convolutional layers learn the important features in the training data, and encapsulate those features within the filter maps.

At this stage, let's pause and clarify exactly what is passed to, and returned from, a convolutional layer. If the convolutional layer is at the start of the network, it is taking an image as input. For a color image represented by RGB values, this is a 3D array: one dimension for the image's height, one dimension for its width, and one dimension for each of the red, green, and blue color channels. The 3D "shape" of the data being passed to the neural network for a 224 x 224 pixel image would be:

```
shape = (224, 224, 3)
```

A convolutional layer may apply more than one filter, which means that it will return a stack of feature maps—one for each time a filter is applied across the input. This means that a convolutional layer might generate more data than it consumes! To reduce the dimensionality (and noise) from the output, a convolutional layer is typically followed by a *pooling* layer. During pooling, small windows of the data are iteratively stepped over (similar to the way the convolution filter "steps" across the image). The data in each window is "pooled" to give a single value. There are several approaches to the pooling step. For example, we might perform pooling by taking the average value of the windowed data, or by taking the maximum value. This latter case of *max pooling* has the effect of shrinking the data and also relaxing the precision of the filtering if the filter wasn't a perfect match by discarding lower values.

Typically, the layers in the first part of a CNN alternate in type—convolution, pooling, convolution, pooling, etc. Layers containing simple ReLU functionality might also be incorporated to remove negative values, and these may be logically combined with the convolutional step. Figure 4-5 shows one way that these layers might be organized.

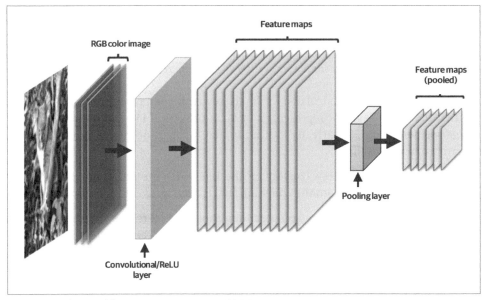

Figure 4-5. Typical layering pattern in a CNN

To see how the convolutional layers might be incorporated in an example image classification, take a look at Figure 4-6. This CNN uses the convolutional–pooling layer combination to extract relevant features from the image. The features extracted by these layers are then passed to the latter part of the network, which has fully connected layers, as used for our simple neural network example in Chapter 3. This is where the calculations are made that ultimately determine the network's predictions and classification of the image.

You'll be beginning to realize that there's a lot of data in the form of multidimensional arrays passing between the layers of a typical DNN. These multidimensional arrays are often referred to as *tensors* (hence the name of the "TensorFlow" library introduced in Chapter 3). Also, Figure 4-6 is simplified for clarity; an image DNN will typically take batches of images as input, rather than a single one.

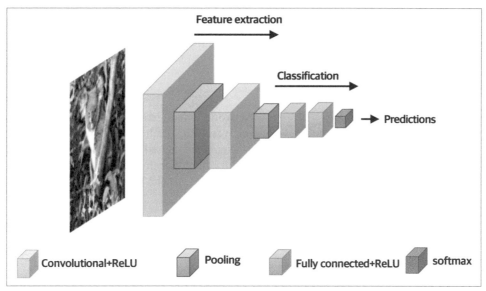

Figure 4-6. An example CNN image classification architecture

This batching is useful during training, when the model is being optimized for high volumes of training instances, and it also makes processing of multiple images simpler when the model is being tested and used operationally. Therefore, the dimensionality of an input tensor for a CNN will be four, not three. For example, if 50 color images of 224 x 224 pixels were passed to a neural network, the shape of this 4D input tensor would be:

```
shape = (50, 224, 224, 3)
```

That's 50 images, each of 224 x 224 pixels, and 3 color channels.

Most image processing neural networks take advantage of convolutional layers, so are classified as CNNs. However, their architectures vary considerably. In fact, one of the interesting challenges in DNN processing over recent years has been to create new architectures that are more accurate, learn faster, or take up less storage. There have been many approaches for image processing, as described in the following note.

Some Examples of Image Processing Neural Networks

Approaches for image processing include the following:

VGG

 The VGG network has a very simple architecture, similar to that depicted in Figure 4-6. The depth of the network is indicated by the number in its name (e.g., VGG16 has 16 layers).

The VGG architecture was first introduced by Simonyan and Zisserman in "Very Deep Convolutional Networks for Large-Scale Image Recognition."[2] At the time of development, VGG16 and VGG19 were considered very deep, but VGG has a problem in that it is slow to train and the deployed model is relatively large (compared to more recent architectures).

ResNet
ResNet (short for "Residual Neural Network") is an extremely deep neural network. ResNet addresses the problem of "vanishing gradients" during training by skipping layers early on. Vanishing gradients are caused by the gradients of the cost function becoming so small during training that the network fails to learn. Again, the number in the name of each flavor of ResNet indicates the number of layers in the architecture.

The ResNet architecture was introduced by He et al. in "Deep Residual Learning for Image Recognition."[3]

Inception
Developed by Google, the initial Inception architecture (called "GoogLeNet") is 22 layers deep and has approximately 4 million parameters. Since this first incarnation, Google has improved the Inception architecture with subsequent versions and has also created a hybrid Inception-ResNet network.

The Inception architecture was introduced by Szegedy et al. in "Going Deeper with Convolutions."[4]

Audio

Sound is our ears' interpretation of pressure waves generated in the environment by anything that causes the air to vibrate. As with any waveforms, sound waves can be characterized by their *amplitude* and *frequency*.

The amplitude of the wave represents the variation in pressure and relates to our perception of the loudness of any noise. As with light, the frequency of the wave is the inverse of the wavelength, measured in Hertz (Hz). Shorter sound waves have higher frequencies and higher pitch. Longer sound waves have lower frequencies and lower pitch. Humans typically are able to hear waves ranging from 20 Hz to 20,000 Hz, and

---

2 K. Simonyan and A. Zisserman, "Very Deep Convolutional Networks for Large-Scale Image Recognition," ImageNet Large Scale Visual Recognition Challenge (2014), *http://bit.ly/2IupnYt*.

3 K. He et al. "Deep Residual Learning for Image Recognition," ImageNet Large Scale Visual Recognition Challenge (2015), *http://bit.ly/2x40Bb6*.

4 Christian Szegedy et al., "Going Deeper with Convolutions," ImageNet Large Scale Visual Recognition Challenge (2014), *http://bit.ly/2Xp4PIU*.

this is what we might classify as "sound." However, for other animals or for digital sensors, this range might be quite different.

The simple characterization of amplitude and frequency fails to grasp the full complexity of sounds. To understand why, take a look at the sound waves in Figure 4-7. Sound wave *a* and sound wave *b* are clearly very different, but they have the exact same amplitude and fundamental frequency.

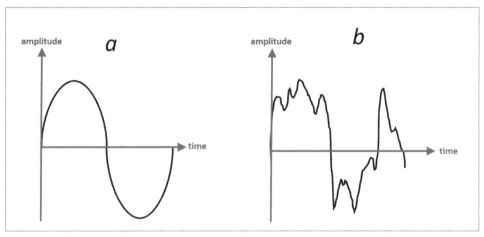

Figure 4-7. Two very different sound waves sharing the same wavelength (frequency) and amplitude

Sound wave *a* illustrates what we might consider a "perfect" simple sound wave representing a single tone. Sound wave *b*, however, is indicative of the messy sound that we hear day-to-day—that is, a wave derived from multiple frequencies from varying sources that bounce off objects and combine into complicated harmonics.

Digital Representation of Audio

Analog sound waves are transformed to digital format by capturing the intensity of the wave at regular sampling intervals. The simplest representation of a digital audio signal is therefore a list of numbers, where each number depicts the intensity of the sound wave at a specific time.

Once again, let's think about precision as this will be important to an adversary in generating adversarial audio. Precision of digital audio depends upon two things: the *rate* at which the samples are taken and the *accuracy* of each intensity value. This is measured in terms of the frequency at which the analog data was sampled and the accuracy with which each sample is encoded—the sample rate and number of bits per sample (or "bit depth"), respectively. The bit depth determines the accuracy with which each sound sample is captured, akin to color resolution in image data. The sampling rate is the audio temporal equivalent to image spatial resolution. This is illustrated in Figure 4-8.

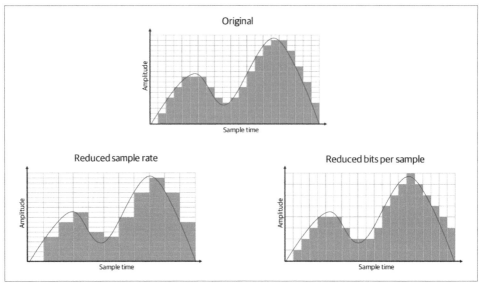

Figure 4-8. The effect of reduced sample rate and bits per sample in digital audio

DNNs for Audio Processing

As with image processing, audio processing existed for many years prior to the prevalence of DNN technology. DNNs remove the requirement to handcraft the features of the audio. However, audio processing using neural networks still often exploits traditional methods to extract low-level feature information common to all tasks.

Very broadly speaking, we might adopt one of two approaches to processing audio data using neural network technology:

- First, we could train the data using the raw digitally encoded audio. The network would then learn to extract the features relevant to its task. This can produce highly accurate models, but the amount of data required for the network to learn from raw, messy audio is vast, so this approach is often not feasible.
- Alternatively, we can give the neural network a head start by exploiting more traditional audio preprocessing steps, then using the preprocessed data to train the network. Preprocessing has the advantage that it reduces the amount of learning required by the network, thereby simplifying the training step and reducing the amount of data required for training.

Audio preprocessing usually uses a *Fourier transform*, which is a really neat mathematical calculation to convert the complicated waveforms that represent many frequencies (as shown earlier in this chapter in Figure 4-7, image *b*) into their constituent frequency parts. This information can then be turned into a *spectrogram*, representing frequencies as they change over time.

To create a spectrogram, the amplitude of each frequency is calculated within consecutive (and possibly overlapping) time windows using a Fourier transform. To create a visual depiction of a spectrogram, these intensities can be represented using color and the frequency time windows concatenated to produce something like the images in Figure 4-9. The image on the left illustrates the concept; the one on the right is a real spectrogram.

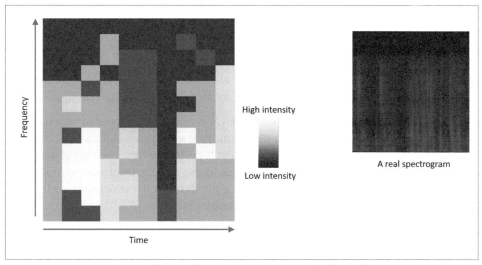

Figure 4-9. A spectrogram depicts changing intensities at different frequencies over time

In some cases, the preprocessing step may also extract only aspects of the audio that are pertinent to the task and discard other information. For example, audio may be transformed to *mel-frequency cepstrum* (MFC) representation to more closely represent the way in which audio data is treated in the human auditory system. This is particularly useful in processing that mimics human comprehension, such as speech processing.

Let's consider a fundamental task in audio processing—classification. This is required as a precursor to other, more complex tasks such a speech processing. As in image classification, the task is to assign an audio clip to a classification based on the audio characteristics. The set of possible classifications will depend upon the test data and the application, but could be, for example, identifying a particular birdsong or a type of sound, such as "engine."

So, how could we do this using a DNN? One method is to repurpose the CNN architecture by simply taking the spectrogram image and essentially turning the problem into one of image processing. The visual features within the spectrogram will be indicative of the audio that produced it, so, for example, a barking dog sound might have visual features that a CNN architecture would extract. This solution is essentially converting the time dimension into a spatial one for processing by the network.

Alternatively, a different type of neural network capable of dealing with *sequences* could be used. This type of network is called a recurrent neural network.

Introducing RNNs

RNNs are able to learn patterns and correlations in sequential data by processing each piece of data in the context of what has been processed before it and what comes afterward. Examples of data with meaning determined by sequence are text and time-based information such as speech. Patterns across *sequences* of data are not going to be detected by a simple feed-forward DNN or CNN because they only consider a single input in isolation. RNNs, however, are able to find correlations or patterns in sequential data by maintaining some kind of memory (or state) between inputs.

The simplest architectural approach for an RNN is for a hidden layer to take its input not only from the previous layer but also from its own output. Put another way, the output from the layer is fed forward to the next layer (as we have seen previously) but also fed *back* into itself, providing some input to the current layer's calculation. This allows the hidden layer's previous output to contribute to the processing of the current input. Figure 4-10 shows a simple illustration of this.

A challenge facing simple RNNs is that they are unable to learn patterns that span across longer sequences; that is, correlations that are separated by other data in the sequence. A good example of this is speech, where the likelihood of a particular phoneme might depend upon the sounds heard a few moments previously. During training of these simple RNNs, the cost function gradients have a tendency to vanish or become infinite. Essentially, the mathematical optimization step isn't able to reach a good solution that accounts for these longer-spaced sequential relationships. This makes it impossible to adequately minimize the cost function so that the RNN performs well.

A more complex type of RNN called a *long short-term memory* (LSTM) network is commonly used to address this problem. The RNN nodes within an LSTM are far more complex units than shown in Figure 4-10, comprising a component that retains state and regulators (called "gates") that control the data flow. This more complex architecture enables the network to both "remember" previous data in the sequence and "forget" previous data that is deemed less important. It's this ability to forget that makes optimizing the network during training possible.

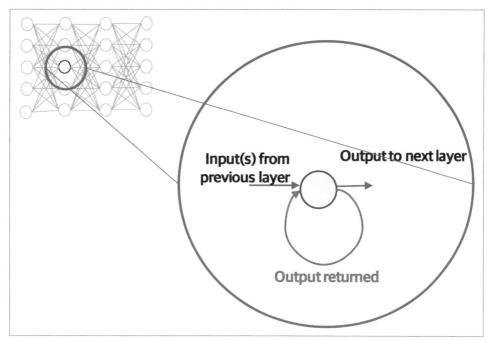

Figure 4-10. Basic concept underpinning RNN architectures

The various types of LSTMs have slightly different LSTM unit designs (for example, different gates). LSTMs have proven very effective across several applications, such as handwriting and speech recognition.

LSTMs are a common architectural choice for audio processing to enable the network to learn audio patterns that span time. This is obviously very applicable to understanding audio where the meaning of its parts depends on what is on either side (such as birdsong or speech). As an example, Figure 4-11 depicts the use of an RNN in processing audio that has been previously converted into a spectrogram. The preprocessed frequency information is a 2D tensor (a 2D matrix) representing the amplitude of each frequency in one dimension and time in the other.[5] In this example, the same number of frames are output from the RNN, each one corresponding to the output of the RNN for a particular input in the sequence—one set of sound frequencies for a particular time generates a set of probabilities of possible sounds.

---

5 This assumes a single audio channel. If the audio contains multiple channels, there is a third dimension representing the channel depth.

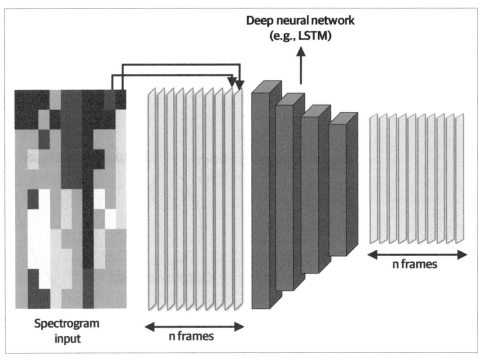

Figure 4-11. Typical processing chain for audio, with spectrogram preprocessing

Speech Processing

Speech processing is a fascinating application of DNNs which has considerable relevance to adversarial audio—many motivations for generating adversarial sound are likely for fooling speech recognition systems.

Speech recognition is a particularly challenging computational task. First, there's the extraction of the sounds that form the building blocks of speech, known as *phonemes*. People are sloppy with their speech, they have different accents, they speak at different speeds and pitches, and there's often background noise. All of this makes correct identification of each individual phoneme difficult. The extracted phonemes must then be mapped to real words and sentences. There may be many possible mappings; the correct mapping will depend on the language and the context.

In speech-to-text processing, the neural network is typically a part of a bigger processing chain. For example, a typical speech-to-text processing chain might look something like this:

1. An LSTM takes an audio MFC spectrogram as input and produces a list of the current probabilities for each of the possible symbols in a text system. This is the

step depicted in Figure 4-11. In English, the probabilities would refer to the probabilities of each of the letters "a" to "z" and the "word space" character.[6]

2. The probability distributions are output from the LSTM at the same rate as they are input. This is a big problem because someone could be speaking really sssslllloooowwwwllllllyyyyy, or they might speakreallyfast. So, the length of the probability sequence indicates the length of the input audio, rather than the length of a phonetic transcription. Working out the alignments of the audio input with the phonetic transcription is another step in the processing.

A commonly used approach is *connectionist temporal classification* (CTC).[7] CTC essentially "squashes" and tidies up the symbol probabilities to create probable phrases. For example, CTC would take a high-probability output such as _cc_aa_t and generate cat.

3. At this stage, there's a list of probabilities for different phonetic transcriptions but no decisive phrase. The final step requires taking the most probable "raw" phrases and mapping them to transcripts appropriate to the language. A lot of this stuff is not possible to learn through generalization (for example, many words in English do not map to their phonetic equivalents). Therefore, this part of the processing likely uses a "language model" that encodes information about the language, probability of sequences, spellings and grammar, and real names.

Video

Video is a combination of moving image and audio. For completeness, in this section we'll have a brief look at moving images, as audio was covered previously.

Digital Representation of Video

Video is simply a sequence of images referred to as *frames*. Precision of video therefore is a combination of image precision and also the number of frames captured per second (the frame rate).

DNNs for Video Processing

It's possible to analyze video simply by considering each image in isolation, which may be perfectly adequate for many scenarios. For example, facial detection and recognition can be performed on a frame-by-frame basis by feeding each frame into the

---

6 There's also a special blank character, different from the space, to represent a gap in the audio.

7 A. Graves et al., "Connectionist Temporal Classification: Labelling Unsegmented Sequence Data with Recurrent Neural Networks," *Proceedings of the 23rd International Conference on Machine Learning* (2006): 369–376, *http://bit.ly/2XUC2sU*.

neural network one by one. However, the additional dimension of time opens opportunities for understanding movement. This allows video understanding to extend to more complex semantic understanding, such as:

Entity tracking
> Tracking the paths of specific objects (such as people or vehicles) over time. This might include inferring positional information when the entity is obscured or leaves the scene.

Activity recognition
> Extending the idea of object recognition to detect activities within a scene using additional information pertaining to movement. For example, this could be understanding gestures used to control a device or detecting behavior (such as aggression) within a scene. The ability to recognize activities within videos enables other higher-level processing, such as video description.

As with image and audio, there are more classical approaches to video processing that do not use neural networks. But, once again, DNNs remove the requirement to hand-code the rules for extracting features.

Unsurprisingly, the element of time will add complexity to processing frames. There are, however, approaches to dealing with this additional dimension using the architectural principles described previously for CNNs and RNNs. For example, one option is to exploit *3D Convolutions*. This extension of the convolutional principles used in image CNNs includes a third temporal dimension across frames which is processed in the same way as spatial dimensions within each frame. Alternatively, it's possible to combine spatial learning of a CNN with sequential learning borrowed from an RNN architecture. This can be done by exploiting the CNN to extract features on a per-frame basis and then using these features as sequential inputs to an RNN.

Whereas color images are passed to a neural network as a 4D tensor, video inputs are represented by a whopping 5D tensor. For example, if we have one minute's worth of video sampled at 15 frames per second, that gives us 900 frames. Let's assume low-definition video (224 x 224 pixels) and color using RGB channels. We have a 4D tensor with the following shape:

```
shape = (900, 224, 224, 3)
```

If there are 10 videos in the input batch, the shape becomes 5D:

```
shape = (10, 900, 224, 224, 3)
```

Adversarial Considerations

This chapter provided an introduction to the variety of neural networks available, with a focus on those commonly used for image, audio, and video processing. Some aspects of these neural networks are defined by the software developer, whereas others are learned during training. Aspects defined by the developer are defined as the *model architecture* and the learned parts of the model as the *model parameters*. It's not important to understand the details of specific DNN architectures and parameters in order to acquire a good conceptual understanding of adversarial examples. However, it is good to appreciate the difference between a model's architecture and its learned parameters because an understanding of the target network architecture and its parameters can be important when generating adversarial examples:

Model architecture

>At the highest level, the model architecture is the types of layers in the model and the order in which they are placed. The model architecture also defines the pre-determined aspects of the configuration of the model. In the code at the end of Chapter 3, we defined the number of layers, the types of layers (ReLU and softmax), and the size of each layer. More complex layers, such as CNN layers, introduce more architectural decisions, such as the size and number of filters in a convolutional layer, the type of pooling, and the pooling window size plus the convolving step movement (the "stride") for each of the pooling and convolutional steps.

Model parameters

>In terms of model parameters, most obvious are the values of the weights and biases, as learned during the training phase in the example in Chapter 3. There are often many other parameters that also must be learned in more complex layers, such as the values that make up each convolutional filter.

While there are not "set" architectures for any particular task, there are certainly reusable architectural patterns, such as convolutional layers or LSTM units.

Adversarial input has primarily been researched in the context of image classification and (to a lesser extent) speech recognition, but other similar types of tasks will also be susceptible to this trickery. For example, while most interest in adversarial imagery has related to fooling image classifiers, the adversarial techniques are also likely applicable to object detection and localization and semantic segmentation, as they are essentially extensions of the more basic classification task.[8] Facial recognition is another example—creating adversarial input to fool a facial recognition system does not, in principle, differ from creating adversarial images for misclassification of other objects. However, there may be other complexities; for example, the adversarial changes may be more difficult to hide on a face. In the audio domain, adversarial examples have been proven for speech recognition, but the same methods could also

---

8 This is demonstrated in Cihang Xie et al., "Adversarial Examples for Semantic Segmentation and Object Detection," *International Conference on Computer Vision* (2017), *http://bit.ly/2KrRg5E*.

be applied to simpler tasks (such as voice verification and more generic audio classification).

Image Classification Using ResNet50

To illustrate image classification, the examples in this book use ResNet50, rather than one of the other models available online. It's a fairly arbitrary decision based primarily on the fact that the model doesn't require much space (approximately 102 MB). All the other current state-of-the-art image classification neural networks have also been proven to be vulnerable to adversarial input.

This section demonstrates how to download the ResNet50 classifier and generate predictions for one or more images. Later, this will be useful for testing adversarial examples.

 You can find the code snippets in the Jupyter notebook chapter04/resnet50_classifier.ipynb (*http://bit.ly/2IpkqQy*) on the book's GitHub repository.

We begin by importing the TensorFlow and Keras libraries and the ResNet50 model:

```
import tensorflow as tf
from tensorflow import keras
from keras.applications.resnet50 import ResNet50
import numpy as np ❶

model = ResNet50(weights='imagenet', include_top=True) ❷
```

❶ We will use NumPy to manipulate the image data as a multidimensional array.

❷ This command instantiates the ResNet50 model that has been trained on ImageNet. include_top=True indicates that the final neural network layers that perform the classification should be included. This option is provided because these classification layers may not be required if the purpose of the model is to extract the relevant features only.

As with the Fashion-MNIST classifier, it's nice to see what the model looks like:

```
model.summary()
```

This generates the following output (the depth of ResNet50 makes the output from this call very lengthy, so only the initial and final layers are captured here):

```
Layer (type)                    Output Shape              Param #  Connected to
================================================================================
input_1 (InputLayer)            (None, 224, 224, 3)  0

conv1_pad (ZeroPadding2D)       (None, 230, 230, 3)  0               input_1[0][0]

conv1 (Conv2D)                  (None, 112, 112, 64) 9472            conv1_pad[0][0]

bn_conv1 (BatchNormalization)   (None, 112, 112, 64) 256             conv1[0][0]

activation_1 (Activation)       (None, 112, 112, 64) 0               bn_conv1[0][0]

pool1_pad (ZeroPadding2D)       (None, 114, 114, 64) 0               activation_1[0][0]

max_pooling2d_1 (MaxPooling2D)  (None, 56, 56, 64)   0               pool1_pad[0][0]


...


activation_49 (Activation)      (None, 7, 7, 2048)   0               add_16[0][0]

avg_pool (GlobalAveragePooling2(None, 2048)              0           activation_49[0][0]

fc1000 (Dense)                  (None, 1000)              2049000  avg_pool[0][0]
================================================================================
Total params: 25,636,712
Trainable params: 25,583,592
Non-trainable params: 53,120
```

Let's get an image to classify (Figure 4-12):

```
import matplotlib.pyplot as plt

img_path = '../images/koala.jpg' ❶
img = image_from_file(img_path, (224,224)) ❷
plt.imshow(img)
```

❶ You'll find a selection of images in the repository, but of course you can try your own as well.

❷ image_from_file is a simple helper utility to open an image and scale it to 244 x 244 pixels for input to the classifier. For brevity, this function is not included here, but it is included as a Python utility in the GitHub repository.

Figure 4-12. Code output

The image needs to undergo some preprocessing before it is passed to ResNet50. Keras provides the preprocessing function (`preprocess_input`):

```
from keras.applications.resnet50 import preprocess_input
normalized_image = preprocess_input(img)
```

This preprocessing step prepares the image so that it is in the same format as the images that were used to train the network. This will depend upon the model being used. For ResNet50, `preprocess_input` transforms the image in the following ways:

Normalization
> Subtracting the mean RGB values for the complete training data centers data around the zero mean for each of the channels. Normalizing the training data in this way helps the network to learn faster. Subsequent test data passed to the network should undergo the same normalization.

Switching channel order
> ResNet50 was trained on images with the channels ordered as BGR, rather than RGB. If the image is in RGB format, the channel order needs to be switched.

> To see the preprocessing steps in detail, visit the Jupyter notebook chapter04/resnet50_preprocessing.ipynb *(http://bit.ly/2WO9rUx)* on this book's GitHub site.

The normalized image can now be passed to the classifier:

```
normalized_image_batch = np.expand_dims(normalized_image, 0) ❶
predictions = model.predict(normalized_image_list)
```

❶   The classifier takes a batch of images in the form of `np.arrays`, so `expand_dims` is required to add an axis to the image. This makes it a batch containing one image.

We now have the predictions that are the vector output from the final layer of the classifier—a big array representing the probabilities for every classification. The top three classifications along with their predictions can be printed out nicely using the following code:

```python
from keras.applications.resnet50 import decode_predictions

decoded_predictions = decode_predictions(predictions, top=3) ❶

predictions_for_image = decoded_predictions[0]
for pred in predictions_for_image:
    print(pred[1],' : ', pred[2])
```

❶   `decode_predictions` is a handy helper utility to extract the highest predictions in the `predictions` array (in this case the top three) and associate them with their associated labels.

Here's the output:

```
koala   :  0.999985
indri   :  7.1616164e-06
wombat  :  3.9483125e-06
```

Superb classification by ResNet50! In the next part of this book, we'll see how the model, when presented with the same image with very minor perturbation, will do considerably worse.

## PART II

Generating Adversarial Input

Part I provided an introduction to adversarial input and its motivations and the fundamentals of deep learning as applied to image and audio data. This section investigates the various mathematical and algorithmic techniques for generating adversarial data.

We'll begin with a conceptual explanation of the ideas that underpin adversarial input in Chapter 5. This chapter considers why DNNs can be fooled by small changes to input that do not affect human understanding of the image or audio. We'll look at how the amount of change required to render an input adversarial can be measured mathematically, and how aspects of human perception might affect the ways in which images and audio can be altered without those changes being noticed.

Chapter 6 then goes into greater depth, explaining specific computational methods for generating adversarial input based on research in this area. We'll explore the mathematics behind some of these methods and the differences in approaches. The chapter also provides some code examples to illustrate the methods in action, based on the neural networks introduced in the code in 3 and 4.

At the end of this section, you'll understand why DNNs can be fooled and the principles and methods that are required for this trickery. This will form the basis for exploring real-world threats in Part III.

## CHAPTER 5

The Principles of Adversarial Input

This chapter looks at some of the core principles underpinning the generation of adversarial examples. We'll hold off on the more detailed mathematics and specific techniques and begin by building upon the ideas presented in the previous chapters. This discussion will use analogy and approximation to provide an intuitive understanding prior to delving into the details. The aim is to understand, at a high level, how the addition of adversarial perturbation or an adversarial patch could cause a DNN to return an incorrect result.

To recap:

Adversarial perturbation
A combination of imperceptible (or nearly imperceptible) small changes distributed across the input data which cause the model to return an incorrect result. For an image, this might be small changes to several disparate pixels across an image.

Adversarial patch
An addition to a specific area (spatial or temporal) of the input data to cause the model to return an incorrect result. An adversarial patch is likely to be perceptible by a human observer, but could be disguised as something benign.

This chapter considers the generation of adversarial perturbation and patches by direct manipulation of digital data. Adversarial patches and perturbation are easier to apply to the input in its digital form, but it may be possible to apply these techniques to the real world (altering traffic signs for autonomous vehicles, for example) to cause the sensor (camera or microphone) to generate digital input that has the adversary's desired effect. Chapter 8 looks at the additional challenges facing the adversary if they do not have access to the digital form of the input.

Very broadly speaking, adversarial attacks can be divided into two types:

Untargeted attacks

An untargeted (or indiscriminate) attack aims to cause the DNN to return an incorrect result, such as a misclassification. An example of this would be to avoid facial detection; so long as an image is not positively identified as a specific person, the actual DNN output is not important.

Targeted attacks

A targeted attack aims to generate a specific output from the DNN processing; for example, to cause an autonomous vehicle to not recognize a stop sign.

It will come as no surprise that an untargeted attack will be easier to achieve than a targeted attack, as the attacker is less fussy about the DNN output and so has greater scope for manipulation of the input data. However, the techniques employed are similar for both cases.

Prior to considering the attacks themselves, let's begin by looking at the raw input presented to a DNN and the features that the model subsequently extracts from that input—those are the characteristics that it deems most important in making its decision. For the purposes of this explanation and those that follow in this chapter, we'll use image classification, the most commonly researched area of adversarial examples. However, the concepts presented here are by no means limited to images; the ideas can be applied to other modalities, such as audio.

 Mathematics Refresher

If you are unfamiliar with (or have forgotten) mathematical notation, examples and explanations of the mathematical symbols used in this book can be found in Appendix A.

The Input Space

DNNs are learned functions that map some complex input to an output. We considered a simple image classification task using the Fashion-MNIST dataset in Chapter 3. Chapter 4 then went on to explain how the principles of deep learning can be applied to other scenarios, such as more complex image recognition, audio classification, and speech-to-text.

All the scenarios presented in the preceding chapters take complex data as input. For example, the ResNet50 classifier presented in Chapter 4 takes ImageNet data cropped to 224 x 224 pixels. Therefore, each image comprises 50,176 pixels in total. The color of each pixel is described by three channels (red, green, blue), so each image is represented by 50,176 x 3 (150,528) values. Each of these values has a value between 0 and 255. This gives a staggering 256^{150528} *possible* images that could be presented to the image classifier!

Using a similar calculation,[1] a relatively low-resolution 1.3 megapixel photograph can encode $256^{3932160}$ possible picture variations. Even the far lower-resolution monochrome Fashion-MNIST classifier has 256^{784} possible inputs.[2]

One way of envisaging all the possible images that could be input to the DNN would be to place each one at its own point in a highly dimensional *input space*. In such a space, one dimension represents one input neuron value (or raw "feature"). This equates to one dimension per pixel value (three values and three dimensions for each pixel if it's in color, one value and one dimension for each pixel if it's in grayscale). For the ResNet50 classifier, the input space would comprise 150,528 dimensions, each of which could have one of 256 values. For Fashion-MNIST, it's 784 dimensions.

We cannot visualize such a complex hyperdimensional space. So, for this discussion, Figure 5-1 presents an outrageous oversimplification to two dimensions for the two example datasets.

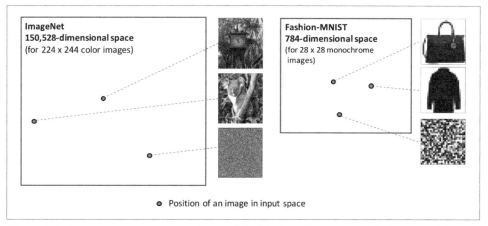

Figure 5-1. Input spaces outrageously simplified to two dimensions (obviously not to scale)

Although the input space is vast, it's worth noting that most of the *possible* images would not represent anything that we would understand as a proper "picture." They might look like random pixel combinations, or perhaps patterns that don't represent anything in the real world. Every possible image has a specific location in the input space, however. Changing one of its pixels will move it in the space along the dimension (or dimensions in the case of a color image) representing that pixel value.

---

1 The number of pixels is 1,280 x 1,024, which equals 1,310,720. There are 3 channels per pixel, giving 3,932,160 pixel values, each between 0 and 255.

2 28 x 28 = 784 grayscale pixels for each image.

As described in Chapter 3, for each image the DNN returns a vector of probabilities —one value within the vector for each possible classification.

In the Fashion-MNIST input space, images falling in one area of the input space might be assigned a high probability of being "Bag," and images falling in another area might be assigned a higher probability of being "Coat" or "Sandal" or one of the other clothing classifications. Every point in the input space has a set of 10 values returned from this image classifier.

Input Space Versus Feature Space

The term *feature space* expresses the same concept of a multidimensional space, but with variation across *features* rather than raw input values. The feature space is therefore the collection of feature combinations used by the ML algorithm to make its predictions.

In more traditional (non-DNN) ML applications, the raw data fed into the learned model represents the features on which the model will make its predictions. Therefore, the feature space can be considered to be the same as the input space.

In contrast, DNNs are usually trained to extract the features from raw data. Therefore, an interpretation of feature space in the context of neural networks would be the lower-dimensional space of more complex features that have been extracted by the DNN to make its predictions. For example, in the case of a CNN performing image classification, this might be the higher-level feature information output from the convolutional layers in the first part of the network.

Strictly speaking, when referring to changes affecting the raw data to create DNN adversarial examples, it may be more correct to use the term *input space*. In practice, however, the two terms are often used interchangeably—the input pixels in an image are, after all, just very low-level features.

A nice way to think of this is in terms of multiple landscapes, each with contours. Higher (darker) ground depicts a more confident prediction for the classification that the landscape refers to ("Coat," "Bag," etc.). Although this landscape analogy is very simple, it forms the fundamental basis of the mathematical explanations of adversarial examples that follow.

For example, if we zoom into the area of the input space where a coat image resides and provide shading to illustrate the probabilities assigned to each of the 10 classes for images in this area, the input space might be visualized as a set of *prediction landscapes*, something like that shown in Figure 5-2. The outrageous simplification of the high-dimensional input space to two dimensions still applies.

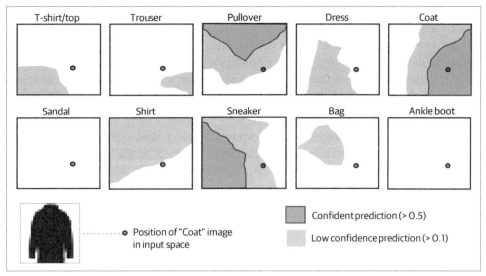

Figure 5-2. A model's prediction landscapes for each classification—zoomed into a tiny area of the complete input space

For each classification, the darker shaded areas represent the areas in the input space where images are confidently predicted to be that classification. Images in lighter shaded areas are less confidently predicted to be that classification.

A single classification for an image can be established based on whichever of the list of predictions is the highest, and possibly with the extra constraint that it must have a minimum confidence. In Figure 5-2, this minimum confidence is 0.5 and is marked with a continuous line. Images falling outside this boundary in the prediction landscape will therefore be assigned a different classification (or be unclassified). In the Figure 5-2 depiction, the image falls within the "Coat" boundary, and is therefore classified correctly.

Generalizations from Training Data

Each of the landscapes in Figure 5-2 represents a mapping from the image position to a specific classification. So this is simply a visual depiction of the formula representing the neural network algorithm:

$$\mathbf{y} = f(\mathbf{x}; \Theta)$$

where the shading represents one of the values in the returned vector **y** for the coat image at location **x**, assuming the DNN has the set of weights and biases represented by Θ.

Cast your mind back to "How a DNN Learns" on page 38, which discussed the process by which a DNN learns by adjusting all the weights and biases represented by Θ. In terms of the contour analogy, this can be thought of as *shifting* the prediction landscapes so that each of the training examples is at (or close to) the relevant height for its true classification. The training examples' **x** values do not change, but the landscape is molded to ensure that the DNN is as accurate as possible for the training data.

The process of gradient descent is readjusting the parameters of the function to shift the contours so that the training data is correctly classified. At the beginning of training, the parameters are randomly initialized, so the landscape is bad for the training examples. During training, you can imagine the landscape gradually morphing as the parameters are altered, optimizing the function for the training set. This is shown in Figure 5-3.

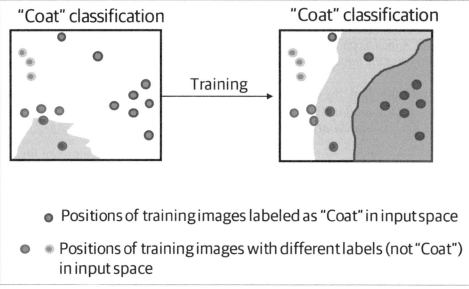

Figure 5-3. *The changing prediction landscape of the input space during training*

At the end of the training the majority of the training samples with the "Coat" label should fall within an area of the input space that allocates a high prediction to "Coat," and similarly for all the other classes. The optimization step might fail to create classification boundaries that allocate all the training images to their correct classes, especially when the image does not have features similar to the others in its class. However, the purpose of the optimization is to *generalize* over patterns and create a best fit for the training data.

The ability of a model to perform accurate predictions for all possible inputs depends upon it learning the correct prediction landscapes for the areas at and around the training examples, and also in areas of the input space where no training examples exist. This is a nontrivial task, as by far the majority of the input space will have no training examples and many areas of the input space will reside outside the set of data with which the network has been reliably trained.

The aim of a DNN is to return accurate results across all possible input data, based on generalization of characteristics, but the accuracy of the model will be highly dependent on the characteristics of the training data on which these generalizations are made. For example, exactly what aspect of a Fashion-MNIST image causes the DNN to allocate it to the "Coat" classification? If the characteristic is not something that a human would use to perform the same reasoning, there's scope for an adversary to exploit this difference.

Furthermore, the training data is unlikely to be representative of all possible types of input. The model is unlikely to perform accurately on data outside the training data distribution, known as *out-of-distribution* (OoD) data, and adversarial examples can exploit this weakness in the algorithm.

Out-of-Distribution Data

OoD data does not conform to the same distribution as the training set. If you consider the number of possible inputs to a DNN, it is unsurprising that the majority of potential inputs for image and audio tasks will lie outside this distribution.

For example, the training data for Fashion-MNIST comprises 60,000 examples. Sounds like a lot? This is actually tiny relative to the 784^{256} possible inputs for a 28 x 28 grayscale image. Similarly, even though there are over 14 million images in the ImageNet dataset, if we restrict the images to resolution 224 x 224, this training set provides a very sparse representation of the complete input space for all possibilities (150528^{256}).

In practice, if the training data represents examples from the real world (such as photographic images), many OoD inputs will correspond to data that would not occur naturally. Random-pixel images, for example, or images that have undergone some weird manipulation would be OoD. Usually these inputs will result in model predictions that are inconclusive, which is behavior that we might expect. Sometimes, however, the model will return incorrect confident predictions for OoD inputs.

Recognizing OoD data is extremely challenging—we'll return to this in Chapter 10 when considering defenses.

Experimenting with Out-of-Distribution Data

It's interesting to experiment with random or unreal images to see what DNN classifiers make of them. Figure 5-4 shows a couple of examples of the predictions returned when random images are presented to the Fashion-MNIST and ResNet50 models.

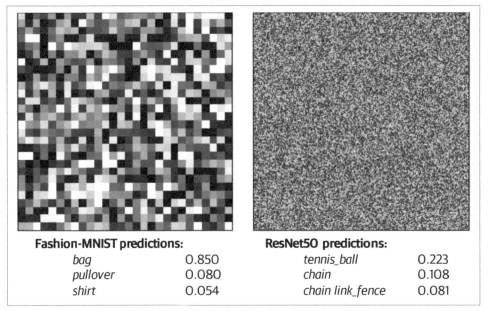

Fashion-MNIST predictions:		ResNet50 predictions:	
bag	0.850	*tennis_ball*	0.223
pullover	0.080	*chain*	0.108
shirt	0.054	*chain link_fence*	0.081

Figure 5-4. Classification predictions for randomly generated images

Code Examples: Experimenting with Random Data

You can test the Fashion-MNIST classifier on random images using the Jupyter notebook chapter05/fashion-MNIST_random_images.ipynb (*http://bit.ly/2KsCMlI*) on this book's GitHub site.

To improve the model, you might like to experiment with retraining it with training images comprising random pixels and an additional classification label of "Unclassified." The Jupyter notebook also includes the code to do this.

The Jupyter notebook chapter05/resnet50_random_images.ipynb (*http://bit.ly/2Flr7Bj*) provides the code for testing ResNet50 on random data.

The confident prediction returned by the Fashion-MNIST classifier on the left is "Bag," and by far the majority (over 99%) of random-pixel images passed to the classifier will have this classification. This indicates that the model has learned to classify most of the input space as "Bag." It's likely that the images of bags are not being identified by specific pixels, but based on the fact that they do not belong to any other classification. ResNet50 at least does not return a confident classification, so has not misidentified the random image..

What's the DNN Thinking?

The mathematical function described by a DNN extracts and quantifies characteristics of the data in order to make its predictions. Perhaps some particular characteristics of the image data are more important to the algorithm than others; for example, a particular combination of pixels in an image might indicate a feature such as a dog's nose, thus increasing the probability that the image is of a dog.

This would make sense, but how could we work out which features a DNN is actually responding to? Put another way, what is the model "seeing" (in the case of image data) or "hearing" (in the case of audio)? Knowing this information might aid in creating adversarial examples.

Once again, this is best illustrated using image classification. Taking each individual pixel in an image, we can calculate the pixel's *saliency* with respect to a particular classification—that is, how much the pixel contributes to a specific classification. A high value means that the pixel is particularly salient to the DNN in producing a particular result and a low value indicates that it is less important to the model for that result. For images, we can view all these values in a *saliency map* to see which aspects of the image the DNN focuses on to make its classification.

Saliency Mathematics

Saliency is estimated by considering the partial derivative of an output with respect to its input:

$$\frac{\partial output}{\partial input}$$

If a small change in the input causes a large change in the output, the input is salient.

So, the saliency of a particular pixel i on a classification j is defined by the following partial derivative:

$$\frac{\partial f(\mathbf{x})_j}{\partial x_i}$$

Conceptually, this is the gradient of the dimension *i* at the point where the image lies in *j*'s prediction landscape. The steeper the gradient, the greater the saliency.

Saliency measured in this way is an estimation as it relies on consistent (linear) gradients. Model linearity will be explored in "Exploiting Model Linearity" on page 105, and we will see in Chapter 6 that saliency scores can be used to create adversarial examples.

Code Examples: Generating Saliency Maps

There are several Python packages available for visualizing image saliency. The code used to generate the images in this chapter uses the Keras-vis Python package (*http://bit.ly/2RmVXhH*).

If you would like to experiment with the code for generating the saliency visualizations described in this chapter, the code and more detailed explanations are included in the GitHub repository. You can experiment using the Fashion-MNIST data in the Jupyter notebook chapter05/fashionMNIST_vis_saliency.ipynb (*http://bit.ly/2FeU69N*) or using the ResNet50 data found in the Jupyter notebook chapter05/resnet50_vis_saliency.ipynb (*http://bit.ly/2XYclaR*).

Figure 5-5 provides an example of an image with its top three classifications using the ResNet50 DNN classifier. To the right of the image is the associated saliency map, which highlights the pixels that were most important in generating the classification. The top three prediction scores returned from the ResNet50 classifier are "analog_clock," "wall_clock," and "bell_cote." (A "bell cote" is a small chamber containing bells.)

ImageNet Data

The ResNet50 model used in these examples was trained on ImageNet data. If you are interested in exploring this training data to see for yourself what the model is learning from, search ImageNet (*http://www.image-net.org/*) for training examples assigned to the different classifications.

The saliency map highlights aspects of the clock face such as the digits, suggesting that ResNet50 deems these to be critical features to its prediction. Look closely and you will see that the classifier is also extracting other "clock" features, such as the hands and the square boxing that may be typical of wall clocks. The third-highest (but nonetheless low) prediction of "bell_cote" might be attributed to the casing below the clock, which has similarities in shape to bell cote chambers.

The aspects of the image in Figure 5-5 that the ResNet50 classifier identifies as salient are what we (as humans) might expect to be most important in the classification. Neural networks are, however, simply generalizing patterns based on training data, and those patterns are not always so intuitive.

ResNet50 predictions:

analog_clock	0.625
wall_clock	0.366
bell_cote	0.005

Figure 5-5. Clock image with associated saliency map (ResNet50 classifier)

Figure 5-6 illustrates this point. Two cropped versions of an identical image return completely different results from the neural network.

Where the candles are more prevalent in the top image, the highest prediction is "candle" followed by "matchstick," and it is clear from the associated saliency map that the DNN's attention is on the flames and the candles. The circle outline of the cake is also extracted by the neural network; this is likely to be a feature common across images of Dutch ovens, explaining the third prediction.

The second image, where the candles have been partially cropped, is misclassified by the DNN as a "puck." The saliency map might provide some explanation for this classification; the disc shape being extracted is similar to that of an ice hockey puck. One of the candles is salient to the DNN, but its flame is not. This may explain the third prediction of "spindle."

Now let's consider the Fashion-MNIST model that we trained in Chapter 3. This was a particularly simple neural network, trained to classify very low-resolution images into one of 10 clothing types. This classifier may be basic in the world of DNN models, but it is effective at achieving its task with high model accuracy.

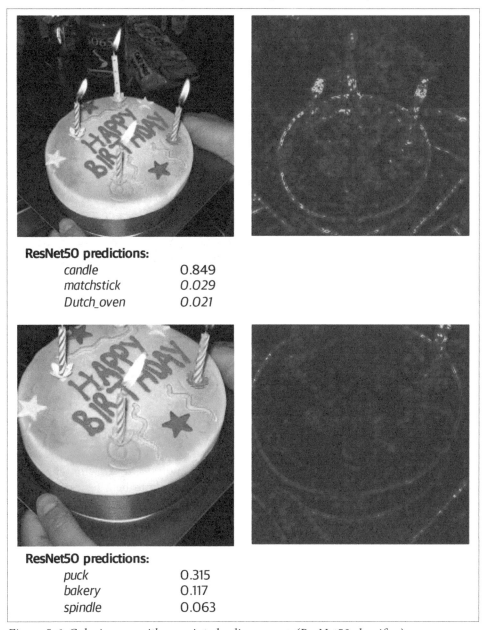

ResNet50 predictions:

candle	*0.849*
matchstick	*0.029*
Dutch_oven	*0.021*

ResNet50 predictions:

puck	*0.315*
bakery	*0.117*
spindle	*0.063*

Figure 5-6. Cake images with associated saliency map (ResNet50 classifier)

Figure 5-7 depicts the pixels that are deemed most important (salient) by the simple model in correctly classifying a selection of images as "Trouser" and "Ankle boot." Unlike with the previously shown saliency pictures, the saliency maps overlay the original images so that the relationship between the pixels and the images is clear. To make the images simpler, the saliency maps also show only the 10 most prevalent pixels in determining the predicted classification.

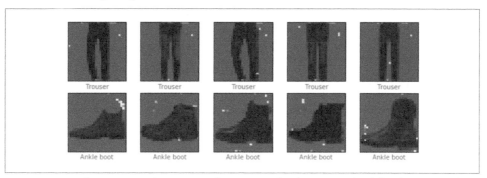

Figure 5-7. Fashion-MNIST images with associated saliency overlaid for the target classification (basic classifier)

Figure 5-7 illustrates that the pixels most salient to a DNN in determining the image classification are not what we might expect. For example, it appears that the model has learned to distinguish trousers based primarily on pixels in the top and bottom rows of the image rather than, for example, the leg shape of the trousers. Similarly, particular pixels around the toes of the boots seem important to the "Ankle boot" classification. Certain clusters of pixels, once again near the edges of the images, also have unexpected relevance. Because the model has been trained to identify the *easiest* method to distinguish categories of clothing, it might not pick out the features that we would intuitively use to categorize clothing. Therefore, the pixels at the edges of the image might be sufficient in discriminating between the different clothing categories for the restricted Fashion-MNIST dataset.

With the concepts of an input space and saliency in mind, let's move on to see how this all relates to the generation of adversarial input.

Perturbation Attack: Minimum Change, Maximum Impact

As you will have gathered from the previous sections, adversarial examples exploit flaws in untested areas of the input space of a DNN model, causing it to return an incorrect answer. These examples introduce a perturbation or patch that would not fool or might not even be noticed by a human.[3] So, whatever alteration changes a benign image into an adversarial one, there's a broad principle that it should result in minimum change to the data, while also maximizing the effect on the result produced by the DNN.

Let's begin by considering the challenge of adding some perturbation—perhaps changing a few salient pixels, or changing many pixels very slightly—to our Fashion-MNIST coat image, to result in a misclassification. Changing a selection of pixels in the image will shift it through the input space to another location, moving it across the landscapes depicted originally in Figure 5-2. This shift is depicted in Figure 5-8 by the arrow going from the original image position indicated by the circle to the adversarial image position indicated by the triangle.

On the one hand, the image must be changed sufficiently so that its position within the input space is no longer within the "Coat" classification area. If this is a targeted attack, there is the additional constraint that the image has moved to an area of the input space that will result in the target classification. In Figure 5-8, the changed image is now classified as "Sneaker." Generation of adversarial perturbation therefore comes down to the challenge of which pixels will cause the most change away from the correct classification, and possibly toward a target classification.

On the other hand, any perturbation required must be minimized so that it is insignificant to the human eye. In other words, ideally the perturbation is likely to be the minimum change to the image required to move it *just* outside the "Coat" classification boundary or *just* inside the target classification boundary.[4] There are a number of approaches; we might focus on changing a few of the pixels that are most critical for the classification change (the most salient ones), or we could change many pixels, but to such a small extent that the overall effect on the image is not noticeable.

The concepts described use a vastly simplified pictorial representation, but they illustrate the fundamental principles of adversarial example generation, regardless of the technique employed. The generation of adversarial examples typically requires altering a nonadversarial example to move it to a different part of the input space that will change the model's predictions to the maximum desired effect.

---

3 As mentioned in Chapter 1, as strictly defined an *adversarial example* does not need to remain unnoticed by a human, as this term may be used to signify adversarial intent. However, for the audio and image discussions in this book, these are the adversarial examples that we are interested in.

4 There is a risk that a less confident adversarial example might creep back to its original (correct) classification if it resides *too* close to the critical boundary that makes it adversarial. This might be the case, for example, if its pixels were changed in a small way during the processing chain prior to it reaching the DNN classifier. An adversarial example with greater robustness might reside more significantly away from the original classification boundary or more comfortably within the target classification area (in the case of a targeted attack).

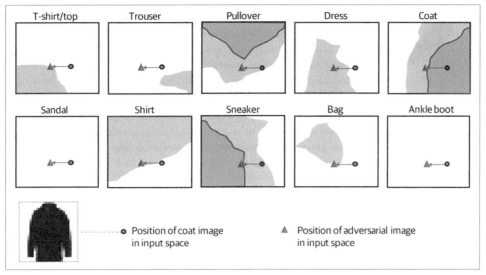

Figure 5-8. Untargeted attack—moving outside the "Coat" classification area of the input space

Adversarial Patch: Maximum Distraction

The principles behind the generation of an adversarial patch are very similar to those employed for a perturbation attack. Once again, the aim is to alter the input in such a way that it moves through the input space, either away from its initial classification (untargeted attack) or toward a target classification (targeted attack) This time, however, a localized area of the image is altered, rather than implementing more general perturbations across the whole picture. The altered area or "patch" must be optimized to "pull" the image toward another part of the input space.

If the target misclassification is "koala," the patch would ideally represent what would be perceived as the perfect koala, encapsulating every characteristic the model deemed to be important to a koala classification. The patch should contain all the salient features of a koala, so it appears to be more koala-like (to the DNN) than anything that you would ever see in the real world—in other words, it should be an excessively "koala-y" koala. This positions it comfortably within an area of the input space such that the features of the unpatched image are overlooked. The very toastery toaster in Figure 1-5 illustrates this nicely.

Optimizing the adversarial example might also consider the size of the patch, its location on the image, and potentially the way it will be perceived by humans. Moving the patch around on the image and resizing it will obviously have an effect on the resulting image's position within the input space and may affect its classification.

Supernormal Stimulus

The concept of distraction through exaggerated, unnatural versions of things in the real world is not unique to AI. Scientists have also proven a similar concept of *supernormal stimulus* in animals and humans.

In the 1950s, ethologist Nikolaas Tinbergen demonstrated that artificially exaggerated versions of natural objects could stimulate innate behaviors in gulls to a greater extent than their natural equivalents.[5] He proved this with false oversized eggs and mock "beaks" made from knitting needles with patterns that exaggerated those on a real beak. Psychologists have since extended these ideas to humans in areas such as junk food, entertainment, and art.

Measuring Detectability

Methods used to generate adversarial perturbation require a measurement of the distance from the benign input to the adversarial. This is a measurement of the distance moved through the input space, as shown by the arrows in Figure 5-8. The mathematics then seeks to minimize this value (minimize the change) while ensuring that the input fulfills the adversarial criteria.

Mathematics provides us with different mechanisms for measuring differences between points across multidimensional spaces, and we can exploit these techniques to provide a quantifiable "difference" between two image positions in the input space. Constraining the amount of difference allowed between an adversarial example and its nonadversarial counterpart ensures that the perturbation is minimized. A high similarity score (a small difference) would imply that it would appear nonadversarial to a human observer, whereas a large change might suggest it is more likely to be noticed. In fact, human perception is more complex than this as some aspects of the input may be more noticeable to a human observer than others, so the mathematical quantification may be too simple.

The next section describes how the difference between a benign and an adversarial input can be measured mathematically, and the section "Considering Human Perception" on page 93 considers the added complexity introduced by human perception.

A Mathematical Approach to Measuring Perturbation

There are several different mathematical approaches to measuring distance in high-dimensional space. These measurements are called the L^p-norm, where the value of p

---

5 Niko Tinbergen, *The Herring Gull's World: A Study of the Social Behavior of Birds* (London: Collins, 1953), 25.

determines how the distance is calculated. Figure 5-9 summarizes these various distance measurements.

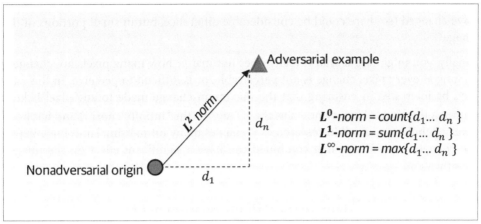

Figure 5-9. A visual depiction of L^p-norm measurements where the number of dimensions is 2

Perhaps the most obvious measurement is the Euclidean distance between the original and adversarial images in the input space. This is simply an application of Pythagoras' theorem (albeit in a highly dimensional feature space) to determine the distance between the two images by calculating the sum of the squared difference in each feature dimension and then taking its root. In mathematical parlance, this difference measurement is called the L^2-norm and belongs to a wider set of approaches for measuring the size of a vector. The vector being considered in measuring adversarial change has its origin at the original image and its end at the adversarial one.

A curious characteristic of high-dimensional spaces is that their dimensionality ensures that all the points in the space are a similar Euclidean distance apart. While the L^2-norm is the most intuitive measure of distance in low two- or three-dimensional spaces that we understand, it turns out that it is a poor measure of distance in high-dimensional spaces. The L^2-norm is often used in the generation of adversarial examples, but it is not necessarily the best measure of perturbation.

An alternative distance measurement is the L^1-norm, which is simply the sum of all the pixel differences. This is sometimes referred to the "taxicab" norm; whereas the L^2-norm measures direct distance ("as the crow flies"), the L^1-norm is akin to a taxicab finding the fastest route through a city that has its streets arranged in a grid plan.

Another approach might be to measure the difference between two images in terms of the total number of pixels that have different values. In input space terms, this is simply the number of dimensions that have different values between the two images.

This measurement is referred to mathematically as the L^0-"norm."[6] Intuitively, this is a reasonable approach as we might expect that fewer pixel changes would be less perceptible than many, but the L^0-norm does not restrict the amount that these pixels have changed (so there could be considerable difference, but in small portions of the image).

Finally, you might argue that it really does not matter how many pixels are changed, so long as every pixel change is not perceivable, or is difficult to perceive. In this case we'd be interested in ensuring that the maximum change made to any pixel is kept within a threshold. This is known as the L^∞-norm (the "infinity" norm) and has been a very popular approach in research as it enables many infinitesimal and imperceptible changes to an image that combined can have a significant effect on the image's classification.

Mathematical Norm Measurements

Here's how L^p-norms are written mathematically.

The generic formula for L^p-norm measurements is:

$$\| \mathbf{d} \|_p = \left(|d|_1^p + |d|_2^p + \ldots |d|_n^p \right)^{\frac{1}{p}}$$

where $|d|_1, |d|_2 \ldots |d|_n$ represents the vector between the two positions in the input space (i.e., the adversarial perturbation or patch).

The absolute bars ensure that an absolute (nonnegative) measurement is returned, regardless of whether the vector is traveling in a positive or negative direction along any of its axes. These are sometimes omitted when p is even, as raising the vector values to an even number will ensure that they are not negative.

When p is 1, the L^1-norm ("taxicab" norm) measurement is:

$$\| \mathbf{d} \|_1 = \left(|d|_1^1 + |d|_2^1 + \ldots |d|_n^1 \right)^1 = |d|_1 + |d|_2 + \ldots |d|_n$$

This is simply the sum of all the absolute values of the pixel changes.

When p is 2, the L^2 (Euclidean norm) measurement is therefore:

---

6 The quotes are deliberate here; see the mathematical explanation in "Mathematical Norm Measurements" on page 92 if you are interested in an explanation.

$$\| \mathbf{d} \|_2 = (|d|_1^2 + |d|_2^2 + \dots |d|_n^2)^{\frac{1}{2}} = \sqrt{|d|_1^2 + |d|_2^2 + \dots |d|_n^2}$$

and when p is ∞, the L^∞-norm resolves to:

$$\| \mathbf{d} \|_\infty = max\{|d|_1, |d|_2 \dots |d|_n\}$$

This is simply the maximum individual pixel change.

Finally, another useful measurement of perturbation is the number of pixels changed (the count of nonzero values). This is sometimes referred to as the L^0-"norm." However, it is not a proper mathematical norm because setting $p = 0$ requires calculating 0^0, which is not defined.

So, which is the best measurement for an adversary to use to ensure an effective perturbation attack? Is it better to change a few pixels (minimize L^0-norm), or to change many pixels but constrain each change to be small (minimize L^∞-norm), or perhaps to minimize the overall distance that the perturbation moves in the input space (with the L^2-norm or L^1-norm)? The answer depends on several factors which will be discussed later in the book, including human perception and the level of robustness required of the adversarial example to data preprocessing.

Considering Human Perception

The challenge of the adversarial example is to generate input that results in incorrect interpretation by the network, but without being detectable as an attack by a human being. This might mean that the change is imperceptible to humans or insignificant enough for a human to disregard it either consciously or subconsciously.

At the most fundamental level, our perception is constrained by the physical limitations to the range of electromagnetic or sound waves that our senses can process. It would seem intuitive, therefore, that the data allowed into neural network technology designed to mimic human decisions about images or audio should be subject to similar restrictions as those imposed on us by our eyes and ears. To a large extent, this constraint is imposed on human-consumable digital data. For example, image formats (PNG, JPEG, etc.) are designed to represent information in the visible spectrum. Similarly, much audio processing is constrained to frequencies that are human-audible or, in the case of speech processing, within the range of sound produced by the human vocal tract. Without these constraints, an adversary might simply augment data with information that humans cannot hear or see to confuse a DNN (see the following note for an example).

Dolphin Attack: Exploiting Ultrasound

In 2017, researchers Zhang et al. demonstrated the efficacy of ultrasound voice commands as a mechanism to add an audio adversarial patch inaudible to humans but discernible by digital assistants (referred to as a "dolphin" attack).[7] While interesting, this type of attack could be easily prevented simply by ensuring that the digital assistant filters out sounds inaudible to humans or, better still, outside the human vocal range. Adversarial attacks that use parts of the electromagnetic spectrum or sound wave frequencies that cannot be perceived by human eyes and ears are unlikely, therefore, to pose a realistic threat.

Assuming all the data presented is within the human sensory range, the problem with the mathematical measurements of the differences described here is that they assign equal weight to each part of the input data. The measurements assume every pixel within an image is perceived equally and contributes equally to a human's perception of that image. This is clearly not the case; it has been proven that people are typically less aware of changes to a busy part of an image. Pixel changes in a simple area (clear sky, for example) are likely to be more noticeable.

For audio, the distortion metric often employed in generating adversarial examples is decibels (dB), a logarithmic scale that measures the *relative* loudness of the distortion with respect to the original audio. This is a good way to ensure that adversarial audio remains imperceptible to humans because it ensures that the changes during quiet points are relatively small with respect to any changes introduced to louder aspects of the audio.

There has been considerable research into the aspects of image or sound that humans pay most attention to. These are the salient features from the human rather than the machine perspective (as previously discussed in "What's the DNN Thinking?" on page 83). Adversarial examples might be improved by skewing perturbations toward aspects of the input data that are less interesting to a human but more interesting to the model. Consider images: humans subconsciously divide image information into constituent parts, paying greater attention to the foreground and less to the background. There may be effective, simple techniques that could enable greater flexibility in creating adversarial input, such as favoring perturbations in busy background areas of the image.

We can turn to psychology for the definition of the *absolute threshold of sensation*: the minimum stimulus required for it to be registered by an individual 50% of the time.

---

7 Guoming Zhang et al., "DolphinAtack: Inaudible Voice Commands," *Proceedings of the 2017 ACM SIGSAC Conference on Computer and Communications Security* (2017), *http://bit.ly/2MWUtft*.

Unsurprisingly, this varies from person to person and also varies for a specific individual depending on aspects such as their physiological state. From the perspective of an adversary, understanding thresholds by which stimuli might be registered by a human may be beneficial in creating adversarial data.

Another interesting consideration is sensory adaptation. Our senses become less responsive to constant stimulus over time, enabling us to notice changes that might be important to survival. In a car, for example, we may stop noticing the sound of the engine after a time. Conversely, we are particularly sensitive to abrupt changes to sensory input, such as sudden noise. From an adversarial perspective, therefore, there may be benefit in gradually introducing perturbation to video or audio to remain undetected.

Summary

This chapter introduced some of the high-level principles underpinning adversarial examples. Prior to getting into more detail about adversarial techniques in Chapter 6, here's the high-level mathematical explanation of adversarial input.

The Mathematics Behind Adversarial Examples

Let's assume that we have a neural network that is a classifier. It takes a vector representing the input data and returns an output:

$$f(\mathbf{x}; \Theta) = \mathbf{y}$$

In this equation, f is the function applied by the DNN algorithm to generate the output. Recall from Chapter 3 that Θ represents all the parameters (weights and biases) of the network. When the network has been successfully trained, these parameters do not change, so we can simplify that equation to:

$$f(\mathbf{x}) = \mathbf{y}$$

where $\mathbf{x}$ identifies the point in the raw input space where the input is located.

What $\mathbf{x}$ and y represent varies with the type of input data and the task that the DNN is addressing. In the case of a monochrome image classifier, $\mathbf{x}$ is a vector of real numbers, each corresponding to the value of a pixel:

$$\mathbf{x} \in \mathbb{R}$$

For a classifier, y is a single classification such as "dog" or "cat" assigned an enumeration derived from the vector of probabilities returned from the DNN's output layer

---

(such as the highest value). So y is not a vector of probabilities in this case, but belongs to the set of numbers from $1 \ldots L$, where L is the number of classifications. This is written as:

$$y \in \{1, 2, \ldots L\}$$

Creating an adversarial example requires a carefully calculated change to the initial input. In simple mathematics, we can express this as follows:

$$\mathbf{x}^{\mathbf{adv}} = \mathbf{x} + \mathbf{r}$$

where:

- $\mathbf{x}^{\mathbf{adv}}$ is a vector representing the updated (adversarial) input data.
- $\mathbf{x}$ is the vector representing the original input data.
- $\mathbf{r}$ is a vector representing a small change to the original input data.

For the input $\mathbf{x}^{\mathbf{adv}}$ to be successfully adversarial, the output of the model (the classification) must differ from that of a nonadversarial equivalent. We can write this as:

$$f\left(\mathbf{x}^{\mathbf{adv}}\right) \neq f(\mathbf{x})$$

If the attack is targeted, we have the additional constraint:

$$f\left(\mathbf{x}^{\mathbf{adv}}\right) = y_t$$

where y_t represents the target adversarial classification.

Whether the attack is a perturbation or a patch, the value of the adversarial change $\mathbf{r}$ must be minimized to make it imperceptible (or less perceptible) to humans. If this measurement is a simple L^p-norm for a perturbation attack, the aim is to find the closest image to $\mathbf{x}$, so we also state that the perturbation $\mathbf{r}$ should be as small as possible. For an untargeted attack, we can write this as:

$$\arg \min_{\mathbf{r}} \left\{ \| \mathbf{r} \|_p : f\left(\mathbf{x}^{\mathbf{adv}}\right) \neq f(\mathbf{x}) \right\}$$

And for a targeted attack, it's:

$$\arg \min_{\mathbf{r}} \left\{ \| \mathbf{r} \|_p : f\left(\mathbf{x}^{\mathbf{adv}}\right) = y_t \right\}$$

The value of p depends on the measurement of distance being used to assess the adversarial example. So, for example, if the adversarial technique exploits Euclidean distance as its measurement, the preceding equation would be written as:

$$\arg \min_{\mathbf{r}} \left\{ \| \mathbf{r} \|_2 : f\left(\mathbf{x}^{\mathbf{adv}}\right) = y_t \right\}$$

The measurement might be more complex, for example incorporating some consideration of the impact of the adversarial perturbation on human perception, but much of the work on adversarial examples uses L^p-norm measurements.

The goal of the adversary is to find the optimal value of $\mathbf{r}$ that satisfies the preceding constraints. Mathematically, this can be done through a constrained optimization algorithm, of which there are several (we will consider some in Chapter 6). The aim of the algorithm selected is therefore to solve the following problem to establish the perturbation $\mathbf{r}$ in order to create the adversarial example:

$$\mathbf{x}^{\mathbf{adv}} = \mathbf{x} + \arg \min_{\mathbf{r}} \left\{ \| \mathbf{r} \|_p : f\left(\mathbf{x}^{\mathbf{adv}}\right) \neq f(\mathbf{x}) \right\}$$

Or, more specifically, for a targeted attack:

$$\mathbf{x}^{\mathbf{adv}} = \mathbf{x} + \arg \min_{\mathbf{r}} \left\{ \| \mathbf{r} \|_p : f\left(\mathbf{x}^{\mathbf{adv}}\right) = y_t \right\}$$

## CHAPTER 6

Methods for Generating Adversarial Perturbation

Chapter 5 considered the principles of adversarial input, but how are adversarial examples generated in practice? This chapter presents techniques for generating adversarial images and provides some code for you to experiment with. In Chapter 7 we'll then explore how such methods might be incorporated into a real-world attack where the DNN is part of a broader processing chain and the adversary has additional challenges, such as remaining covert.

Open Projects and Code

There are several initiatives to bring the exploration of adversarial attacks and defenses into the public domain, such as CleverHans (*http://bit.ly/2N7t7mG*), Foolbox (*https://foolbox.readthedocs.io*), and IBM's Adversarial Robustness Toolbox (*http://bit.ly/ 2XZ7EgW*). These projects are detailed further in Chapter 10.

For consistency, all the code in this book uses the Foolbox libraries.

Before considering the methods for creating adversarial input, you might wonder—how difficult is it to create an adversarial example simply by trial and error? You might, for example, add some random perturbation to an image and see the effect it has on the model's predictions. Unfortunately for an adversary, it isn't quite so simple. During its learning phase, the DNN will have generalized from the training data, so it is likely to have resilience to small random perturbations; such changes are therefore unlikely to be successful. Figure 6-1 illustrates that even when every pixel color value has been incrementally perturbed by a significant random amount, the ResNet50 classifier still makes a correct classification. Misclassification only occurs when the perturbation is visible.

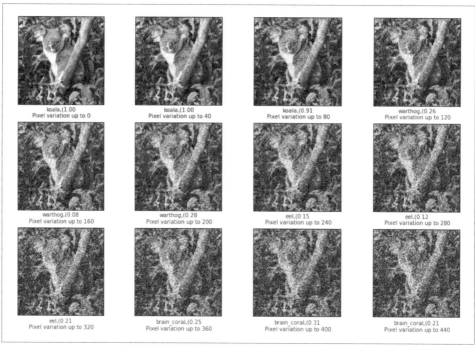

Figure 6-1. Resulting ResNet50 predictions for an image with random variation added; maximum amount of perturbation per pixel is shown for each iteration.

To effectively generate adversarial examples, an adversary will need to be far more cunning. There are several approaches that they might take, each assuming a different level of knowledge of the DNN algorithm. We can categorize the methods for generating adversarial input as follows, based on the attacker's level of access to the model:

White box

These methods exploit complete knowledge of the DNN model to create adversarial input.

Limited black box

These methods refine adversarial input based on an output generated from the model or from the system in which it resides. For example, the output might be simply a final classification.

Score-based black box

These methods refine adversarial input based on the raw predictions (scores) returned from the DNN. Score-based methods may have access to all of the scores or just the highest (for example, the top 10) scores. Score-based methods lie somewhere between white box and limited black box methods; they require access to more detailed responses than a limited black box attack, but do not require access to the model algorithm as a white box attack does.

A Naive Approach to Generating Adversarial Perturbation

To experiment with the code used for Figure 6-1, use the Jupyter notebook chapter06/resnet50_naive_attack.ipynb (*http://bit.ly/2FlGCZN*) on the book's GitHub site.

For the Fashion-MNIST classifier, use the Jupyter notebook chapter06/fashionMNIST_naive_attack.ipynb (*http://bit.ly/2WSB1oO*).

The information available to the attacker for each of these three methods is depicted pictorially in Figure 6-2.

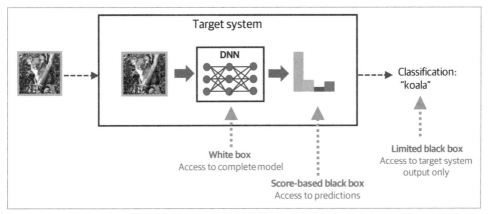

Figure 6-2. Information available in white box, score-based black box, and limited black box methods

The remainder of this chapter considers each of these methods in turn.

Using a Model Substitute: Replica or Transfer Attacks

It's possible (and, as we shall see, sometimes preferable) to use a substitute DNN that serves as a copy or an approximation of the target DNN to develop and test the adversarial input. In this way, an attacker might use white box or score-based black box methods on a substitute network to develop an attack, prior to launching the attack on the actual target.

This approach has the advantage of allowing the adversary to remain covert during refinement of the attack (querying the actual model may alert suspicion). This is also the only available option if the attacker does not have access to the actual model.

When the substitute model is identical to the target model, this is called a *replica* attack. When the model is an approximation of the target, it is called a *transfer attack* because the adversarial input must *transfer* to the target algorithm to be successful.

The methods described in this chapter (white box, score-based black box, and limited black box) may be used on either the end target or a substitute and therefore are not necessarily indicative of the adversary's access to or knowledge of the actual target DNN under threat. This is explained in greater detail in Chapter 7.

White Box Methods

White box methods involve complete knowledge of the DNN model (its parameters and architecture) and use mathematical optimization methods to establish adversarial examples based on calculating the gradients within the input space landscape that was discussed in Chapter 5. Such techniques are particularly interesting because they provide insight into the weaknesses inherent within DNNs. This section explains how these white-box methods work.

Searching the Input Space

Chapter 5 introduced the notion of moving an image across classification boundaries in the input space through carefully selected perturbations. The aim was to minimize the movement in the input space (as measured by one of the L^p-norms) as well as achieving the required adversarial goal—be it a targeted or untargeted misclassification. Let's reconsider the Fashion-MNIST example from that chapter and the impact that altering a coat image has on the predictions returned from the DNN. We'll focus on the "Coat" prediction landscape, as highlighted in Figure 6-3.

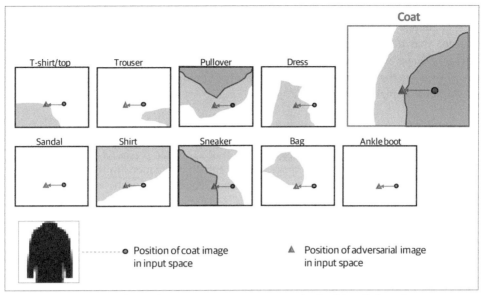

Figure 6-3. Untargeted attack—moving an image outside the "Coat" classification area of the input space

Perhaps the most obvious approach to finding a position in the input space that achieves the adversarial goal is to simply search outward from the initial image. In other words, start with the image, test a few small changes to see which move the predictions in the required direction (i.e., which lower the strength of the "Coat" prediction in our example), then repeat on the tweaked image. This is essentially an iterative search of the input space, beginning at the original image and moving outwards until the predictions change in such a way as to alter its classification, as shown in Figure 6-4.

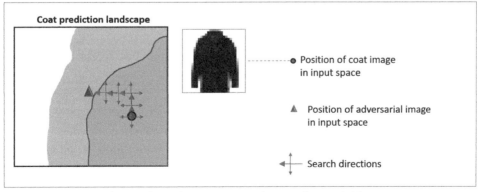

Figure 6-4. Iteratively searching the input space for an adversarial location

Although this might appear to be a pretty simple task, this search is in fact a considerable challenge in itself. There are simply so many different pixel changes and combinations that need to be explored. One option might be to get the answer by brute force, perhaps experimenting with all the possible small perturbations to an input to see what gives the best result. However, this is not computationally feasible, as the following note explains.

Many Possible Perturbations

Let's assume an image resolution of 224 x 224 pixels. Say we want to generate all the possible very small permutations to that image by minimizing the change to any specific pixel to be a value of either plus or minus ε, where ε is a small amount. If we could generate all these permutations, perhaps we could test each one to see whether any fulfilled our adversarial criteria. But how many variations would there be to test?

Recall from Chapter 5 that a low-resolution (224 x 224) color image is represented by 150,528 pixel values (where each pixel has 3 values for red, green, and blue).

For each possible perturbation that we want to generate from the original image, an individual pixel value might remain the same, increase by ε, or decrease by ε.

Therefore, there are $3^{150,528}$ combinations of perturbation whereby each pixel can only change by exactly ε from its original value. To be pedantic, we should subtract 1 from this value so we don't count the possible perturbation where every pixel remains the same. Try putting this into your calculator and you will get an overflow error. Alternatively, pop it into a Jupyter notebook cell using:

```
pow(3,150528) - 1
```

(The number returned is too large to include here.)

The search approach may be computationally intractable, but access to the DNN algorithm grants the attacker a huge privilege; they can use the algorithm to generate a mathematical approximation to this search, which reduces the number of search combinations.

In their initial paper,[1] Szegedy at al. use the Limited-memory Broyden-Fletcher-Goldfarb-Shanno (L-BFGS) algorithm to speed up the exploration of the area surrounding the original image to find adversarial examples. The L-BFGS algorithm is a

---

1 Szegedy et al., "Intriguing Properties of Neural Networks."

mathematical technique that allows more effective searching of the input space by approximating the probability gradients in the input space near a particular point. The "limited-memory" aspect of the algorithm is a further approximation to reduce the amount of computer memory required during the iterative search.

The L-BFGS algorithm proved to be effective in establishing adversarial examples, but it's still incredibly slow and computationally expensive.[2] To optimize the search further, we need to understand more about the characteristics of DNN algorithms and the shapes of the prediction landscapes that they define.

Exploiting Model Linearity

In 2015, some of the same authors of the original research into adversarial examples reconsidered the problem. They proved a simple algorithm—the Fast Gradient Sign Method (FGSM)[3]—to be effective in generating adversarial examples.

The FGSM algorithm was never intended to be the *best* approach to finding adversarial input. Rather, its purpose was to demonstrate a characteristic of DNN algorithms that makes the problem of creating adversarial input far simpler. Let's begin by looking at the algorithm itself, and then consider what it tells us.

The FGSM algorithm calculates the direction in the input space which, at the location of the image, appears to be the fastest route to a misclassification. This direction is calculated using gradient descent and a cost function similar in principle to that for training a network (as explained in "How a DNN Learns" on page 38). A conceptual explanation is to simply think of the direction calculation as being an indirect measure of the steepness of the contours in the prediction landscape at the location of the image.

The adversarial direction is very crudely calculated, so each input value (pixel value or, put another way, axis in the multidimensional input space) is assigned in one of two ways:

Plus

Indicating that this input value would be best being increased to cause a misclassification

Minus

Indicating that this input value would be best decreased to cause a misclassification

---

2 Optimizations have since been made to this approach to generate more effective perturbations, such as those described in Nicholas Carlini and David Wagner, "Towards Evaluating the Robustness of Neural Networks" (2016), *http://bit.ly/2KZoIzL*.

3 Ian J. Goodfellow et al., "Explaining and Harnessing Adversarial Examples" (2015), *http://bit.ly/2FeUtRJ*.

This simple allocation of "plus" or "minus" may appear counterintuitive. However, FGSM isn't concerned with the *relative* importance of any particular change, just the direction (positive or negative) of the change. If, for example, increasing one input value would have a greater adversarial effect than increasing another, the two values would still both be assigned a "plus" and treated equivalently.

With the direction established, FGSM then applies a tiny perturbation to every input value (pixel value in the case of an image), adding the perturbation if the value's adversarial direction of change has been deemed positive, and subtracting the perturbation otherwise. The hope is that these changes will alter the image so that it resides *just* outside its correct classification, therefore resulting in an (untargeted) adversarial example.

FGSM works on the principle that every input value (pixel) is changed, but each one only by a minuscule amount. The method is built on the fact that infinitesimal changes to every dimension in a high-dimensional space create a significant overall change; changing lots of pixels each by a tiny amount results in a big movement across the input space. Cast your mind back to the L^p-norm measurements and you'll realize that this method is minimizing the maximum change to a single pixel—that's the L^∞-norm.

The surprising aspect of FGSM is that it works at all! To illustrate this point, take a look at the two scenarios in Figure 6-5, where the input space of two different DNN models is depicted. Both images show very zoomed-in pictures of the input space, so the arrow depicting the difference between the position of the original and new image generated by the FGSM algorithm represents the very small movement in each dimension.

The boundary for the "Shirt" classification area is depicted by the same thick line in both cases, but you can see that the model on the left has far more consistent gradients. The contours suggest a smooth, consistent hill, rather than the inconsistent, unpredictable landscape on the right.

The direction of the perturbation calculated by FGSM is determined by the gradient at the point of the original image. On the left, this simple algorithm takes us successfully to an adversarial location because the gradients remain roughly the same as the image moves away from the original. In contrast, using FGSM with the gradients on the right fails to place the image in an adversarial location because the gradient near the original image location is not indicative of the gradients further away. The resulting image still lies within the "Shirt" classification area.

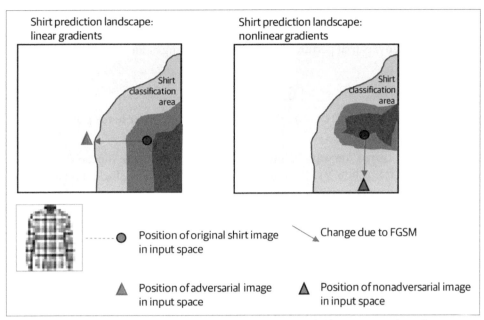

Shirt prediction landscape: linear gradients

Shirt prediction landscape: nonlinear gradients

Shirt classification area

Shirt classification area

⊙ --- Position of original shirt image in input space

↘ Change due to FGSM

▲ Position of adversarial image in input space

▲ Position of nonadversarial image in input space

Figure 6-5. The Fast Gradient Sign Method assuming model linearity and nonlinearity

The whole premise of the success of FGSM assumes that the steepness of the slope in a particular direction will be maintained. Put in mathematical terminology, the function that the model represents exhibits *linear* behavior. With linear models, it's possible to vastly approximate the mathematics for generating adversarial perturbation by simply looking at local gradients.

FGSM will not generate the *best* adversarial input, but that isn't the purpose of this algorithm. By showing that the FGSM approach worked across state-of-the-art image classification DNNs, the researchers proved the fundamental characteristic of linearity was inherent to many of these algorithms; DNN models tend to have consistent gradients across the input space landscape, as shown in the figure on the left in Figure 6-5, rather than inconsistent gradients as shown on the right. Previous to FGSM, it was assumed that DNN algorithms comprised more complex nonlinear gradients, which you could envisage as landscapes with continually varying steepness, incorporating dips and hills. This linearity occurs because the optimization step during training will always favor the simplest model (the simplest gradients).

Model linearity makes the mathematics for generating adversarial examples with white box methods far simpler as it's possible to greatly approximate the mathematics for generating adversarial perturbation by simply looking at local gradients.

FGSM Mathematics

Here's the basic mathematics behind the FGSM algorithm. Refer to the paper[4] for further details.

"How a DNN Learns" on page 38 introduced the notion of a "cost function" that provided a measure of how well a network was performing for a single input. This is written as:

$$C(f(\mathbf{x}; \Theta), \mathbf{y})$$

where:

> C represents the cost function for the DNN f given input $\mathbf{x}$ and its correct output probability vector $\mathbf{y}$.[5]

> The weights and biases of f are represented by Θ.

The purpose of training the neural network is to minimize the cost (represented by the preceding function) across all the training examples by adjusting the weight and bias parameters. Θ is altered until the network performs well for the training data.

Consider this cost function from a different perspective—the neural network has been trained and its parameters are not going to change. So the weights and biases represented by Θ must remain static. Changes to the input data (image) represented by $\mathbf{x}$, however, will also affect the cost value. Therefore, we are reusing this notion of a cost function to measure the effect of moving the image within the prediction landscape, rather than to change the prediction landscape itself, as was done during training.

If the change to $\mathbf{x}$ increases the confidence of the correct prediction, the cost function will return a smaller value. Conversely, if the change to $\mathbf{x}$ decreases the confidence of the correct prediction, the cost will increase.

The adversary's goal is to change $\mathbf{x}$ to *increase* the cost returned by this function, because increasing this cost value moves the prediction *away* from the correct prediction.

---

4 Goodfellow et al., "Explaining and Harnessing Adversarial Examples."

5 A classifier collapses this probability vector to a single value that represents the most probable classification.

It is possible to calculate gradients of the cost function from the original image using differential calculus. Then, taking the sign of the gradients in each direction gives a direction of travel for the perturbation. This is expressed mathematically as:

$$sign(\nabla_x C(f(\mathbf{x}; \Theta), \mathbf{y}))$$

Basically, this is a vector of the same size as the input vector with a "plus" or a "minus" allocated to each of its values.

Finally, the perturbation to create the adversarial example using FGSM is calculated by multiplying the direction by a small distance measurement, ε:

$$\mathbf{x^{adv}} = \mathbf{x} + \varepsilon \cdot sign(\nabla_x C(f(\mathbf{x}; \Theta), \mathbf{y}))$$

Even with the tiny perturbations spread across the image, FGSM can overstep. Hence, it can be improved by iteratively adding very small perturbations until the image is just past the classification boundary and therefore becomes adversarial. While we're at it, we might as well recheck the gradient direction on each iteration just in case the model is not entirely linear. This technique is referred to as the *basic iterative method*.[6]

The following code snippet demonstrates the FGSM attack on the Fashion-MNIST classifier that we created in Chapter 3. We'll use the openly available Foolbox library for this example.

Code Example: Gradient Attack

To experiment with the FGSM code in this section, see the Jupyter notebook chapter06/fashionMNIST_foolbox_gradient.ipynb (*http://bit.ly/2FiRQhO*).

To begin, import the required packages:

```
import numpy as np
import matplotlib.pyplot as plt

import tensorflow as tf
from tensorflow import keras
```

---

6 Alexey Kurakin et al., "Adversarial Machine Learning at Scale" (2016), *http://bit.ly/31Kr3EO*.

Load the model previously saved in Chapter 3 and run the test images through it:

```
fashion_mnist = keras.datasets.fashion_mnist
_, (test_images, test_labels) = fashion_mnist.load_data()
test_images = test_images/255.0

model = tf.keras.models.load_model("../models/fashionMNIST.h5") ❶

predictions = model.predict(test_images) ❷
```

❶ Load the Fashion-MNIST classifier that was saved in Chapter 3.

❷ Get the model's predictions for the test data.

Select an original (nonadversarial) image and display it (see Figure 6-6) along with its prediction:

```
image_num = 7 ❶

class_names = ['T-shirt/top', 'Trouser', 'Pullover', 'Dress', 'Coat',
               'Sandal', 'Shirt', 'Sneaker', 'Bag', 'Ankle boot']

x = test_images[image_num]
y = np.argmax(predictions[image_num])
y_name = class_names[y]

print("Prediction for original image:", y, y_name)

plt.imshow(x, cmap=plt.cm.binary)
```

❶ Change this number to run the attack on a different image.

This output is generated:

```
Prediction for original image: 6 Shirt
```

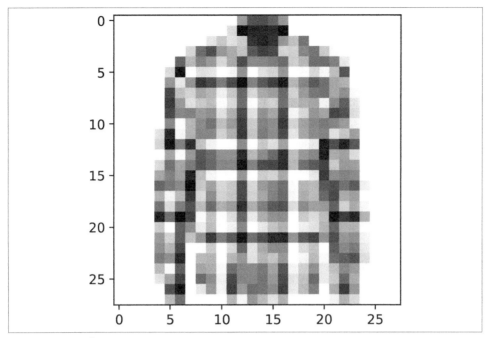

Figure 6-6. Code output

Next, create a Foolbox model from our Keras one:

```
import foolbox
from foolbox.models import KerasModel
fmodel = foolbox.models.TensorFlowModel.from_keras(model, bounds=(0, 255))
```

Define the attack specificity:

```
attack_criterion = foolbox.criteria.Misclassification()  ❶
distance = foolbox.distances.Linfinity                    ❷
```

❶ The `attack_criterion` defines the specificity of the attack. In this case, it is a simple misclassification.

❷ The perturbation distance will be optimized according to the L^{∞}-norm.

Define the attack method:

```
attack = foolbox.attacks.GradientSignAttack(fmodel,
                                            criterion=attack_criterion,
                                            distance=distance)
```

And run the attack:

```
x_adv = attack(input_or_adv = x,
               label = y,
               unpack = False) ❶
```

❶ Specifying unpack = False means that a foolbox.adversarial.Adversarial object is returned, rather than an image. The image and other information about the adversarial example (such as its distance from the original) can be accessed from this object.

Now, let's print out the results (see Figure 6-7):

```
preds = model.predict(np.array([x_adv.image]))  ❶

plt.figure()

# Plot the original image
plt.subplot(1, 3, 1)
plt.title(y_name
plt.imshow(x, cmap=plt.cm.binary)
plt.axis('off')

# Plot the adversarial image
plt.subplot(1, 3, 2
plt.title(class_names[np.argmax(preds[0])])
plt.imshow(x_adv.image, cmap=plt.cm.binary)
plt.axis('off')

# Plot the difference
plt.subplot(1, 3, 3)
plt.title('Difference')
difference = x_adv.image - x
plt.imshow(difference, vmin=0, vmax=1, cmap=plt.cm.binary)
plt.axis('off')

print(x_adv.distance)  ❷

plt.show()
```

❶ This line gets the predictions for the adversarial example. x_adv.image represents the adversarial image part of the Adversarial object.

❷ x_adv.distance is an object representing the perturbation required to generate the adversarial image.

This generates the following output:

```
normalized Linf distance = 1.50e-04
```

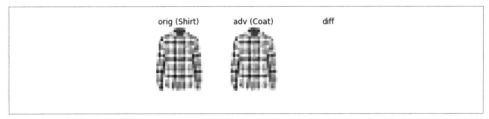

Figure 6-7. Code output

The code has optimized for the L^∞-norm. If you look carefully at the difference, you can see that many pixels have been changed slightly.

Before moving on, there's an important caveat to this discussion about model linearity with respect to audio. Preprocessing such as MFCC and the recurrent nature of LSTMs that are often part of speech-to-text solutions (see "Audio" on page 58) introduce nonlinearity to the model. Therefore, to successfully establish adversarial distortion using a technique such as FGSM on a speech-to-text system will require iterative steps rather than a single-step approach. In addition, the complex processing chain in speech-to-text systems makes generating a loss function more difficult than in the image domain. It requires minimizing loss for an audio sample over the complete end-to-end chain (including steps such as MFCC and CTC), which in turn requires more challenging mathematics and increased compute power.[7]

Adversarial Saliency

"What's the DNN Thinking?" on page 83 introduced the concept of *saliency maps* that enable us to visualize the aspects of input data most important in determining the DNN's predictions. This concept is not unique to DNN processing; these maps have been used for many years as a method of depicting the pixels (or groups of pixels) most relevant to a particular computer vision recognition task.

Saliency calculations can also be exploited in generating adversarial examples. Knowing the most relevant features in determining a classification is bound to be useful if we wish to restrict perturbation to the areas that will have the most influence in moving a benign input to an adversarial one. The Jacobian Saliency Map Approach (JSMA)[8] demonstrates this approach.

The JSMA involves calculating the *adversarial saliency* score for each value that makes up the input. Applied to image data, this is a score for each and every pixel value (three per pixel in the case of color images) indicating its relative importance in

7 Carlini and Wagner, "Audio Adversarial Examples."

8 Nicolas Papernot et al., "The Limitations of Deep Learning in Adversarial Settings," 1st IEEE European Symposium on Security & Privacy (2016), *http://bit.ly/2ZyrSOQ*.

achieving the adversarial goal. Changes to pixels with a higher score have greater potential to change the image to an adversarial one than pixels with a lower score.

The adversarial saliency for a particular pixel considers two things:

- The effect of the change on *increasing* the predicted score for the target classification (in a targeted attack)
- The effect of the change on *decreasing* the predicted score for all other classifications

The changes to input that are likely to have the greatest effect on achieving the adversarial goal will have a high value for both, so these are the changes that will be made first.

The JSMA selects the pixels that have the greatest impact and changes them by a set amount in the relevant direction (i.e., either increases or decreases their values). Essentially, this is moving a set distance along carefully chosen directions in the multidimensional input space in the hope of bringing the image to a location in the prediction landscape that satisfies the adversarial criteria. If the goal is not achieved, the process is repeated until it is.

The JSMA minimizes the number of pixel value changes to the image, so it's the L^0-norm measurement that's being used this time as a measure of change.

JSMA Mathematics

Computing the saliency score requires knowing the relative impact that a small change to *every* input has on *every* one of the output predictions.

Say we have n input values and m output classifications. All these relative changes can be expressed in a large matrix—called a Jacobian matrix—of dimensions $m * n$. For each pixel value and prediction, this matrix contains a value indicting the impact that changing the pixel value will have on a particular prediction.

Each of these values is the forward derivative of the DNN function f for a prediction j with respect to a change in a particular value i:[9]

$$\frac{\partial f(\mathbf{x})_j}{\partial x_i}$$

---

9 Once again, as with backpropagation, derivatives are calculated using the chain rule: the mathematical technique that enables the derivative to be calculated by considering $f(\mathbf{x})$ as composition of the functions in each DNN layer.

The expression for the complete matrix is therefore:

$$S_{mn} = \frac{\partial f(\mathbf{x})_m}{\partial x_n}$$

The forward derivatives calculated for every pixel-prediction pair in the Jacobian matrix enable us to calculate the saliency for each pixel with respect to a target output using the following logic.

For an adversarial target classification of t, the saliency of input value i *increasing* is calculated as follows:

- If increasing the value of the input will reduce the target prediction score, the derivative

$$\frac{\partial f(\mathbf{x})_j}{\partial x_i}$$

will be less than 0. In this scenario the input is not adversarially salient and is simply set to 0:

$$\text{if} \quad \frac{\partial f(\mathbf{x})_t}{\partial x_i} < 0 \quad \text{then} \quad s_{adv} = 0$$

- Similarly, if increasing the input value causes an overall increase in all the other (nontarget) class predictions, this won't aid the adversarial goal. This is the sum of all the derivatives for all predictions other than the target with respect to the input. If this sum is greater than 0, then once again the input value is set to 0 and the input value is not considered adversarially salient:

$$\text{else if} \quad \sum_{j \neq t} \frac{\partial f(\mathbf{x})_t}{\partial x_i} > 0 \quad \text{then} \quad s_{adv} = 0$$

- Otherwise, the input value is adversarially salient, so we just need to quantify this saliency to enable comparison against the other input values. This can be done by taking the product of the partial derivative calculated in the first step and the value of the partial derivative sum calculated in the second step. The first part must be positive and the second part must be negative due to the constraints mentioned previously, so we negate this product to make the answer positive:

otherwise $s_{adv} = -\dfrac{\partial f(\mathbf{x})_t}{\partial x_i} \cdot \displaystyle\sum_{j \neq t} \dfrac{\partial f(\mathbf{x})_t}{\partial x_i}$

Written out in full, we can create a "saliency map" S^+ that represents the influence an increase in each input will have in causing the desired prediction:

$$
S^+(x_i, t) = \begin{cases} 0 & \text{if} \quad \dfrac{\partial f(\mathbf{x})_t}{\partial x_i} < 0 \quad \text{or} \quad \displaystyle\sum_{j \neq t} \dfrac{\partial f(\mathbf{x})_t}{\partial x_i} > 0 \\[2em] -\dfrac{\partial f(\mathbf{x})_t}{\partial x_i} \cdot \displaystyle\sum_{j \neq t} \dfrac{\partial f(\mathbf{x})_t}{\partial x_i} & \text{otherwise} \end{cases}
$$

This saliency map represents the adversarial saliency across inputs if they were *increased*. The JSMA also involves calculating to establish which pixels would have the greatest impact in creating a misclassification if they were *decreased*. This requires slight changes to the logic to create another saliency map, S^-:

$$
S^-(x_i, t) = \begin{cases} 0 & \text{if} \quad \dfrac{\partial f(\mathbf{x})_t}{\partial x_i} > 0 \quad \text{or} \quad \displaystyle\sum_{j \neq t} \dfrac{\partial f(\mathbf{x})_t}{\partial x_i} < 0 \\[2em] -\dfrac{\partial f(\mathbf{x})_t}{\partial x_i} \cdot \displaystyle\sum_{j \neq t} \dfrac{\partial f(\mathbf{x})_t}{\partial x_i} & \text{otherwise} \end{cases}
$$

(Note the greater-than and less-than operators have switched position for this case.)

The JSMA takes the single most salient pixels from each of the maps S^+ and S^- to provide a pair of pixels that are each changed by a small amount in their relevant directions. The whole process is then repeated until the input is classified as adversarial.

The following code snippet demonstrates the Foolbox `SaliencyMapAttack` on the ResNet50 classifier that we created in Chapter 4.

Code Example: Saliency Attack

The complete code for this attack can be found in the Jupyter notebook chapter06/resnet50_foolbox_saliency.ipynb (*http://bit.ly/2KpRKsL*).

Let's begin by selecting our original nonadversarial photograph and running it through the classifier:

```
original_image_path = '../images/koala.jpg'
x = image_from_file(original_image_path, [224,224]) ❶
```

❶ This helper utility is in the GitHub repository. It reads in the file and resizes it.

Import the relevant libraries and the ResNet50 model. We'll pass the nonadversarial image to the model to check the prediction returned from ResNet50:

```
import tensorflow as tf
from tensorflow import keras
from keras.applications.resnet50 import ResNet50
from keras.applications.resnet50 import preprocess_input
from keras.applications.resnet50 import decode_predictions

model = ResNet50(weights='imagenet', include_top=True)

x_preds = model.predict(np.expand_dims(preprocess_input(x), 0))
y = np.argmax(x_preds)
y_name = decode_predictions(x_preds, top=1)[0][0][1]

print("Prediction for image: ", y_name)
```

This generates the following output:

```
Prediction for image:  koala
```

Now let's create the Foolbox model from the ResNet50 one. We need to articulate the preprocessing required:

```
import foolbox

preprocessing = (np.array([103.939, 116.779, 123.68]), 1) ❶
fmodel = foolbox.models.TensorFlowModel.from_keras(model,
                                                   bounds=(0, 255),
                                                   preprocessing=preprocessing)
```

❶ The Foolbox model can perform preprocessing on the image to make it suitable for ResNet50. This involves normalizing the data around the ImageNet mean RGB values on which the classifier was initially trained. The preprocessing variable defines the means for this preprocessing step. The equivalent normalization is done in keras.applications.resnet50.preprocess_input—the function that we have called previously to prepare input for ResNet50. To understand this preprocessing in greater detail and try it for yourself, take a look at the Jupyter notebook chapter04/resnet50_preprocessing.ipynb (*http://bit.ly/2WO9rUx*).

As mentioned in "Image Classification Using ResNet50" on page 68, ResNet50 was trained on images with the channels ordered BGR, rather than RGB. This step (also in keras.applications.resnet50.preprocess_input) switches the channels of the image data to BGR:

```
x_bgr = x[..., ::-1]
```

Next, we set up the Foolbox attack:

```
attack_criterion = foolbox.criteria.Misclassification()
attack = foolbox.attacks.SaliencyMapAttack(fmodel, criterion=attack_criterion)
```

and run it:

```
x_adv = attack(input_or_adv = x_bgr,
                          label = y,
                          unpack = False)
```

Let's check the predicted label and class name of the returned adversarial image:

```
x_adv = adversarial.image[..., ::-1] ❶

x_adv_preds = model.predict(preprocess_input(x_adv[np.newaxis].copy()))
y_adv = np.argmax(x_adv_preds)
y_adv_name = decode_predictions(x_adv_preds, top=1)[0][0][1]

print(print("Prediction for image: ", y_adv_name))
```

❶ Get the adversarial image from the `foolbox.adversarial` object and change the channels back to RGB order.

The output is:

```
Prediction for image:  weasel
```

Finally, we display the images alongside each other with their difference (Figure 6-8):

```
import matplotlib.pyplot as plt

plt.figure()

# Plot the original image
plt.subplot(1, 3, 1)
plt.title(y_name)
plt.imshow(x)
plt.axis('off')

# Plot the adversarial image
plt.subplot(1, 3, 2)
plt.title(y_adv_name)
plt.imshow(x_adv)
plt.axis('off')

# Plot the difference
plt.subplot(1, 3, 3)
plt.title('Difference')
difference = x_adv - x

# Set differences that haven't changed to 255 so they don't show on the plot
difference[difference == 0] = 255 ❶
plt.imshow(abs(difference))
```

```
plt.xticks([])
plt.yticks([])

plt.show()
```

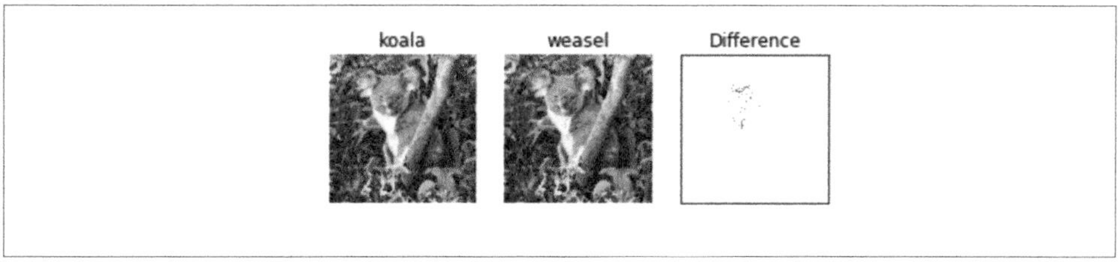

Figure 6-8. Code output

The difference image in Figure 6-8 shows that a relatively small number of pixels have been changed. You may be able to see the perturbation on the adversarial image in the center.

Increasing Adversarial Confidence

The FGSM and JSMA methods generate adversarial examples, but because these attacks generate input close to classification boundaries, they attacks may be susceptible to preprocessing or active defense by the target system. For example, a minor change to the pixels of an adversarial image might change its classification.

Creating input that is more confidently adversarial allows the adversary greater robustness. Carlini and Wagner proposed an alternative attack method which does exactly this.[10] The attack iteratively minimizes the L^2-norm measurement of change, while also ensuring that the difference between the confidence of the adversarial target and the next most likely classification is maximized. This gives the adversarial example greater wiggle room before it is rendered nonadversarial. This attack is referred to as the *C&W attack*.

---

10 Carlini and Wagner, "Towards Evaluating the Robustness of Neural Networks."

Carlini and Wagner Attack Mathematics

Assuming a targeted attack:

$$f\left(\mathbf{x^{adv}}\right) = y_t$$

where y_t represents the target adversarial classification (and the classification is derived from the output probability vector).

The L^2-norm version of the C&W attack minimizes the L^2-norm.

Taking the square of the L^2-norm reduces the computational complexity because it removes the requirement to calculate the square root. Therefore, the distance measurement between the adversarial and the nonadversarial image is defined as:

$$\| d \|_2^2 = \| \mathbf{x^{adv}} - \mathbf{x} \|_2^2$$

The C&W attack ensures robustness by creating an adversarial example that maximizes the difference between the target adversarial class prediction and the next likely class prediction. The predictions are the logits returned in the layer prior to softmax processing. These logits are expressed as:

$$Z\left(\mathbf{x^{adv}}\right)$$

Assuming the highest prediction for the adversarial example is logit t, the second-highest prediction for the adversarial example is expressed as follows:

$$\max\left\{Z\left(\mathbf{x^{adv}}\right)_i : i \neq t\right\}$$

Subtracting the target prediction gives the difference between it and the second-highest value:

$$\max\left\{Z\left(\mathbf{x^{adv}}\right)_i : i \neq t\right\} - Z\left(\mathbf{x^{adv}}\right)_t$$

This returns a negative number indicating the confidence of the example. The more negative it is, the greater the confidence in the example.

We can provide a way to adjust the confidence required by adding a parameter k. This value serves as a mechanism to define the confidence required when we take the maximum of the preceding difference calculation and the negation of k. An increased value of k results in a more confident example:

$$\max\left\{\max\left\{Z\left(\mathbf{x}^{\mathbf{adv}}\right)_i : i \neq t\right\} - Z\left(\mathbf{x}^{\mathbf{adv}}\right)_{t'} - k\right\}$$

We'll call the confidence loss function for the adversarial example l. Putting it all together gives:

$$\text{minimize} \quad \left\{ \parallel \mathbf{x}^{adv} - \mathbf{x} \parallel_2^2 + c \,.\, l\left(\mathbf{x}^{\mathbf{adv}}\right) \right\}$$

where:

$$l\left(\mathbf{x}^{adv}\right) = \max\left\{\max\left\{Z\left(\mathbf{x}^{\mathbf{adv}}\right)_i : i \neq t\right\} - Z\left(\mathbf{x}^{\mathbf{adv}}\right)_{t'} - k\right\}$$

If you look carefully, you may notice an extra parameter c has snuck into the equation. This "balances" the two aspects of the equation—the distance measurement, which is positive, and the confidence measurement, which is zero or negative—so that the confidence measurement does not dominate the equation at the risk of the distance (perturbation) becoming too large. The value for c is determined using a binary search algorithm.

Variations on White Box Approaches

This section has introduced a few of the available white box approaches for generating adversarial examples. There are other methods, and undoubtedly more will be developed.

All white box approaches share the same aim: to optimize the search of the input space by using some computationally feasible algorithm. Either directly or indirectly, all the methods exploit knowledge of model gradients to minimize the required adversarial perturbation. Optimizing the search may involve some approximation or random step, and that may incur a trade-off in terms of a larger perturbation than is absolutely necessary. In addition, due to the variation in how the algorithms search the input space, different approaches will return different adversarial examples.

Limited Black Box Methods

Limited black box query methods iteratively refine the adversarial perturbation based on output returned from the model. This could be, for example, the final classification of an image ("cat" or "dog") or the text output from a speech-to-text translation. With these methods, the adversary has no access to the model itself or to the raw scores (predictions) from its output layer. Essentially, there's a level of indirection; the output of the DNN model has been processed and simplified in some way to provide a result and it is only this result that the attacker has access to.

It's not immediately obvious how an adversary might effectively search the input space in the limited black box scenario. One approach would be to iteratively make a small change to the input, run it through the model, and check the classification to see whether it has altered. However, this is unlikely to be an effective strategy because there is no way of knowing whether the small change is moving the image toward the required nefarious part of the input space until the classification changes. This brute-force method will be too slow and clumsy; the adversary will need a better plan.

The *boundary attack* proposed by Brendel et al.[11] is a clever strategy that is pleasantly simple in its approach. A targeted boundary attack is depicted in Figure 6-9. It is seeded with the original image (in this case, a sneaker) and a sample image (in this case, a sandal), as shown by the circle and square, respectively. The sample is an image that is classified by the model as the target classification. So, in this case, we want the sneaker image to look like a sneaker but be classified as a sandal.

The boundary attack begins with the sandal image rather than the original sneaker image. It iteratively moves the image closer to the sneaker, while never allowing each iterative step to alter the adversarial classification by straying across the classification boundary.

The algorithm begins with an initialization step. The sample image from the adversarial target class is overlaid with a diluted version of the original to create an input that is *just* adversarial. This is done by overlaying the sample sandal image with selected pixels from the original sneaker image until the resulting image is located just on the adversarial side of the classification boundary. This will take quite a few iterations; overlay, test, and repeat until any further changes would make the image nonadversarial. At this point, the image has moved *just* across the classification boundary and is classified as a sneaker. It's gone a little too far, so the input from the original image is reduced *very slightly* to return it to the adversarial (sandal) classification.

Conceptually, this is moving the image from the sample toward the original, then stopping at the boundary just before it takes on the original classification. The location of the image at the end of the initialization step is shown in Figure 6-9 as the triangle marked with a "1."

---

11 Wieland Brendel et al., "Decision-Based Adversarial Attacks: Reliable Attacks Against Black-Box Machine Learning Models," *Proceedings of the International Conference on Learning Representations* (2018), *http://bit.ly/2Y7Zi6w*.

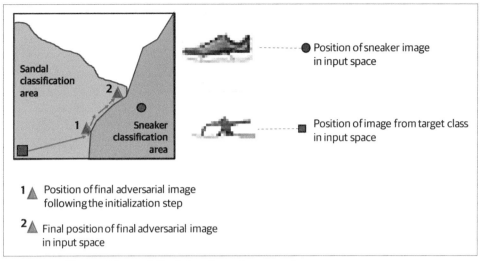

1 ▲ Position of final adversarial image
following the initialization step

2 ▲ Final position of final adversarial image
in input space

Figure 6-9. Targeted limited black box boundary attack

At the end of the initialization step, the current image is *just* within the adversarial boundary. However, it is unlikely to be sufficiently close to the original for the perturbation to be hidden. In this case, it most likely still looks like the sandal. The algorithm then creeps along the edge of the boundary, at each step testing random perturbations that would bring the input closer to the original sneaker. Each time, the input is submitted to the target DNN; if it steps outside the adversarial boundary, it is discarded. Each iteration to bring the sample image closer to the original may therefore take multiple steps. At some point, the image is deemed close enough to the original to look like it, and yet retain the adversarial classification of the sample.

Let's take a look at the code for a targeted boundary attack on Fashion-MNIST. We'll try to turn the sneaker into a sandal, as illustrated in Figure 6-9.

> **Code Example: Saliency Attack**
>
> The complete code for this attack can be found in the Jupyter notebook chapter06/fashionMNIST_foolbox_boundary.ipynb (*http://bit.ly/2L2x61i*).

The code for the boundary attack requires specifying an original image (x) and starting point image. First we'll specify the original image, establish its classification, and display it (see Figure 6-10):

```
original_image_num = 9

x = test_images[original_image_num]
y = np.argmax(predictions[original_image_num]) ❶
```

```
y_name = class_names[y]

print("Prediction for original image:", y, y_name)

plt.imshow(x, cmap=plt.cm.binary)
```

❶ y is the original (nonadversarial) prediction.

This output is generated:

```
Prediction for original image: 7 Sneaker
```

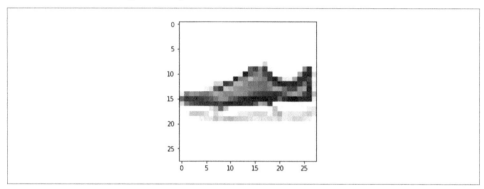

Figure 6-10. Code output

Next, we select the starting point image, establish its classification, and display it (see Figure 6-11). This image has the required adversarial classification:

```
starting_point_image_num = 52

starting_point_image = test_images[starting_point_image_num]
y_adv = np.argmax(predictions[starting_point_image_num])      ❶
y_adv_name = class_names[y_adv]

print("Prediction for starting point image:", y_adv, y_adv_name)
import matplotlib.pyplot as plt

plt.imshow(starting_point_image, cmap=plt.cm.binary)
```

❶ y_adv is the target adversarial prediction.

This generates the following output:

```
Prediction for starting point image: 5 Sandal
```

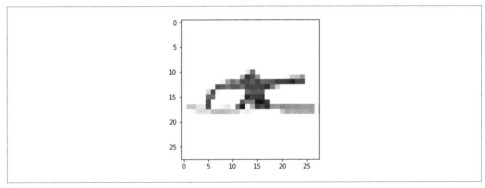

Figure 6-11. Code output

Now we prepare the Foolbox attack:

```
import foolbox

fmodel = foolbox.models.TensorFlowModel.from_keras(model, bounds=(0, 1))
attack_criterion = foolbox.criteria.TargetClass(y_adv) ❶
attack = foolbox.attacks.BoundaryAttack(fmodel, criterion=attack_criterion)
```

❶ This is a targeted attack, so we use the `TargetClass` criteria.

And issue the attack:

```
x_adv = attack(input_or_adv = x,
               label = y,
               starting_point = starting_point_image,
               unpack = False,
               log_every_n_steps = 500)
```

Which generates this output:

```
run with verbose=True to see details
Step 0: 5.60511e-02, stepsizes = 1.0e-02/1.0e-02:
Step 500: 1.44206e-02, stepsizes = 1.5e-02/2.0e-03:
Step 1000: 3.43213e-03, stepsizes = 1.5e-02/1.3e-03: d. reduced by 0.26% (...)
Step 1500: 1.91473e-03, stepsizes = 6.7e-03/5.9e-04: d. reduced by 0.12% (...)
Step 2000: 1.54220e-03, stepsizes = 3.0e-03/1.7e-04: d. reduced by 0.03% (...)
Step 2500: 1.41537e-03, stepsizes = 8.8e-04/5.1e-05: d. reduced by 0.01% (...)
Step 3000: 1.37426e-03, stepsizes = 5.9e-04/2.3e-05: d. reduced by 0.00% (...)
Step 3500: 1.34719e-03, stepsizes = 3.9e-04/2.3e-05:
Step 4000: 1.32744e-03, stepsizes = 3.9e-04/1.5e-05: d. reduced by 0.00% (...)
Step 4500: 1.31362e-03, stepsizes = 1.7e-04/1.0e-05:
Step 5000: 1.30831e-03, stepsizes = 5.1e-05/2.0e-06:
```

The attack is stopped by default when the algorithm converges or after 5,000 iterations. At this point we hope that we have crept around the decision boundary to a
position close enough to the original image for it to look the same. Let's take a look
(see the output in Figure 6-12):

```
preds = model.predict(np.array([x_adv.image]))

plt.figure()

# Plot the original image
plt.subplot(1, 3, 1)
plt.title(y_name)
plt.imshow(x, cmap=plt.cm.binary)
plt.axis('off')

# Plot the adversarial image
plt.subplot(1, 3, 2)
plt.title(class_names[np.argmax(preds[0])])
plt.imshow(x_adv.image, cmap=plt.cm.binary)
plt.axis('off')

# Plot the difference
plt.subplot(1, 3, 3)
plt.title('Difference')
difference = x_adv.image - x
plt.imshow(difference, vmin=0, vmax=1, cmap=plt.cm.binary)
plt.axis('off')

plt.show()
```

Figure 6-12. Code output

Figure 6-13 shows the image after every hundred iterations (up to 1,200 iterations) during the attack. The sandal changes to be increasingly similar to the original image without changing its classification. The sandal prediction is in brackets under each image—you'll see that it creeps around the boundary with the prediction close to 0.5 throughout the optimization. The code to generate Figure 6-13 is also in the Jupyter notebook chapter06/fashionMNIST_foolbox_boundary.ipynb (*http://bit.ly/2L2x61i*).

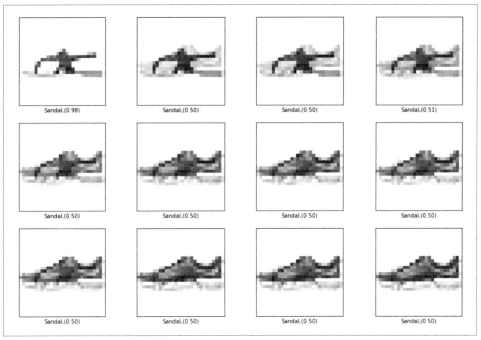

Figure 6-13. The boundary attack begins with an image from the target class and gradually moves it closer to the original

The boundary attack is a very powerful attack able to effectively create adversarial input. However, it is likely to take thousands of iterations, and each iteration may involve several queries to the DNN.

Score-Based Black Box Methods

Score-based methods fall somewhere between the white box and limited black box categories. Sometimes in research literature score-based models are termed *black box*, but the term *score-based* is used throughout this book to clearly distinguish between the two.

Score-based methods require access to the output class probabilities of the model; that is, the attacker can submit an input and receive the predicted scores from which the final decision (such as the classification) will be made by the DNN. It's worth noting that the scores available to the attacker may be limited (for example, the top five probabilities).

Score-based methods might appear closer to limited black box methods; after all, the adversary only has access to input and output. However, access to the scores could be considered "privileged," as typically an attacker would not have access to the raw

DNN output. The score-based methods are therefore closer in characteristics to white box approaches. They approximate the model's algorithm through output predicted scores and then perform an intelligent search to establish the perturbation required to achieve the adversarial goal. But unlike in a white box attack, the attacker does not have access to the model algorithm. Therefore, they cannot compute the algorithm gradients that are required for the white box methods presented previously. (There are other ways of searching for the adversarial example, such as using a genetic algorithm, as explained in the following note.)

Genetic Algorithm Approach to Search

Genetic algorithms are commonly used in software to search for good solutions among many possibilities. They exploit the notion of an ever-evolving population of possible options where each successive generation aims to be an improvement on the previous one.

Applied to adversarial generation, the genetic strategy begins with a population of nonadversarial inputs, each generated by adding some random perturbation to the original benign sample. In the context of audio, this population can be generated by selecting several random subclips from the original audio clip and adding a small random perturbation to each.[12] Each sample is scored in terms of its adversarial fitness based on the result returned when it is passed to the network.

A next generation of samples is then created by a process that requires selection, cross-over, and mutation. First, a subset of the existing generation is selected to be "parents," with preference given to those with a higher fitness score. The adversarial aspects of the parents are combined (cross-over) and some additional random noise (mutation) added to create the children that will form the next generation. Once again, each member of the new generation is scored for adversarial fitness based on the scores returned from the network.

The process completes either when an adversarial example is created, or when the number of generations exceeds a maximum threshold (in which case the genetic algorithm has failed to produce a result).

At this point, you might be wondering why any organization that cared about the security of its model would make the scores available. For example, if an image was automatically deemed to contain inappropriate content on a social media website and therefore qualify for removal, the individual who uploaded the image would receive

---

12 M. Alzantot et al., "Did You Hear That? Adversarial Examples Against Automatic Speech Recognition," Conference on Neural Information Processing Systems, Machine Deception Workshop (2017), *http://bit.ly/2ITvtR3*.

at best a warning or notification that their image had been censored. They would not receive the detailed output scores depicting the classification probabilities that the DNN assigned to the image. So, no, an organization wouldn't make the scoring information available in scenarios such as this. However, there are a number of open APIs created for the benefit of showcasing and advancing DNN technology that do make the scores available. While the security of these models themselves is not a risk, as we shall see in Chapter 7, openly available model APIs could be exploited as a model substitute, saving the adversary the effort of creating their own model.

Summary

This chapter has considered a selection of methods for the generation of adversarial perturbation. There are many other variations on these methods, and new methods are regularly proposed.

Although these methods were discussed in the context of images, the fundamental techniques are just as applicable to audio or video. Also, don't assume mathematical optimization approaches are always required to generate adversarial input; very simple methods might also be exploited if there is no mitigation in place at the target. For example, it has been shown[13] that algorithms performing video search and summarization can be fooled by simply inserting occasional still images into the video. The still images contain content that results in the network returning an incorrect result, but they are inserted at a sufficiently low rate to not be noticed by humans.

As we have seen, the algorithms to generate adversarial perturbation are essentially mathematical optimizations. When considering defenses in Part IV, it will become clear that many approaches to defending against adversarial examples involve changing or extending the model's algorithm. Creating adversarial examples that thwart the defenses thus remains an optimization problem, just against a different algorithm. Many defenses, therefore, succeed in constraining the methods available to the adversary, but are not guaranteed defenses.

This chapter has considered the mathematical approaches for generating adversarial examples against DNN models. Next, Part III explores how an attacker can use these theoretical approaches against real-world systems that incorporate AI.

---

13 Hosseini Hossein et al., "Deceiving Google's Cloud Video Intelligence API Built for Summarizing Videos" (2017), *http://bit.ly/2FhbDxR*.

## PART III

Understanding the Real-World Threat

Part II explored the mathematical and algorithmic methods that can be used to develop input capable of fooling DNNs. Part III uses these methods to consider the threat posed in real-world scenarios where the targeted DNN forms part of a broader computer system. This broader system might be, for example, a voice controlled device, web filtering software, or an autonomous vehicle.

Chapter 7 explores the methods that an adversary might use to launch an adversarial attack when they have restricted access to the target. In this chapter, we'll consider what might make it more challenging (or easier) for an adversary to launch an attack and look at a variety of possible attack patterns: direct, replica, and transfer. We'll also explore whether it's possible for an attack developed against one target to work on another.

In Chapter 8, we'll consider the additional complexities posed to the adversary in generating physical-world attacks. In these scenarios the attack moves away from the purely digital realm to adversarial objects or adversarial sounds that are created and exist in the physical world. This chapter will explore how these physical-world examples might be created in such a way that they are adversarial regardless of changes in the environment or the positioning of the camera or microphone capturing the data.

Understanding the threat is a fundamental part of securing any system. This part lays the foundations for examining defenses in Part IV.

## CHAPTER 7

Attack Patterns for Real-World Systems

In this chapter we explore the various attack patterns that could be used to generate adversarial input, taking into account the attacker's goals and capabilities. These patterns exploit the methods described in Chapter 6, and as we will see, the selected approach will depend on factors such as the access that the adversary has to the target to test and develop adversarial input and their knowledge of the target model and processing chain. We'll also consider whether an adversarial perturbation or an adversarial patch could be reused across different image or audio files.

Attack Patterns

Chapter 6 considered different techniques for generating adversarial examples. These methods have been proven in a "laboratory" environment, but how do they play out in real-world scenarios where the adversary has limited knowledge of or access to the target model and broader system? Creating adversarial input that is effective in a real-world scenario will pose a significant challenge to any attacker.

There are several different patterns that might be exploited to generate adversarial input and subsequently launch an attack. These patterns vary in terms of complexity and the resources needed to generate adversarial examples. In addition, some approaches require greater knowledge of, or access to, the target system han others. The pattern selected may also depend upon the required robustness and covertness of the attack.

Broadly speaking, we can categorize these approaches as follows:

Direct attack
    The attacker develops the attack on the target system itself.

Replica attack

The attacker has access to an *exact* replica of the target DNN in order to develop the attack.

Transfer attack

The attacker develops the attack on a substitute model which *approximates* the target.

Universal transfer attack

The attacker has no information about the target model. They create adversarial input that works across an ensemble of models that perform similar functions to the target in the hope that it will also work on the target DNN.

Figure 7-1 provides a summary of the four approaches.

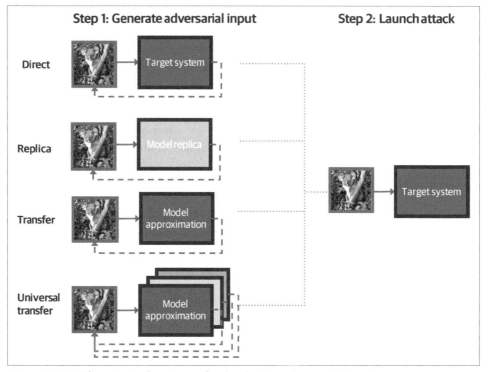

Figure 7-1. Different attack patterns for developing adversarial input

In the following sections we explore each of the patterns in greater detail. We'll assume at this stage that the adversary can manipulate the digital content; physical-world adversarial examples will be considered in Chapter 8.

Attack Pattern Terminology

Many different terms are used across the literature to describe the various attack patterns. The lack of consistently adopted terminology can make things quite confusing.

For example, you may come across the term *black box* used to refer to a direct attack. Similarly, a replica attack using white box methods may be referred to elsewhere simply as a "white box attack."

To avoid ambiguity, the terms *white box* and *black box* have not been used in this book to refer to attack patterns because these terms also imply the use of a specific algorithmic method.

Consider, for example, a replica attack. As the attacker has complete knowledge of the model, the model architecture, and its parameters, it may seem logical to use a white box method to generate adversarial input. However, the adversary could use a black box method (such as the boundary attack), possibly because it is more robust against defenses, or maybe just because it's easier to implement. Similarly, although transfer attacks are sometimes referred to as "black box," such an attack could use white box or black box methods on the substitute model.

Direct Attack

In a direct attack, the attacker is able to submit inputs to the actual target and receive corresponding results, enabling accurate feedback to refine adversarial input.

In such an attack, the adversary is unlikely to have access to more detail than the restricted responses that the target system returns.[1] Additionally, the feedback may not be direct but inferred; for example, failure of a video to be successfully uploaded might suggest that it has been classified as containing violent content, although the adversary did not receive this classification explicitly. Creation of adversarial input will therefore require a black box approach. As discussed in "Limited Black Box Methods" on page 121, black box approaches iteratively refine queries submitted to the system based on the responses returned to morph the input and move it to the required adversarial area of the input space.

A direct attack poses a significant problem. Finding that perfect adversarial input using a black box approach such as a boundary attack takes many iterations (tens of thousands). Each iteration also requires a handful of queries to the target DNN. That's a lot of queries, which are unlikely to go unnoticed by the defending organization! What's more, the throughput and latency of a commercial deployment will slow

---

1 In real-world systems where there might be a motivation for an attack, the adversary will not receive the raw probabilistic scores from the target.

the rate at which these queries can be processed. In fact, the target system might also limit queries or introduce latency to responses specifically to protect against such an attack. If the attacker is fortunate enough to have access to the scores returned from the target, it may be possible to reduce the query volume through more intelligent strategies, such as the genetic algorithm approach described in "Score-Based Black Box Methods" on page 127. However, as discussed previously, access to the scores is likely to be limited.

The direct approach considers the complete processing chain and any active defenses being employed by the system, not only the DNN. So, although an attacker may use one of the other nondirect approaches to develop an attack, an element of direct experimentation on the target is likely to be critical to ensure the adversarial robustness of the input.

Replica Attack

An obvious approach to developing adversarial input is to use an exact replica of the target to finesse the adversarial input, prior to launching it on the target. We'll consider a couple of scenarios: when the attacker has access to a replica of the complete target, and when the attacker has access to just the DNN algorithm.

Replica system

It is possible for the attacker to have a local copy of the complete target system to experiment with. For example, a commercially purchased digital voice assistant or perhaps an autonomous vehicle. An attacker could develop their own adversarial input on their local target by repetitive simulation queries and monitoring of the responses using a black box method.[2]

In practice, target systems that are commercially available to buy (not web hosted) will often not accept input digitally and return a digital response. For example, a commercially purchased digital assistant is unlikely to provide a nice programming interface to its internal processing chain for the attacker to use to iteratively refine the adversarial input based on repeated queries. Rather, it will take audio input and return audio (speech) or instigate some digital command (such as an online purchase). Automating the generation of adversarial input will be more challenging when the interaction (request or response) is not digital.

Similar to the black box attack, access to a complete replica enables the attacker to test their attack against the complete processing chain, not just against the target DNN.

---

2 The local copy may send information back to a centralized backend for processing, as is often the case for voice controlled audio assistants.

Replica DNN

Armed with information about all aspects of the trained DNN under attack (that is, the model architecture and all its parameters), the attacker is in a strong position to generate adversarial input. In traditional software terms, it's akin to having knowledge of the source code of an internal algorithm in a target system. With this knowledge and sufficient capability, the attacker can create a replica of the DNN and use any method they wish on the replica to create adversarial examples that exploit flaws in the target DNN exactly.

Using a copy of the target to develop adversarial input might seem like a no-brainer, but where would an attacker get access to a replica? Surely a security conscious organization would never knowingly share any algorithm that it uses internally? This isn't necessarily true—as DNNs typically require large amounts of labeled data, computational resource, and a data scientist to train effectively, it would not be unreasonable for an organization to use a pretrained model obtained commercially or through open source, simply to save on time and resources. If the attacker was aware of the model being used and has some access to an identical one (either by creating a replica or using an existing published copy) they would be able to launch a replica attack. Even if the attacker had no insider knowledge of the model being used, they might be able to infer likely models from those publicly available and through educated guesswork about the target organization's internal processing.

Transfer Attack

When the adversary does not have access to the DNN algorithm used by the defending organization, it might be possible to use a good-enough approximation of the target DNN to develop adversarial input prior to launching it on the target. This is called a *transfer attack*.

The transfer attack strategy is likely to be the most feasible approach in many real-life scenarios where the internal DNN implementation is unknown outside the defending organization. This approach is also preferable to a direct attack because the development of the adversarial example is performed without querying the target. Thus, it does not arouse suspicion and is not subject to any limitations on or throttling of queries.

In a transfer attack, the adversary creates a substitute model to develop the adversarial input based on some limited knowledge of the target DNN. They use white box, score-based black box, or limited black box methods on this substitute to refine the adversarial example, prior to submitting it to the target. As with a replica attack, they may not need to create their own substitute model, or they might be able to exploit an existing one (for example, an online model with open API access).

There is, of course, an obvious problem for the attacker: the substitute needs to be behave in a similar way to the target, at least on the adversarial input. So, without access to the *exact* model, how easy would it be to create something that was close enough to work?

Creating something akin to the target system's DNN might appear to be an insurmountable problem. Think of the complexity of a DNN: how many layers does it have, what activation functions does it use, what's its structure, and what are its possible outputs? Is it really possible to create adversarial input using an approximate model substitute that will transfer effectively to the target system?

The answer is quite surprising. It turns out that, with limited access to information about the model, it is sometimes possible to create an imitation close enough to the original to develop adversarial examples that will transfer between the two models.[3] To understand why this is the case, consider what defines a DNN:

Input and output mappings
> This includes the format and precision of the input and the allowable outputs. In the case of a DNN classifier, there's the set of classifications and potentially the hierarchical structure of those classes (e.g., "dog" is a subset of the "animal" class).

Internal architecture
> The network type (for example LSTM or CNN), its layers, and number of nodes for each layer. This includes details of the activation function(s); basically, the aspects of the model defined prior to training.

Parameters
> The weights and biases established during training.

The adversary might be able to make an educated guess regarding certain aspects of these. For example, for the DNN architecture, it's likely that image classification is performed with some type of convolutional network. The adversary may also be able to guess the resolution of the input and possible output predictions (even without information on the exhaustive list of classifications).

Given that the attacker has made some informed guesswork about the network architecture and input/output mappings, let's consider the case where they have access to some, or all, of the training data. This is not an unreasonable assumption as, due to the cost of generating and labeling training data, training sets are often shared online.

Knowing the training data can enable the attacker to create a good approximation of the target model, even if they're able to infer very little about its architecture. Put

---

3 Florian Tramèr et al., "The Space of Transferable Adversarial Examples" (2017), *http://bit.ly/2IVGNfc*.

another way, two models with different architectures are likely to be susceptible to similar adversarial examples if they have been trained with the same data. This idea is illustrated in in Figure 7-2. Two completely different models trained on the same data are likely to establish similar prediction landscapes. This is as you would expect because the training data itself is obviously instrumental in defining the model parameters.

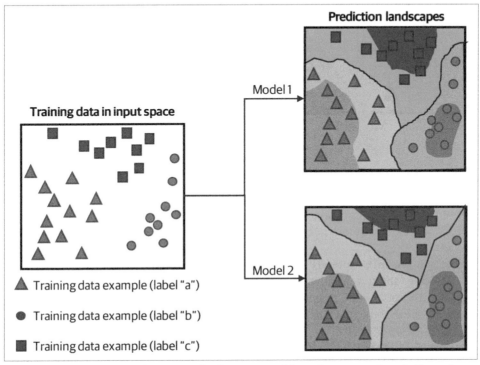

Figure 7-2. Input spaces of target and substitute models with training data indicated

Regions of the input space where the model returns an incorrect result are known as *adversarial subspaces*. These subspaces are where the training step has failed to generalize correctly. Therefore, they are likely to be at similar locations in models that share training data. Therefore, it's probable, but not guaranteed, that an adversarial example would transfer successfully if the substitute model shared its training data with its target.

To illustrate the notion of similar adversarial subspaces across models, Figure 7-3 depicts this idea using the prediction landscapes of the two models shown in Figure 7-2. The models have similar adversarial subspaces as they are based on the same training data. Hence, adversarial examples are likely to transfer across these models.

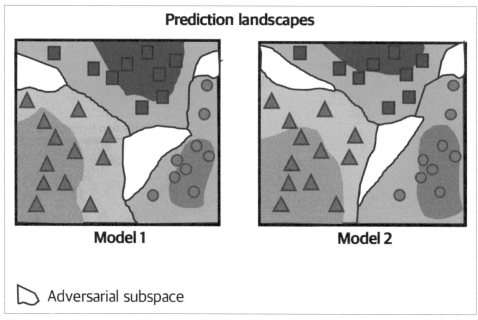

Figure 7-3. Input spaces of target and substitute models with adversarial subspaces indicated in white

As we will see in Chapter 10, the ability to approximate a DNN model based on knowledge of the training data has important implications for information security. Training datasets should therefore be considered sensitive artifacts as they indirectly imply behavior of the machine learned models that they are used to train.

Universal Transfer Attack

A universal transfer attack is a method exploited when the adversary has no knowledge of the target DNN or its training data. In this scenario, the adversary creates adversarial input using an ensemble of substitute models. If the example works across a variety of substitutes, it may be flexible enough to transfer to the target.

It's interesting that although training datasets may differ, they are likely to populate similar areas of the input space if they are derived from information representing the natural world. The areas of the model where there is a lack of representative data (corresponding to OoD data[4]) are likely to be similar *regardless* of the training dataset. Training datasets are also likely to bear similarities to each other due to (for example) common camera angles or common voice characteristics. In other words, different

---

4 Out-of-distribution data was introduced in "Generalizations from Training Data" on page 79.

training datasets may have similar distributions in terms of characteristics, features, and, most importantly, adversarial subspaces.

Universal adversarial subspaces make a universal transfer attack possible. It is (unsurprisingly) more difficult to achieve, but the ability to launch a universal transfer attack is very powerful to an adversary. Adversarial input that works across models also allows an attack across a group of DNNs (such as multiple search engines). Once again, in practice an attacker might combine a universal transfer attack with direct experimentation (see the following sidebar for an example).

Hypothetical Example: Circumventing Video Classification

A video curation web company wishes to improve the classification of its videos to ensure that content can be filtered according to the viewer. The company develops an automated DNN algorithm able to classify videos (for example, "contains violence" or "features use of drugs") based on a combination of audio and image information.

An adversarial organization is incentivized to manipulate video content that is being uploaded so that it is viewed by a wider audience. The organization creates a substitute model and uses white box methods to develop adversarial input based on that model. The substitute is an approximation based on the (correct) assumption that the target web company will have used a neural network architecture trained with open data.

The adversarial organization then uses the direct attack pattern in combination with the transfer approach to test and refine the generated adversarial examples so that they transfer effectively and are robust to the processing chain.

A most interesting application of the universal attack is in cases where the attacker receives no feedback from the target because the target organization is processing the data for its own purposes (market analysis, for example). We could consider this a "black hole" attack; the adversary may never know whether it succeeded and will need a high degree of tolerance to failure.

Reusable Patches and Reusable Perturbation

Imagine the possibility of creating reusable adversarial alterations that could be shared across different input data. For example, adversarial perturbation or a patch that could work effectively on *any* image, or adversarial distortion applicable to *all* audio files. This create-once-and-reuse approach would undoubtedly open an exciting opportunity for our adversary. No longer would they need to regenerate fresh adversarial content for every image or audio file; they could instead simply overlay a patch or perturbation that they had prepared earlier, saving on cost, time, and queries to the target system.

In "Adversarial Patch," researchers Brown et al.[5] generated patches that could be reused on different images. The size or location of the patch on the target image that it is being added to will affect its effectiveness, but these patches really do work across images. This instinctively makes sense; if you can find some super-salient patch that is able to distract a neural network, it's likely to work across multiple images.

Experimentation with Reusable Patches

If you'd like to try a reusable patch on your own images, head over to the Jupyter notebook chapter07/reusable_patch.ipynb (*http://bit.ly/2WSCgnY*) in this book's GitHub repository.

Intuitively, you might assume that reusable adversarial perturbation is unlikely to be achievable because the adversarial change is generated to achieve its aims based on the characteristics of a specific image or specific piece of audio. Put another way, adversarial perturbation is a movement from a location in the input space that is unlikely to work from a different starting point. Figure 7-4 illustrates this point. The illustration shows an imaginary input space zoomed out, and two images sharing the same classification but in different locations. When the adversarial perturbation calculated to move image 1 to a misclassification is applied to image 2, the second image still resides comfortably within the correct classification area.

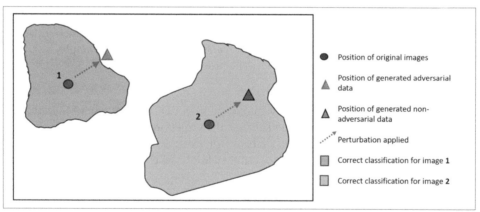

Figure 7-4. Transferring adversarial perturbation to a different image

Although it might seem unlikely, researchers Moosavi-Dezfooli et al.[6] have proven that it is possible to generate perturbations that are universal. This is achieved by

---

5 Brown et al., "Adversarial Patch."

6 Seyed-Mohsen Moosavi-Dezfooli et al., "Universal Adversarial Perturbations," IEEE Conference on Computer Vision and Pattern Recognition (2017), *http://bit.ly/2WV6JS7*.

optimizing adversarial perturbation using a formula that considers a sample of images from a distribution, rather than a single image in isolation.

The technique works as follows. An adversarial perturbation is calculated for an initial image to take that image outside its classification boundary. The same perturbation is then applied to a second image in the sample. If the second image is correctly classified (in other words, remains nonadversarial) after the perturbation has been applied—as shown in Figure 7-4—the perturbation has failed to demonstrate that it works across both images. An additional delta to the original perturbation is calculated that is sufficient to misclassify the second image. As long as this second delta does not return the first image to its correct classification, the resulting perturbation will succeed across both images. Figure 7-5 depicts this second delta.

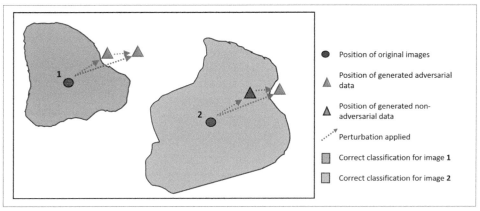

Figure 7-5. Calculating universal adversarial perturbation

This is repeated over a distribution of realistic images with the constraints that the resulting perturbation must be kept within a minimally quantified change (as defined by an L^p-norm) and that a specified proportion of the images must be fooled (termed the *fooling rate*). Obviously, a higher fooling rate may require more perturbation and therefore may be more noticeable, but the results are impressive. Although the perturbation is not guaranteed to work over all images, the researchers proved it possible to create perturbations that are imperceptible and work over 80% or 90% of images. They also proved that these perturbations transferred well across different models. The universal perturbations are untargeted; they change any image from its correct classification to another, unspecified one, and the resulting adversarial classification may differ between images.

Similar methods to those described above are likely to be applicable to audio. In the same way that the location and size of an adversarial patch on an image might affect its perceptibility and effectiveness, an audio patch may need to be located at a particular point within audio or have its loudness adjusted to work optimally. In addition to the benefits of reusability, universal adversarial audio distortion could be potentially played in any environment to, for example, maliciously control audio devices with hidden voice commands in waveforms. Adversarial audio reproduced in the physical world is discussed in "Adversarial Sound" on page 155.

Adversarial alterations that are designed to work across multiple inputs are unlikely to be guaranteed to succeed. However, they are low-cost, so may be suitable for cases where robustness is not paramount (the following sidebar for a hypothetical example). Perhaps the most interesting aspect of this approach is that it potentially allows for the sharing of adversarial capability between different threat actors. For example, a group or individual could sell adversarial patches online with simple software to attach them to images.

Hypothetical Example: Beer Branding

A brewing company has created a beer and would like to increase its association with a more popular brand to increase its profile.

As part of brand (mis)management, the company digitally develops an adversarial patch which causes some image search engines to confidently classify images of their beer as the more popular beer. The patch is not sufficiently visually similar (to a human) to breach copyright law.

By incorporating the patch on their cans and digital advertising content online, they hope to make the new brand of beer appear in searches for the more established brand.

The brewing company develops the adversarial patch with score-based black box methods using openly available APIs provided for research purposes. Due to latency and query restrictions incorporated into these systems, this takes a few weeks. But they have patience and refreshments.

While the attack is detectable by these open APIs, the purpose is not known and the attack is not against the open API–owning organization itself, so there is no need for covertness. The generated patch is incorporated in subsequent digital marketing material with the aspiration that it will transfer across images and to online search engines. The patch does not need a 100% success rate; occasional success should ensure that the aims are reached.

Bringing It Together: Hybrid Approaches and Trade-offs

In practice, a real-world attack is likely to comprise a combination of approaches. Perhaps the adversary will initially develop adversarial examples on a substitute model, then occasionally test them on the target system to get the best of all worlds.

As with all cyberattacks, preparation is key. Generating effective adversarial input prior to the attack is likely to involve experimentation on the target system to establish what works and what doesn't. So there's often a trade-off between covertness and robustness; developing a robust adversarial example may require more queries to the target. Running more queries, however, increase the chance of detection.

Adversarial examples that perform well in a theoretical environment may be susceptible to processing in the broader system. For example, as we will see in Chapter 10, adversarial examples often exploit the accuracy and resolution of digital data, so preprocessing that reduces data resolution may reduce adversarial effectiveness. Therefore, unless the adversary has an exact copy of the complete system under attack (that is, the complete processing chain, not just the DNN), they are likely to need to perform at least some experimentation on the target system.

Covertness during the generation of adversarial examples boils down to minimizing the number of queries to the target system. The replica, transfer, and universal transfer attacks all use substitute models to develop the attack prior to launching it. Access to a substitute model in these cases grants the adversary a luxury; it removes requirement to submit inputs to the target system until the actual attack, making it easier for the attacker to remain undetected.

In addition to all these challenges, unfortunately for our adversary, the defending system may not simply be an implementation that processes all input passively; there may be active defenses in place. We'll get to these in Chapter 10.

Knowledge of the target is always beneficial to an attacker. As we will also see in Chapter 10, the DNN models, or data that could be used to derive them, such as training data, should be treated as sensitive assets of an organization.

There is no "standard" threat. This chapter has presented several approaches to generating adversarial examples, but in practice, a combination of approaches that consider this trade-off depending on the target system and the adversarial goals will be most effective.

## CHAPTER 8

Physical-World Attacks

The previous chapters focused on how adversarial input might be generated through, for example, perturbation of a digital image or distortion of digital audio data. However, there are many occasions when an attacker does not have access to a digital format of the data; the attacker may only be able to affect the physical world from which the data will be generated. The distinction depends on whether the target processing system takes its input from the outside world in the form of digital content (uploads to a social media site, for example) or directly from a sensor (such as a surveillance camera). The resulting threat in the physical-world scenario is quite different from the digital scenarios previously discussed.

Generating adversarial examples in the physical world poses a new set of challenges to the adversary. Now the attacker needs to create, or alter, something that exists in real life so that it incorporates a physical manifestation of an adversarial perturbation or patch. In the case of adversarial data received via a camera, the thing being altered may be a 2D print or a 3D object. Similarly, a microphone might receive adversarial distortion from crafted audio samples that are played in the environment, perhaps through a digital device such as a computer or television. How, for example, does the attacker ensure that an adversarial object remains robust to lighting conditions or camera position? Or how could it be possible to fool a digital assistant with hidden voice commands without a guarantee of the proximity of the assistant to the generated adversarial content, or with other competing noises present in the environment?

Access to the digital data obviously enables finer-grained control in creating adversarial input. Changes to digital images, for example, can be made at very fine pixel granularity. Physical-world attacks typically require a blunter approach, as detail may be lost during the fabrication of the adversarial object or the production of the adversarial sound. The ability of the sensor (camera or microphone) to accurately capture the required perturbation or distortion will affect the ease with which a robust attack can be launched. The unconstrained physical environment also introduces noise and varying conditions—any physical world adversarial example will require additional robustness to cater for this unpredictability. And, of course, the attacker is severely limited in terms of the changes that may be made to the physical environment due to access or detectability, depending on who will perceive the changes and under what circumstances.

To consider the threat presented by physical-world attacks, let's begin by examining how an attacker might create objects that produce adversarial results when captured on camera. We'll then explore the feasibility of generating sounds—specifically speech commands—that are adversarial. For both modalities there are some core challenges facing the adversary:

Creation of the adversarial input
> The fabrication of the adversarial object or the production of adversarial sound from the digitally calculated perturbation or distortion.

Capture of the adversarial input in digital format
> The capture of the adversarial object on camera or adversarial sound by microphone and its translation to digital format.

Effects of positioning and proximity of adversarial input with respect to the sensor
> How the position of the camera or microphone affects the likelihood that an object or sound will attain its adversarial goal.

Environmental conditions
> The uncertainty of the environment, such as changing lighting, weather, or room acoustics.

Attack constraints
> The constraints specific to the attack placed upon the adversary in creating the physical adversarial input. This might be what the attacker is able to change while also remaining undetected, or possible camouflage to hide the adversarial attack.

Adversarial Objects

There are many motivations for creating adversarial objects in the physical world. For example, the increasing use of autonomous systems (such as autonomous vehicles) that utilize image data captured through cameras raises the potential prospect of adversarial objects that confuse these systems. Automated processing of data from surveillance cameras by DNN technology will be increasingly required to process footage, such as for monitoring events. Such systems incur the risk of adversarial attack if it is possible to create physical adversarial objects.

This section considers the challenges and feasibility of creating physical-world adversarial objects. Let's start by considering the basic problem of fabricating adversarial objects and capturing the adversarial features digitally through a camera ("Object Fabrication and Camera Capabilities" on page 149). We'll then consider complicating factors of the environment and viewing angles ("Viewing Angles and Environment" on page 151).

Object Fabrication and Camera Capabilities

As a most basic question, we might begin by asking: is it possible for the camera to capture the adversarial aspects of a printed object sufficiently in its digital rendition? To establish the answer to this question, a first step would be to print the adversarial perturbed image and see whether a camera can feasibly extract the perturbation and generate a digital representation that is rendered adversarial. This basic experiment is depicted in Figure 8-1. Notice that at this stage we're not worrying about complexities such as camera angle or lighting; we're simply interested in whether the adversarial information can be successfully transferred via printing and then a camera sensor.

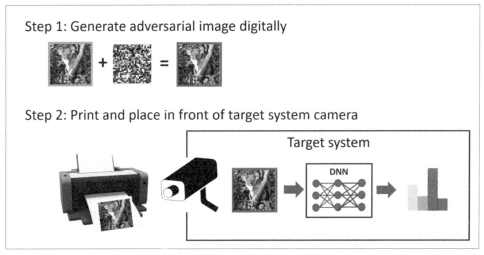

Figure 8-1. Highly constrained physical-world adversarial attack using a printed image

Although this is a fairly simple experiment, it's an important first step and has been successfully proven to be possible.[1] So, yes, adversarial examples generated digitally can still remain adversarial after passing through the extra printing–camera step. There are several considerations, however, including the following:

---

1 See Brown et al., "Adversarial Patch," and Alexey Kurakin, Ian J. Goodfellow, and Samy Bengio, "Adversarial Examples in the Physical World," International Conference on Learning Representations (2017), *http://bit.ly/ 2x0S0pq*.

Object fabrication (2D or 3D printing)

The attacker must have the tools to print the perturbation or patch at the level of detail required. This could present a problem as the range of colors that a printer is capable of producing (its *color gamut*) is a subset of all the possible colors that can be represented by RGB digital data rendition. If the adversarial perturbation or patch is captured in RGB values that cannot be reproduced by the printer, the attack will not be successful. Similarly, the printer must be capable of printing to the pixel granularity required for the adversarial attack.

The colors also require *reliable* reproduction for adversarial perturbation to work effectively. This is surprisingly difficult due to inconsistencies and inaccuracies of image color reproduction by printers. One approach to solving this challenge is to map possible RGB pixel values to their actual printed color. It's then possible to quantify a "printing error" over a complete picture by taking the difference between the correct and actual values. A requirement to minimize the printing error is then incorporated as an additional constraint within the adversarial cost function, with the result that the adversarial perturbation produced is optimized to use colors that are more accurately rendered by the printer.[2] In practice, this approach is not particularly robust as printing errors are inconsistent, varying not only between printers and but also between printouts from a single device. A more effective approach is to create the adversarial example that places less reliance on any specific colors, ensuring robustness of the adversarial example to color inaccuracies. This method is discussed further in the following section,[3] as it also caters to other problems such as the effect of lighting.

Camera capabilities

The precision with which the adversarial information is captured will always be limited by the sensitivity and accuracy attainable by the camera. Perturbation encoded within single pixels on a printed image, for example, will be lost unless the camera is capable of capturing that pixel precision at the distance at which it is placed from the object.

Data precision and the treatment of image noise and distortion are a consideration in the preprocessing chain for both physical-world and digital attacks, so we'll consider these challenges in further detail in "Preprocessing in the Broader Processing Chain" on page 203.

---

2 This technique is demonstrated in Sharif et al., "Accessorize to a Crime."

3 Specifically, in the context of the research in Anish Athalye, Logan Engstrom, Andrew Ilyas, and Kevin Kwok, "Synthesizing Robust Adversarial Examples," International Conference on Machine Learning (2017), *http://bit.ly/2FktLXQ*.

Viewing Angles and Environment

Now let's up the game and consider a less constrained and more realistic environment, perhaps with the goal of adding some adversarial perturbation to a road sign in the hope that it's misclassified, as illustrated in Figure 8-2. This time the adversary decides that they want to go further and alter or create an object in the real 3D world, where camera angles and conditions are no longer guaranteed.

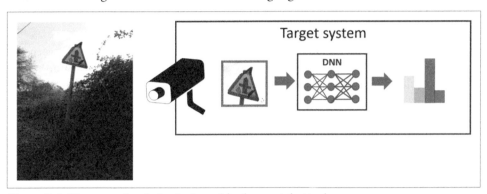

Figure 8-2. Unconstrained physical-world adversarial attack

The first obvious challenge with adversarial objects in the physical world is that they, or the camera capturing them, may move. For example, the images in Figure 8-3 were all taken within a few minutes of each other, at different camera angles. Notice the significant changes in angles, lighting, and exposure. If adversarial perturbation was added to the sign using the methods described so far, it would fail to transfer between these images. Initially, this challenge of transferability was assumed to indicate that creating robust physical-world examples would not be feasible.[4]

Figure 8-3. The effect of camera angles and light on objects in the physical world

---

4 See J. Lu et al. "No Need to Worry about Adversarial Examples in Object Detection in Autonomous Vehicles," Conference on Computer Vision and Pattern Recognition (2017), *http://bit.ly/2XracqU*.

You'll notice a similarity to the problem facing the adversary in generating image-agnostic reusable adversarial perturbation, as discussed in "Reusable Patches and Reusable Perturbation" on page 141. The adversarial change must be sufficiently flexible to work across different images. Broadly speaking, the challenges encompass:

Viewing angles and distances

Let's consider the relative camera position and its settings first, and the many potential resulting transformations to the image. Considerations here include:

Zoom

The image may be magnified (due to varying relative distance between the camera and the target object or as a result of camera magnification). As a result, the object may occupy a large or smaller area of the overall camera view.

Translation and rotation

The object may move with respect to the camera, or the camera may move with respect to the object. The result is that the object moves within the camera frame and the angle at which it is viewed varies.

Skew (or shear)

The position of the camera with respect to the object and the camera's focal length may result in image distortion.

Lighting and environment

For an algorithm to be robust across viewpoints, it must also consider the position of the object in relation to any light sources, other objects, and environmental conditions.

The angle of the light combined with the object's colors and textures will affect how the image is captured by the camera. Even the contrast between stark sunlight and a cloudy day can have an immense effect on the clarity and colors in an image captured on camera.

Objects scatter light differently. The way that the light bounces of an object's surface depends on the material of the surface—its texture, color, diffusion, and reflectance. On nonreflective surfaces, light rays are diffused and bounce off in different directions, giving a more "matte" appearance. Conversely, on reflective surfaces (such as metals), light rays bounce off at the opposite angle to that at which they hit the object. This mirror-like behavior is known as *specular reflection*.

Light will also be affected by the position of other objects and environmental conditions. The adversarial object may become partially hidden or its reflective properties may change (for example, due to rain).

Photographic capture also incurs the risk of introducing noise. Photographs captured in low light may be susceptible to unwanted noise across the image—random variation of color or brightness—manifesting as "specks" in the image. Software in the sensor or data processing steps prior to the neural network processing stage may remove noise introduced during the data collection stage. However, this is unlikely to be helpful to the adversary as noise cleaning steps will not reintroduce subtle adversarial perturbation that was originally masked by the noise.

Attack constraints

Finally, the placement of the adversarial perturbation or patch might be constrained by what the attacker is able to change in the physical environment. Depending on the scenario, the adversarial change may be required on a specific object that already exists, or alternatively may be fabricated in a new object that is placed in the environment. Although the aim may not be to entirely hide the perturbation, the level to which any change can be made while still appearing nonadversarial to onlookers will be a key consideration of the attacker. The adversary may consider camouflaging the attack, for example, as a logo. Alterations to specific areas, colors, or textures may be restricted, and there may be restrictions as to what is physically accessible to change.

With all these challenges, you might assume it impossible to create adversarial objects in the real world. However, in 2018, researchers proved that it is possible to create adversarial examples that are robust over a realistic distribution of viewing and lighting conditions.[5] To achieve this, they used a combination of techniques. Firstly, they exploited wire-mesh 3D images rather than 2D images. These 3D models are wireframe descriptions of a 3D object that can be digitally manipulated and rotated in 3D space. They also have associated colors and textures, so it's possible to digitally synthesize the effects of varying lighting conditions on the object.

Armed with a far richer representation of objects in the real world, the researchers then created functions that could be applied to the object to simulate how it might be transformed. This included rendering from 3D to 2D, lighting, rotation, and translation. The cost function used to calculate adversarial perturbation was then updated to consider these transformations. Using white box methods, rather than establishing a cost gradient for the target prediction with respect to changes in a single 2D image, changes were considered over a distribution of transformations of 3D textured models. This technique is referred to by the authors as *Expectation over Transformation* (EOT).

---

5 Athalye, Engstrom, Ilyas, and Kwok, "Synthesizing Robust Adversarial Examples."

The images in Figure 8-4 are taken directly from the paper by Athalye et al. and depict the results of photographing and classifying a 3D-printed adversarial turtle.

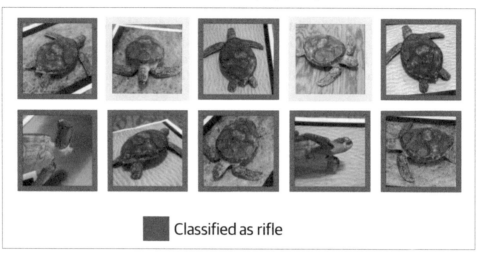

Classified as rifle

Figure 8-4. 3D-printed turtles misclassified as rifles

It's worth noting that this research also has significance to digital adversarial examples. Creating transformation-resilient adversarial perturbations using 3D modeling and then rendering to 2D would be an effective approach to creating adversarial examples that are more robust to preprocessing and defenses (which we'll discuss in Chapter 10).

As discussed in Chapter 1, Eykholt et al.[6] use a similar approach of incorporating transformations into a 2D image to cause a DNN to misinterpret its meaning (for example, misinterpreting a stop sign as a speed limit sign thanks to the use of adversarial stickers, as shown in Figure 8-5). The researchers also go a step further in capturing physical-world changes to the road sign on camera and including these in the adversarial calculation.

The two examples presented (the 3D-printed turtles and the stickers on the stop sign) highlight the differing constraints placed on the attacker when introducing an adversarial perturbation or patch into the environment. The first approach introduces a complete object over which the adversary has complete control. There is flexibility in where adversarial change is added to this object and the shape of the object itself. Of course, an attacker will aim to create an object that appears benign within the environment in which it will be placed, as described in the hypothetical example presented in the following sidebar.

---

6 Kevin Eykholt et al., "Robust Physical-World Attacks on Deep Learning Visual Classification."

Figure 8-5. Physical perturbation applied to a stop sign (image from Eykholt et al. 2018)

With the stop sign example, alterations were restricted to the existing sign itself. To generate adversarial alterations that appear innocuous, the researchers limited the perturbation calculation to only some parts of the image, making them more likely to be overlooked by a human observer as dirt or graffiti.

Hypothetical Example: Surveillance False Positives

A large public venue receives vast amounts of surveillance video from its multiple cameras, which are impossible for the security staff to continually monitor. To respond quickly to any potential threat, the image data is processed in real time to extract and alert to the presence of firearms. Alerts are then passed to the human security team to discount false positives and respond swiftly to any real issues.

With the motivation of causing confusion within the venue during an event, an organization creates bags with seemingly innocuous logos containing adversarial perturbations that result in misclassification as firearms. The adversarial perturbation is designed to be robust to transformations and lighting and to be transferable across multiple image-processing models.

These bags are indirectly distributed to street vendors prior to an event at the venue. They are then openly sold to individuals attending the event, who innocently display them within the venue.

The resulting increased false-positive alerts mean that the threat level is increased and the security team is required to undertake significantly more bag searches on attendees in the venue, resulting in long queues and event disruption. Additional armed police officers are dispatched to the venue before the hoax is detected.

Adversarial Sound

The ubiquity of voice interfaces for control of smartphones, tablets, wearables, digital assistants, and other devices means that adversarial sound is particularly interesting in the context of speech recognition systems. Many devices that use this technology are always listening, even when not in active use, providing an open attack vector at all times. Devices could be at risk not only from sounds played in public spaces but also from television, digital content, and music that we stream into our homes and workspaces. It is possible to hide inaudible voice commands within seemingly benign sounds, but how easy would it be to launch an adversarial attack using these techniques in a physical environment against, for example, a smartphone digital assistant?

As with the previous section, we'll begin with the simple problem of reproducing adversarial audio in the physical world and capturing it digitally through a microphone. We'll then consider complicating factors of the environment and the relative positioning of the speaker and microphone ("Audio Positioning and Environment" on page 157).

Audio Reproduction and Microphone Capabilities

As with image, let's begin by considering the simplest possible scenario: a microphone within close proximity of the sound coming from a single speaker (Figure 8-6). We'll assume a "perfect" sound environment with no other noises.

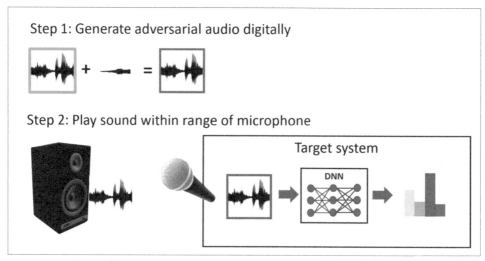

Figure 8-6. Physical-world adversarial attack using sound

Limitations to be aware of include:

Reproduction of digital audio (speakers)
    As with printing adversarial objects, the most basic requirement is to reproduce the digital audio as sound waves at the precision required for adversarial distortion to be effective. This will depend on the precision and capabilities of the speakers.

An interesting aspect of this threat is that, in many scenarios, the attacker does not control the speakers used to render the digital audio to sound. The quality of the sound of an audio adversarial attack shared online, for example, will be at the mercy of the speakers that the playing device is using. This could vary from high-quality speakers for playing audio in a room to low-quality speakers on a basic smartphone.

Speakers translate digital audio to sound waves through vibration of some flexible material (the speaker membrane). In the same way that it is not possible for printers to produce every possible digital RGB combination, the pitch of the sounds that can be produced by a speaker is restricted by the speed at which the speaker membrane can physically move. Digital adversarial audio that requires pitches outside this limit will not be reproduced.

Microphone capabilities

Data capture through the microphone incurs the risk of introducing noise or distortion. Similar to the "specks" introduced when an image is captured, audio may include "static" introduced during the initial rendering of the sound to data by unwanted electronic fluctuations. The microphone or preprocessing chain is also very likely to perform preprocessing (such as MFCC—see "Audio" on page 58) to extract the relevant features and remove data that is not pertinent to the task.

It has been proven possible to reproduce unrecognizable adversarial commands over the air and successfully capture them using a smartphone,[7] so this basic ability to generate adversarial distortion and capture it digitally is feasible.

Audio Positioning and Environment

Now let's consider the additional complications brought about by the environment and relative positioning of the speaker/audio:

Environment

A fundamental challenge to launching a physical adversarial audio attack is that adversarial sounds will need to compete with other sounds in the environment. In many threat scenarios, the attacker will have no control over the amount of other noise in the environment; however, there are some cases where they may have some control, or at least some prior knowledge. Consider, for example, generating voice commands intended to be adversarial to a voice control system incorporated in a car. The attacker may not have knowledge of all the possible competing sounds, but would be able to consider the relatively predictable impact of the car's engine noise during the generation of the attack.

---

7 Tavish Vaidya et al., "Cocaine Noodles: Exploiting the Gap Between Human and Machine Speech Recognition," USENIX Workshop in Offensive Technologies (2015), *http://bit.ly/2FldYIj*.

We are all aware of how sound changes in timbre and character in different environments. There's significant difference between sounds when heard outside, for example, versus when they are heard inside. Inside, waves reflect and reverberate off the walls and indoor surfaces. Objects such as furnishings and room content potentially dampen and spread sound waves. The sound will have been reflected, resonated, and attenuated by nearby objects prior to reaching the microphone. Clearly, the position of the sound source relative to the target device microphone will also have a massive effect on the sound and its quality. Creating adversarial sound that is robust to different environments and speaker/microphone positioning will be challenging, but the attacker may focus on a subset of scenarios (such as a small room) or, if creating the sound in a public space, may even control the speaker and its positioning.

Feedback and confirmation

Digital assistant technology usually supports some form of audio or visual feedback as an assurance of user intent—especially when commands have greater security risk (such as an online purchase). The assistant, for example, might light up or might generate a voice response to request verification. While the actual verification could be included within the adversarial command (such as a carefully timed, inaudible "yes"), the attacker has the problem of ensuring that the audio feedback (such as "are you sure you wish to go ahead with that evil plan?") is not overheard by a bystander.

If the attacker has constructed the adversarial distortion in audio over which they have complete control (music in a video shared online, for example), they could simply increase the volume of the benign sound at the expected point in time of the digital assistant's response. More likely, it may not actually matter if the attack does not always work; sometimes it's thwarted because someone happens to hear it, but occasionally when no one is around or noticing, it might succeed.

Constraints

As with adversarial objects, the success of an adversarial sound attack may depend on the extent to which the attacker can make changes to the audio while the distortion remains undetected. It may be more difficult for the attacker to hide adversarial commands within existing audio than in audio that they control. For example, if the attacker adds audio distortion in some music or speech that they also create, they have far greater control over the audio that masks the attack. The other question is: does the adversarial sound need to be completely hidden? So long as people ignore or overlook the sound as unrecognizable, it may not need to be disguised as normal music or speech.

Attacks with inaudible voice commands are possible even in more challenging environmental conditions. A likely approach would be to repurpose the EOT method for generating adversarial 3D models (as introduced in "Adversarial Objects" on page

148) in the audio domain, considering audio transformations and restrictions of speaker reproduction of sound.

Hypothetical Example: Discredit Voice Assistant Technology

In an attempt to discredit a tech company producing voice assistants, an adversarial group embeds commands into a seemingly benign music track. This is a targeted attack: the commands are specific, such as a request to perform an online order with a corresponding confirmation (following a delay for the voice assistant to request confirmation). The adversarial group then distributes this adversarial audio within video content across several social media channels.

Development of the adversarial audio goes unnoticed. The adversarial group uses a substitute DNN to develop the attack and then tests it on their own local copy of the voice assistant.

Use of an identical replica of the system during development ensures that the attack is robust, subject to correct physical conditions. However, the attack has a low success rate as it relies upon a voice assistant being within close range of the played audio in a quiet environment. Despite the low success rate, the attack is successful, as reported cases reduce consumer confidence in the product and the company that produces it.

The Feasibility of Physical-World Adversarial Examples

Generating adversarial objects and sounds is undoubtedly more difficult than creating adversarial examples digitally. The attacker is presented with the additional challenges of:

- Retaining adversarial information in the physical rendition of the example
- Ensuring that the adversarial information is captured by the sensor and its processing
- Catering for variations in physical positioning and environmental conditions

While it's unlikely that an adversary will be able to generate physical adversarial examples that will always succeed, there is still motivation for physical-world attacks in cases where the attack does not require a high success rate. The hypothetical examples given in "Hypothetical Example: Surveillance False Positives" on page 155 and "Hypothetical Example: Discredit Voice Assistant Technology" on page 159 illustrate such motivations.

## PART IV

Defense

Building on the previous chapters, this section examines the approaches to defending DNNs in real-world systems against adversarial input.

Chapter 9 begins by examining how we model the adversarial threat—this is critical to evaluating any defense. The chapter will then look at how the robustness of neural networks can be evaluated, both empirically and theoretically.

Chapter 10 considers some of the most recent thinking in the area of how to strengthen DNN algorithms against adversarial input, as well as open source projects committed to developing better defenses against adversarial attacks. We'll consider DNN assurance from a broader perspective to examine whether it's possible to establish the sets of inputs over which a DNN can safely operate. The chapter includes code examples to illustrate defenses and defense evaluation, building on examples first presented in Chapter 6. We'll also take a more holistic approach to Information Assurance (IA) and consider the effect that the broader processing chain and organizational procedures might have on reducing the risk of adversarial input.

Finally, Chapter 11 looks at how DNNs are likely to evolve in forthcoming years and the effect that this may have on the ease with which they can be fooled.

Evaluating Model Robustness to Adversarial Inputs

To begin the exploration of defenses, this chapter looks at evaluating the robustness of DNN models against adversarial examples. This will provide the foundations for understanding the effectiveness of the defenses described in Chapter 10.

Evaluating robustness of individual DNN components enables objective comparison of models and defense approaches. For example, this might be for research purposes, to see whether a new defense approach is more or less effective than previous approaches. Alternatively, evaluation may be necessary to ensure that the most recently deployed model in your organization is equally or more secure than the previous version.

Model evaluation requires a consistent methodology and consistent measures to ensure that the metrics used for comparison are objective. Unfortunately, generating metrics that indicate a neural network's ability to defend against adversarial examples is not simple. We need to initially answer the question: defense against *what*? Therefore, based on Chapter 7 and Chapter 8, we will begin by considering how we model the threat that is being defended against. This is the *threat model* discussed in "Adversarial Goals, Capabilities, Constraints, and Knowledge" on page 165.

Complete Knowledge Evaluation

When evaluating defenses, it's important to bear in mind that keeping the workings of the target system secret should never be viewed as defense in itself. Information security practice does not adhere to the "security by obscurity" principle,[1] so any evaluation of adversarial attacks should assume the adversary has complete knowledge of the DNN and any defense mechanisms in place. This is sometimes referred to as the "complete knowledge" attack scenario.

Evaluation against consistent threat models is critical for the objective comparison of defenses. In "Model Evaluation" on page 171 we'll look at techniques for evaluating a model's robustness to adversarial examples.

"Empirically Derived Robustness Metrics" on page 172 examines the role of the threat model during testing and considers some of the empirically derived metrics that can be used to establish model robustness.

We'll then consider whether it is possible to use theoretical approaches to determine a model's robustness in "Theoretically Derived Robustness Metrics" on page 176. A formal proof of a model's robustness has the advantage that it would enable us to derive metrics relevant to a model but independent of the threat.

"Summary" on page 177 summarizes this chapter before we delve into the defenses in Chapter 10.

Red-Blue Teaming

Red-blue teaming assumes that the individuals evaluating the defense by attacking (the red team) are not those who developed it (the blue team). The red team emulates the behaviors of the adversary, and the blue team emulates the defending organization. Separating the roles of the attacker and the defender ensures a different mindset in attack methodology, making it more likely you'll find weaknesses in the system.

Red teams should attempt to exploit adversarial example vulnerabilities using methods such as those described in Chapter 7 and Chapter 8 to emulate the best possible attack. Unlike in model evaluation, the red team should not be given complete knowledge of the target system as this may cause them to miss vulnerabilities by biasing their thinking (for example, not considering attacks where they know there are defenses in place).

---

1 In accordance with Shannon's maxim (*http://bit.ly/2ZvOAHq*), "the enemy knows the system."

The evaluation of a model (including any defense built into the model) is important, but not the whole story. Used in real systems, DNNs are simply components in a broader chain. An evaluation of a model in isolation is useful for model comparison and for assuring the individual component, but the system should also be tested as a whole. Assuring required levels of *system* robustness to adversarial examples requires broader system security testing, including adversarial examples as a potential vulnerability. A common approach to cybersecurity testing of systems is red-blue teaming.

Adversarial Goals, Capabilities, Constraints, and Knowledge

When the attacker's profile is systematically scrutinized in the context of a target system, this articulation of the threat is known as a *threat model*. Threat modeling is a detailed analysis of the threat actor, attack vectors, and risks, and is specific to the organization and scenario. This chapter is not intended to provide a complete threat model. Rather, it describes some of the key information that should be captured when modeling the threat of adversarial examples—information that could be used in a broader threat modeling scenario.

It may not be feasible to model or anticipate all possible threats, but it is prudent to consider different possible threat scenarios. An understanding from the attacker's perspective will aid the design of secure defenses against adversarial input.

The adversary is is often modeled in terms of *goals*, *capabilities*, *constraints*, and *knowledge*.

Goals

Let's start with the goals—what is the attacker trying to achieve, and how does this define the nature of the adversarial input that will be presented to the system?

At the highest level, you can view the threat goals as what the attacker is trying to achieve by fooling the system. This takes us back to the initial motivations presented in Chapter 2. More nebulous reasons such as "because I can" shouldn't be overlooked. Such motivations can result in less specific goals and less obvious threat models.

The high-level motivations determine the goals. These goals can be defined by the required specificity of the attack, minimum success rate, and maximum perturbation limit (Figure 9-1):

Specificity
> The required specificity of the attack refers to whether the aim is simply to create a false prediction from the DNN (an untargeted attack) or to create a *specific* false prediction (a targeted attack). This is determined by the motivation of an attack. For example, it may be sufficient for an evasion attack to be untargeted if it does

not matter what the DNN's interpretation of the input is, as long as it evades a specific interpretation. Conversely, an attack to create confusion may require that the DNN interprets the input in a targeted way to generate a specific false positive.

Success rate
The attack success rate refers to the confidence of the adversary that the attack will achieve its aim of fooling the classifier to the required specificity.

The rate at which the attacker requires attacks to be successful will be determined by the consequences of the input failing to achieve its aim. An evasion attack typically warrants greater confidence in success than a false-positive attack, for example. If failure to evade the AI might result in prosecution, the stakes would be higher and more effort would be invested into methods that will ensure that the adversarial input is robust to failure. Conversely, if the motivation is to cause confusion with large quantities of adversarial input resulting in false positives, it may not matter much if the attack fails some of the time. While motivations such as evasion from detection might appear obvious, other motivations, such as creating a denial of service (DoS), causing confusion, or simply discrediting an organization, should not be overlooked. These types of attacks may not require high success rates, which makes it far easier for the adversary to launch an attack.

Perturbation limit (perceptibility)
The perturbation limit is the maximum perturbation acceptable to the attacker and is an indirect measurement of perceptibility. The acceptable perceptibility of the adversarial input depends on the attack motivation and context. In some cases, there may not even be any need to disguise the adversarial alteration. Take, for example, an adversarial patch added to the corner of an image. The human sender and human recipient of the image may both be aware that the patch has been added, so the sender doesn't need to disguise the patch if it does not affect the main image content. In other scenarios, minimizing perceptibility may be very important. For example, if adding a malicious voice command to audio, it is likely to be important that it is not noticed.

Although perturbation is generally measured in terms of L^p-norms, there's no reason why another measure of change might not be used. Perhaps it will incorporate a more complex algorithm that takes into account the nuances of human perception or the context in which the adversarial example will be seen: for example, giving a higher perturbation value to a change that a person might notice than to one that's not obvious, even if they have the same "digital distance." In the context of an adversarial patch, the perturbation threshold will include the constraint that the perturbation may be measured in terms of L^0-norm (simply the number of pixels changed) with additional constraints on the location of the pixels in the image (such as near the edge of the image).

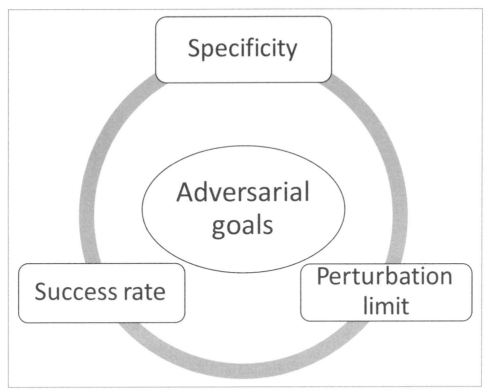

Figure 9-1. The goal of the adversary can be described in terms of required specificity, success rate, and perceptibility (perturbation limit).

There's an obvious tension between success rate and perturbation; the success rate of an attack will increase as the constraints on perturbation are lessened. If we were to plot the success rate of a specific attack against the allowed perturbation for a particular input x, it might look something like Figure 9-2. This graph illustrates the ease with which adversarial examples can be created for a specific input as the allowed perturbation varies. Notice that there is a minimum perturbation required to create an adversarial example. The shape of the plot and the minimum perturbation will depend on the network, the original image, and the perturbation measurement. Hold this thought because this plot and its associated metrics are useful for evaluating the robustness of neural networks too. We'll revisit this type of graph, and the code needed to generate it, in Chapter 10.

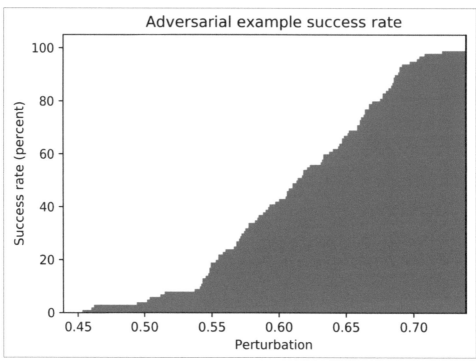

Figure 9-2. Allowing greater perturbation increases the success rate for an adversarial example.

The specificity of the attack is varied by increasing or lessening the constraints of the logic used to generate the adversarial input. Targeted attacks impose tighter constraints on the adversarial input generated, so are likely to be more difficult to achieve and therefore have a lower success rate.

The attack goals are encapsulated in the mathematical and logical constraints used to generate the adversarial example. For example, consider the C&W attack summarized in Figure 9-3. (The complete mathematics is detailed in "Increasing Adversarial Confidence" on page 119.)

You can see how this algorithm articulates the adversarial goals. The specificity (in this case targeted) is captured by the restriction that the DNN returns a target class for the adversarial input. The perturbation is calculated to minimize the distance from the original image by including the L^2-norm measurement between the adversarial example and the original, defined by $\| x^{adv} - x \|_2^2$. This is addressing the goal of ensuring that the image remains within the required perceptibility. The additional robustness requirement $c \cdot l(x^{adv})$ affects the likely success rate.

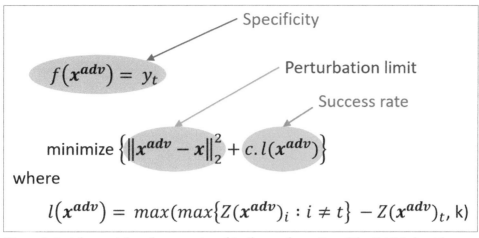

Figure 9-3. Adversarial goals are captured in the mathematics of the C&W algorithm

The methods for generating attacks shown in Chapter 6, including the C&W attack, allow an attacker to create an attack that adheres to their goals, but only consider the neural network algorithm on its own. The threat is against the complete processing chain and any defense mechanisms in place, so achieving the required specificity, success rate, and perturbation on the actual target will require more mathematical modeling and/or experimentation on the complete target. In other words, generating the adversarial example using an algorithm such as the one in Figure 9-3 on a DNN in isolation doesn't ensure that the specificity, success rate, and perturbation goals hold when the example is tried on the complete system.

Capabilities, Knowledge, and Access

The ability of the attacker to attain these goals will depend on several factors: their capabilities, their knowledge of the target, and their ability to affect the input data to make it adversarial. The latter two can be interpreted as potential constraints on the attack; less knowledge will constrain the attacker in achieving their goals, as will a lack of ability to alter the input data. This is summarized in Figure 9-4.

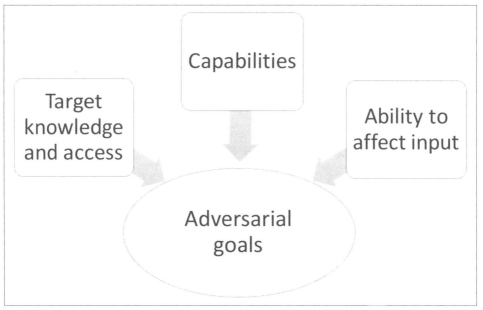

Figure 9-4. Adversarial goals are constrained by target knowledge and access, adversarial capability, and the attacker's ability to affect the input.

Consider each of the factors in turn:

Capabilities

The success of an attack is constrained by the resources (skills, software, hardware, and time) available to the adversary. The resources required will depend greatly on the goals of the attack. A simple, low-cost attack could be adding an adversarial patch that has been shared online to a digital image. At the other extreme, developing a robust perturbation using an ensemble of models and large compute capacity will require greater expenditure, time, and expertise.

The capability of lone threat actors should not be underestimated. Hackers may work alone, but they are likely to be highly knowledgeable and can utilize public cloud and online resources to develop attacks.

Ability to affect the input

The extent to which an attacker is able to alter the data may restrict their ability to create adversarial input. For example, the level to which changes might impact human perception may restrict the ways digital image content can be altered.

In a physical-world attack, the adversary has no access to the digital data, placing significant constraints on the creation of adversarial content. The attacker may be hindered by very low-tech challenges, such as physical access to the required location of the sensor.

Knowledge of or access to the target

Knowledge of the DNN model itself is a significant aid in creating adversarial examples, enabling (for example) a more powerful replica attack for developing the adversarial input. Knowledge of the target should not be solely seen in terms of the ability of the attacker to replicate the model, however. Successfully launching a robust adversarial example attack ideally requires knowledge of the complete processing chain and all its defenses.

Where an attacker does not have complete knowledge of the target, it may be possible to infer the target's behavior through analyzing its responses to queries. Experimenting directly with the target system will increase the robustness of an adversarial example, but will incur the trade-off that it might be detected if the target is checking for suspicious input. Therefore, target access during attack preparation will be constrained by a need to remain undetected. The attacker may need to ensure queries do not look suspicious (for example, by slowing the rate at which they are submitted or by submitting queries from multiple IPs to make them appear unrelated).

If the attacker has their own copy of the target (for example, a digital assistant), they have unlimited access to experiment with, and gain knowledge about, the system. However, systems that take data from the physical world and respond directly through nondigital means are more difficult to perform automated experimentation on. For example, there is no programmable interface for interaction with a digital assistant. In these cases, it's more likely that the attacker would generate the adversarial data on a substitute model, then perform refinement testing on the physical copy before launching it on the target device(s).

Model Evaluation

An interesting question is whether it is possible to quantify a model's robustness to adversarial examples. This would enable comparisons and assurances of models deployed to operational environments. For example, it might be useful to quantify the effect that a particular defense has on the DNN's robustness, especially if the defense resulted in a trade-off regarding model accuracy. Alternatively, it may be useful to objectively compare defenses to establish which were most effective in assuring the safe operation of the model.

It's not currently possible to create DNNs that perform completely flawlessly across all possible inputs. Even a network taking low-resolution (224 x 224 pixel) color images, for example, would need to be proven to perform correctly over 256^{150528} different possible images. We know that DNNs can provide results with outstanding accuracy across inputs that are representative of the training dataset and not deliberately adversarial, but it is computationally infeasible to assure the network's integrity across all input.

An evaluation of defenses can be done empirically (by testing) or theoretically (by mathematical calculations). When evaluating a defense, either empirically or theoretically, it is critical that the effect of the defense on the model's accuracy on nonadversarial data is not overlooked. There are two aspects to this:

- Model accuracy on nonadversarial data must be retested when the defense is in place. The tolerance to a reduction in model accuracy will depend very much on the operational scenario.

- In developing defenses to augment existing models, care must be taken not to inadvertently reduce the model accuracy for *good* data. An overzealous adversarial defense mechanism might wrongly predict benign data as adversarial (in other words, placing inputs in the "false positive" categorization, rather than "true negative").

Let's consider the empirical and theoretical approaches to robustness evaluations in turn.

Empirically Derived Robustness Metrics

The problem with adversarial examples is that they are *deliberate* attempts to fool the model. It is very difficult to create appropriate adversarial tests and consistent robustness metrics because:

- The nature of the adversarial data is very difficult to predict. Adversarial data generated using one attack method may have totally different characteristics from adversarial data generated using another method.

- The likelihood of data that fools the model occurring during normal operations may appear very low; however, if an attacker is going to deliberate lengths to fool the model, the probability of that data fooling the model will be far higher.

Establishing accurate and useful comparative robustness metrics for a particular network requires a clear definition of the threat model, attacks, and test data against which the model robustness is being evaluated:

Threat model
The threat model includes the goals—the specificity (targeted versus untargeted), success rate, and perceptibility threshold (such as the L^p-norm measurement being used and its acceptable bounds). It may also include the ability of the attacker to affect the input (considering, for example, physical-world constraints). The evaluation is meaningless without a clear definition of the threat model; it defines the scope of adversarial tests applied during the evaluation.

The selected threat model will depend on the reason for the evaluation. For example, from a research perspective, you might evaluate a defense with the aim of creating better and more robust DNNs. In this case, you may choose to use common threat models to enable direct comparison with other defenses. Alternatively, you might want to evaluate a defense for a specific operational deployment; you might then choose to focus on specific threat models and test scenarios (for example, particular targeted attacks) because they pose greater risk to your organization. In practice, you may choose to perform multiple evaluations against different threat models.

Attack methodology

A comprehensive description of the attack methods, including any parameters used, forms part of the evaluation. You should assume complete knowledge of the system and its defenses when generating the evaluation adversarial examples.

Proving that a defense works for one attack does not guarantee its effectiveness against another, stronger method. The evaluation should therefore encompass a variety of attacks; while it is not possible to know all the attacks, the attacks should include the strongest known at the time. The aim is to evaluate the defense against the best attacks possible, and this includes attacks that adapt to circumvent the defense.

Test data

The evaluation of a defense's robustness will relate to the test attack data used during experimentation. This data is defined by the method of attack used (including its parameters) and also the data from which the test adversarial examples were generated by this method. Varying the original data used for generating test adversarial examples may affect the success rate of an attack.

Evaluating robustness to adversarial examples is part of the broader problem of evaluating the veracity of the model over inputs. Therefore, evaluating defenses is part of the broader task of establishing the model's accuracy. Assuming that the test data has a similar distribution to the training data, there are commonly used methods for empirically evaluating model accuracy.

The code presented back in Chapter 3 that created a classifier for the Fashion-MNIST dataset demonstrated a very basic evaluation of the model:

```
test_loss, test_acc = model.evaluate(test_images, test_labels)
print('Model accuracy based on test data:', test_acc)
```

This generates the following output:

```
10000/10000 [==================] - 0s 35us/sample - loss: 0.3623 - acc: 0.8704
Model accuracy based on test data: 0.8704
```

This evaluation states that approximately 87% of all the test examples presented to the model were classified correctly. We can perform a more detailed examination of the model's accuracy through a *confusion matrix*. Figure 9-5 is a confusion matrix for the classifier in Chapter 3.

Code Example: Confusion Matrix

The code for producing this matrix is included in the Jupyter note-book chapter03/fashionMNIST_classifier.ipynb (*http://bit.ly/31JsseI*).

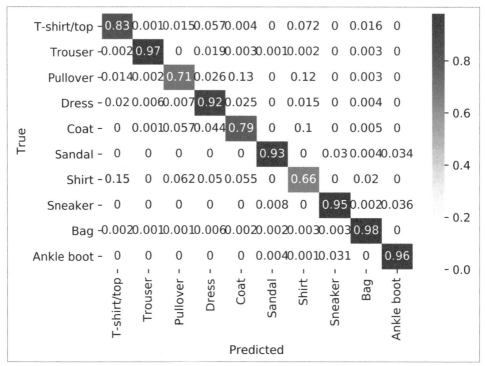

Figure 9-5. A confusion matrix for the Fashion-MNIST classifier provides a summary of the model's performance for each of the fashion labels.

Each row in the matrix corresponds to the test images with that row's particular (true) label. The top row, for example, refers to the test data that is labeled "T-shirt/top." The cells contain the proportion of the test data that was predicted according to the column label. So, the proportion of T-shirt/tops that were correctly labeled is 0.83 (83%). The proportion of T-shirt/tops that were mislabeled as "Shirt" is 0.07 (7%). If the model was performing perfectly against the test data, the cells of the diagonal would all be 1.0 and all others would be 0.

You can learn quite a lot about a classifier model from its confusion matrix. For example, Figure 9-5 indicates that shirts are the most likely to be misclassified—11% of the time they are misinterpreted by the model as T-shirts/tops. Similarly, the model is most accurate when classifying the trouser, bag, and ankle boot examples in the test data (98%). As we will see in Chapter 10, a confusion matrix can be useful in indicating how adversarial test data is misclassified.

To use the confusion matrix for evaluation, we need to create the appropriate attack methodology and generate adversarial test data. To evaluate the efficacy of a specific defense, the testing is performed on the nondefended model and then repeated on the model with the defense in place. The evaluation should be performed with the strongest attacks possible that deliberately aim to defeat any defense mechanism in place. This is extremely difficult because new attacks are constantly evolving, so evaluation of adversarial robustness is a point-in-time assessment that may require subsequent recalculation when further attacks are created. Once again, we may just be interested in the difference in perturbation required to achieve a specific success rate. Or, the metric of greatest interest might be the change in minimum perturbation for an adversarial example. We'll take a look at using a confusion matrix for defense evaluation in a code example in Chapter 10.

Another metric is how difficult (in terms of perturbation required) it is to create adversarial examples against a particular target network. This takes us back to the image presented earlier Figure 9-2 and repeated in Figure 9-6.

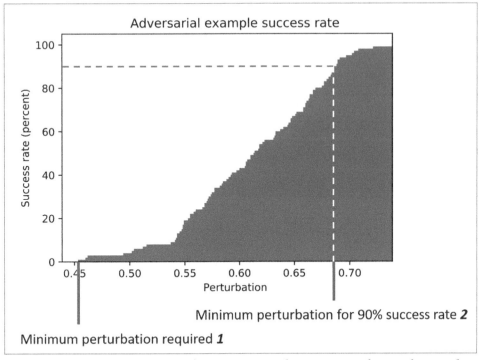

Figure 9-6. Allowing greater perturbation increases the success rate for an adversarial example.

For measuring the robustness of a network to any attack, we might want to take the worst case (from the defender's perspective), which is the smallest perturbation required for an attack to be successful (label 1 on the plot). If the threat model does not place any constraints on the perceptibility boundaries, then the evaluation of the defense is just the point at which the success rate is sufficiently high to achieve the threat model goal (label 2 on the plot). We'll take a further look at how graphs of this type are generated in a code example in Chapter 10.

Evaluation of a Defense Applied Across Models

It's important to realize that the evaluation of a defense on one model is not guaranteed to hold across other models. In particular, a defense approach tested on a model trained with a "toy" dataset such as Fashion-MNIST may not hold for models trained on data with more realism.

It may be acceptable to perform the evaluation on a single model before and after the defense has been added if you wish to evaluate the robustness of one network only (for example, to test a model to be deployed operationally). However, for a more general evaluation of a defense (for example, for research purposes), performing the evaluation across a variety of models with the defense in place will give a better indication of the defense's effectiveness.

Theoretically Derived Robustness Metrics

Empirical robustness measurements are subject to ambiguity because there are so many variables associated with the evaluation method. They are also not guaranteed measures of a network's robustness because increasingly effective attack methods for generating adversarial examples are continually being developed.

A mathematical, rather than empirical, measurement of robustness opens the possibility of a more consistent and reliable metric. Mathematically calculated metrics for software assurance are particularly relevant for the evaluation of safety-critical systems. In the context of adversarial examples, theoretical evaluation may be required to ensure the adequate assurance of a component in an autonomous vehicle, for example. Theoretically derived metrics based wholly on the model (not the threat), also offer the advantage of being attack-agnostic.

One approach is to mathematically calculate the minimum perturbation required to generate an adversarial example. To date, researchers have been able to prove that no adversarial examples can be generated within a defined distance of each of a specific set of inputs. So, assuming there is a "safe zone" around "normal" inputs where no adversarial examples lie, can we establish the minimum (worst case) safe zone for all such inputs? The idea behind this is illustrated in Figure 9-7.

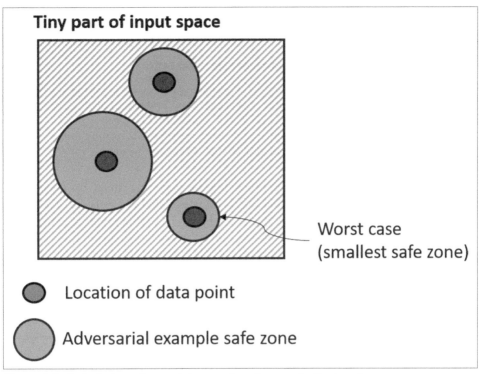

Figure 9-7. Calculating adversarial example safe zones in the input space

The metric that is being calculated is the minimum perturbation required to generate an adversarial example across all correctly classified in-distribution inputs (the smallest safe zone). This is a nontrivial calculation because of the vastness of the input space and the complexity of the prediction landscape. However, researchers have proposed methods using mathematical approximation to establish a robustness metric with a high level of accuracy.[2] At the time of writing, this is nascent research. However, theoretically derived metrics such as this are likely to play an increasingly important part in DNN network security evaluation.

Summary

This chapter has considered the threat model and explored different methods for evaluating robustness to adversarial examples. Although it is difficult to achieve consistent approaches to model evaluation, there is considerable interest in establishing

---

2 Tsui-Wei Weng et al., "Evaluating the Robustness of Neural Networks: An Extreme Value Theory Approach," International Conference on Learning Representations (2018), *http://bit.ly/2Rn5THO*.

standard empirical measures for evaluating model robustness through open projects that are enumerated in Chapter 10.

Open Project for Evaluating Adversarial Robustness

Developing methodologies for evaluating adversarial robustness is a new area and subject to change. "On Evaluating Adversarial Robustness" (*http://bit.ly/2IT2jkR*) is a living document produced by Carlini et al.[3] to solicit and share contributions relating to the evaluation of neural network defenses in an open forum.

Any empirical evaluation of a model holds only for a specific threat. To make comparisons between models requires that the threat considered is consistent. The possibility of theoretically derived metrics based on the model itself is appealing, and more research in this area will hopefully lead to more approaches to generating objective metrics by which models can be compared.

The next chapter investigates different approaches that have been proposed to defend against adversarial input. We'll refer back to the evaluation methods in this chapter when exploring defenses.

---

3 Nicholas Carlini et al., "On Evaluating Adversarial Robustness" (2019), *http://bit.ly/2IT2jkR.*

## CHAPTER 10

Defending Against Adversarial Inputs

In this chapter, we'll consider some of the methods that have been proposed for detecting and defending against adversarial example attacks. The good news is that some defenses can work. The bad news is that each defense has limitations, and if the attacker is aware of the method being used, they may be able to adapt their attack to circumvent the defense.

This chapter considers three broad approaches to defense:

Improve the model

> In the first part of this chapter, we'll focus on the model itself and techniques that have been proposed for creating more robust neural networks.

Remove adversarial aspects from input

> In "Data Preprocessing" on page 202, we'll then look at whether it's possible to render adversarial input benign before it's submitted to the model.

Minimize the adversary's knowledge

> Next, "Concealing the Target" on page 207 will consider ways in which the adversary's knowledge of the target model and broader processing chain might be reduced to make it more difficult to create successful adversarial examples. As highlighted in Chapter 9, target concealment should not be relied upon as a defense.

There's currently no single solution to this problem, but it is an active area of research. Table 10-1 summarizes the capabilities of the defense techniques described in this chapter at the time of writing.

Table 10-1. Summary of defenses

Defense	Improve model robustness	Remove adversarial data characteristics	Minimize the adversary's knowledge
Gradient masking (in "Improving the Model" on page 180)	Limited	N/A	N/A
Adversarial training (in "Improving the Model" on page 180)	Limited	N/A	N/A
Out-of-distribution confidence training (in "Improving the Model" on page 180)	Promising but not guaranteed	N/A	N/A
Randomized dropout at test time (in "Improving the Model" on page 180)	Promising but not guaranteed	N/A	N/A
Data preprocessing (in "Data Preprocessing" on page 202)	N/A	Limited	N/A
Target concealment (in "Concealing the Target" on page 207)	N/A	N/A	Limited

In practice, the capability of an adversary to successfully launch an adversarial attack will be constrained by several factors imposed by the broader processing and its security. This chapter will consider both the model and the system in which it is a component.

The chapter concludes with some practical advice for developing robustness against adversarial examples in real-world systems, in "Building Strong Defenses Against Adversarial Input" on page 209.

Improving the Model

Let's start by exploring what can be done to protect the model itself from adversarial examples. For example, can the DNN be retrained so that it is robust to adversarial input? Are there characteristics shared by adversarial examples that we could use to detect an attack? Alternatively, could we predict when the algorithm is likely to perform incorrectly and therefore reduce the confidence of results that are less certain?

It's important to remember that any alteration to the model for the purpose of defense must not unacceptably impact the algorithm's accuracy; we must consider the effect of any defense mechanism on the *good* data as well as on adversarial input.

We'll consider four approaches:

Gradient masking
    This approach alters the model to hide the gradients in the prediction landscape to make it difficult to create adversarial examples.

Adversarial training

This involves training (or retraining) the network so that it learns to distinguish adversarial input. This is done by including adversarial examples in the training data.

Out-of-distribution (OoD) detection

Here we look at whether it is possible to train the network to return not only a prediction, but also a confidence measure of how sure it is of that prediction, based on whether the data lies within the distribution that the network is able to operate over with high accuracy.

Randomized dropout uncertainty measurements

Finally, this approach adds a training technique called *randomized dropout* to the model post-training into introduce uncertainty to the network's predictions. This is based on a premise that adversarial inputs result in greater uncertainty and so it may be possible to detect them.

Gradient Masking

Gradient masking[1] is a technique that has been proposed to make the calculation of adversarial examples more difficult. The idea is to either hide the gradients of the DNN algorithm's prediction landscape, or smooth them in such a way as to make them useless to an attacker.

Of course, this approach is only beneficial in scenarios where an attacker has sufficient access to the DNN algorithm, enabling the use of the model's gradients to develop the attack. Most obviously, it is prudent to conceal the algorithm from an attacker (see "Concealing the Target" on page 207) to prevent attacks that exploit model gradients. These types of attacks include the white box gradient-based methods applied to the target ("White Box Methods" on page 102) and score-based methods ("Score-Based Black Box Methods" on page 127). Score-based methods use predictions to infer gradients, so unless there is a necessity to return a network's scores to a user, this information should not be exposed directly or indirectly through a response.

A technique called *defensive distillation* has been suggested to disrupt the ability to generate adversarial examples using methods that use gradients.[2] This approach repurposes a technique called *distillation* that had been initially proposed to reduce the size of neural networks. Distillation of a neural network re-creates the DNN func-

---

1 This term was initially coined by Nicolas Papernot et al., in "Practical Black-Box Attacks Against Machine Learning," Sixth International Conference on Learning Representations (2018), *http://bit.ly/2IrqeJc*.

2 Nicolas Papernot et al. "Distillation as a Defense to Adversarial Perturbations Against Deep Neural Networks" (2016), *http://bit.ly/2KZXfOo*.

tion (its parameters) so that the gradients on the prediction landscape near the training points are smoothed.

How to Distill a Neural Network

To "distill" a network, it is initially trained as usual using labels. The model is then used to create predictions for the training dataset. Next, a new "distilled" version of the model is trained using the training data and predictions (probabilities), rather than the initial hard labels.

Neural networks that are trained on discrete labels have less smooth prediction landscape gradients than those trained on probabilities. The smoothing of the distillation process has the effect of reducing the size of the model, but may also reduce the model's accuracy. This trade-off may be justifiable; a smaller footprint may be useful to run a model where there are hardware constraints, such as on a mobile device.

The idea of network distillation is depicted in Figure 10-1. The image illustrates the prediction landscape for a particular classification before and after distillation. From a position in the input space near the training data points in the distilled network, there are no obvious gradients, so methods that extrapolate gradients from a specific point in the input space will not work. The most likely direction of change to create an adversarial example is not obvious.

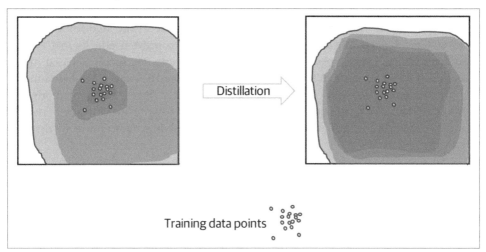

Figure 10-1. The effect of distillation on the prediction landscape around training points for a particular classification

Smoothing of model gradients has limited potential for defending against adversarial attacks, because the defense assumes that the gradients are important to establishing the adversarial input. Consider the methods introduced in Chapter 6. The gradients are important for attacks such as FGSM and JSMA. However, they are not important for methods that explore the search space without the use of gradients, such as the white box L-BFGS attack, or limited black box methods such as the boundary attack. An attacker can also circumvent gradient masking, even when using one of the gradient approaches, by introducing a random step in the algorithm to move the input to a location in the input space that avoids masked gradients.

Smoothing of gradients also provides no protection against transfer attacks. In fact, adversarial examples created using gradient-based approaches on a substitute model that has not been subjected to gradient masking can transfer to a target model whose gradients have been masked.

Adversarial Training

Adversarial training is perhaps the most intuitive approach to strengthening a neural network against adversarial examples. After all, the network can be trained to distinguish complicated features and patterns, so surely there are some features of adversarial examples that will enable them to be spotted by the model?

Adversarial input indicates a flaw in the DNN algorithm illustrating that the DNN is unable to generalize over all inputs. Therefore, detecting adversarial input and treating it correctly as such would improve the robustness of the algorithm. If we can detect adversarial input, we can respond appropriately, perhaps by reducing the confidence of the output prediction or by flagging the input as "adversarial" to trigger additional verification or actions (essentially, introducing an additional classification for this input). An alternative approach is to train the network to correctly classify adversarial data with its original (nonadversarial) label.

As discussed in Chapter 7, most adversarial examples are believed to lie within adversarial subspaces—continuous regions of misclassification within the input space. Surely, then, we could just train (or retrain) the model with many labeled adversarial examples so that it learns to generalize correctly over these subspaces? Figure 10-2 illustrates this idea.

This notion of training the model using adversarial examples has been explored from several perspectives.[3] Unfortunately, although this technique can appear to be a good defense, the trained model is only robust to adversarial examples generated by the same or a similar method as the adversarial training data.

---

3 See for example Goodfellow et al., "Explaining and Harnessing Adversarial Examples."

Prediction landscape

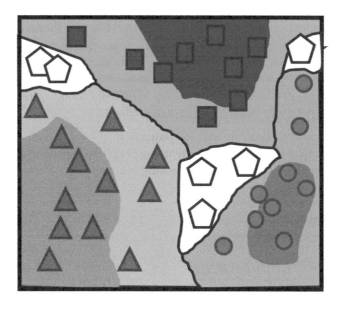

 Adversarial subspace

 Adversarial training data

Figure 10-2. Prediction landscape for a model trained with adversarial examples

To understand the limits of adversarial training, think about how the adversarial training data needs to be generated. Performing the training requires the generation of large quantities of training examples, through the methods described (or similar to those) in Chapter 6. Some of these techniques are computationally expensive or require many iterations, so this places a constraint on the ability to generate this data at scale. Take, for example, the iterative boundary attack. That takes thousands of iterations to generate an adversarial example, so it's going to be too slow to create a whole adversarial training dataset. For this reason, there's an obvious benefit to using quick adversarial generation methods that use simple approximations (such as FGSM and its variants) to generate the training set.

However, you are simply training the network to recognize a certain type of adversarial example. If, for the sake of speed and resources, the adversarial training data is generated using white box methods that approximate model gradients, you will end up with a DNN only able to recognize the features of adversarial examples generated using similar methods. As soon as an attacker uses a different method to generate examples (such as a boundary attack that doesn't use gradients), the defense will fail. Furthermore, if an attacker uses the same simple gradient approaches on a (different) substitute model and then performs a transfer attack, the defense will have poor ability to detect adversarial examples because it has learned what looks "adversarial" using a different set of gradients.

"OK," you might say, "so just create adversarial training data using the boundary attack method too." But therein lies the problem—new methods for adversarial generation are continually being devised, so you can never be sure that your DNN is entirely robust. Adversarial training will only catch similar adversarial input drawn from training data created with similar methods; it is not guaranteed to protect against methods that you have not thought of or not had time to generate training data for, or methods that have not yet been devised.

Jupyter Notebooks for Adversarial Training

The code snippets in this section are from the following:

The Jupyter notebook /chapter10/fashionMNIST_adversarial_training.ipynb (*http://bit.ly/2x3CA3A*) contains the code to train a network with adversarial data.

And the Jupyter notebook chapter10/fashionMNIST_adversarial_training_evaluation.ipynb (*http://bit.ly/2x3mwiv*) contains the code to experiment with and evaluate the adversarially trained network.

A proposed method to improve the defense is to use *ensemble adversarial training*.[4] This technique still uses low-cost methods such as FGSM and JSMA to generate the training data. However, by generating the adversarial training data using different models with different parameters and therefore gradients, you ensure that the model learns adversarial examples that are not tightly coupled to its parameters. This results in greater diversity in the adversarial training data perturbations and a model that exhibits greater ability to recognize adversarial input.

The fact that adversarial training is not guaranteed to create a model able to correctly classify all adversarial examples does not make it worthless. If the model is able to correctly classify even some adversarial inputs, that is likely to be beneficial. Adversarial training should not be relied upon for defense, however.

---

4 Florian Tramèr et al., "Ensemble Adversarial Training: Attacks and Defenses," International Conference on Learning Representations (2018), *http://bit.ly/2XldcFh*.

Let's try doing some adversarial training to see whether it improves the Fashion-MNIST model's robustness to adversarial examples.

The first step is to create some adversarial training data. For the purposes of demonstration, we'll generate this using images from the original training dataset using a weak attack the simple `GradientSignAttack` provided with Foolbox).

First, define the attack:

```
import foolbox
fmodel = foolbox.models.TensorFlowModel.from_keras(model, bounds=(0, 1))

attack_criterion = foolbox.criteria.Misclassification()
attack_fn = foolbox.attacks.GradientSignAttack(fmodel,
                        criterion=attack_criterion,
                        distance=foolbox.distances.Linfinity)
```

Augment the training data with 6,000 extra adversarial images and retrain the model:

```
x_images = train_images[0:6000, :]
predictions = model.predict(x_images)

x_train_adv_images, x_train_adv_perturbs, x_train_labels =
                generate_adversarial_data(original_images = x_images,
                                        predictions = predictions,
                                        attack_fn = attack_fn) ❶
```

❶ `generate_adversarial_data` is a helper utility included in the repository. It iterates through the provided images to create one adversarial example for each (assuming an adversarial example can be found). It also returns as output additional information on the perturbation distances and labels, which we'll use.

This produces the following warnings:

```
Warning: Unable to find adversarial example for image at index:  2393
Warning: Unable to find adversarial example for image at index:  3779
Warning: Unable to find adversarial example for image at index:  5369
```

There were 3 images out of the 6,000 for which the algorithm was unable to find an adversarial example. We still have 5,997, which will be plenty for training.

Next, augment the training data with these examples and retrain the model:

```
train_images_adv = np.concatenate((train_images, x_train_adv_images),
                        axis=0)
train_labels_adv = np.concatenate((train_labels,
                            np.full(x_train_adv_images.shape[0],
                                    adversarial_label)),
                        axis=0)

model_adv = keras.Sequential([keras.layers.Flatten(input_shape=(28,28)),
                        keras.layers.Dense(56, activation='relu'),
                        keras.layers.Dense(56, activation='relu'),
```

```
                    keras.layers.Dense(10, activation='softmax',
                                       name='predictions_layer')
        ])
model_adv.compile(optimizer=tf.keras.optimizers.Adam(),
              loss='sparse_categorical_crossentropy',
              metrics=['accuracy'])

model_adv.fit(train_images_plus_adv, train_labels_plus_adv, epochs=6)
```

Which generates the following output:

```
Epoch 1/6
65996/65996 [================] - 5s 72us/sample - loss: 0.5177 - acc: 0.8151
Epoch 2/6
65996/65996 [================] - 4s 67us/sample - loss: 0.3880 - acc: 0.8582
Epoch 3/6
65996/65996 [================] - 4s 67us/sample - loss: 0.3581 - acc: 0.8677
Epoch 4/6
65996/65996 [================] - 5s 69us/sample - loss: 0.3310 - acc: 0.8763
Epoch 5/6
65996/65996 [================] - 4s 58us/sample - loss: 0.3141 - acc: 0.8839
Epoch 6/6
65996/65996 [================] - 4s 64us/sample - loss: 0.3016 - acc: 0.8881
Out[29]:
<tensorflow.python.keras.callbacks.History at 0x181239196a0>
```

The first thing to check is whether our new adversarially trained model performs as
well as the original on the original test data:

```
test_loss, test_acc = model.evaluate(test_images, test_labels)
print('Original model accuracy based on nonadversarial test data:', test_acc)
test_loss, test_acc = model_adv.evaluate(test_images, test_labels)
print('Adversarially trained model accuracy based on nonadversarial test data:',
      test_acc)
```

This produces the following output:

```
10000/10000 [================] - 0s 37us/sample - loss: 0.3591 - acc: 0.8699
Original model accuracy based on nonadversarial test data: 0.8699
10000/10000 [================] - 1s 53us/sample - loss: 0.3555 - acc: 0.8707
Adversarially trained model accuracy based on nonadversarial test data: 0.8707
```

Not bad! It actually performs slightly better, so the training doesn't appear to have
affected the model's accuracy.

Now we need some adversarial test data. For a proper evaluation, we should assume
that the attacker has complete knowledge of the defense and, therefore, the adversarially trained model. However, let's take a naive approach to begin with for comparison
and use the original (nonadversarially trained) model to create the test data.

Define the attack:

```
import foolbox
fmodel = foolbox.models.TensorFlowModel.from_keras(model, bounds=(0, 1))
```

```
attack_criterion = foolbox.criteria.Misclassification()
x_images = test_images[0:600, :]

attack_fn = foolbox.attacks.GradientSignAttack(fmodel,
                          criterion=attack_criterion,
                          distance=foolbox.distances.Linfinity)
```

Then generate the test dataset. We'll call this x_test_adv_images1:

```
(x_test_adv_images1, x_test_adv_perturbs1, x_test_labels1) =
                generate_adversarial_data(original_images = x_images,
                        predictions = model.predict(x_images),
                        attack_fn = attack_fn)
```

Take a look at the confusion matrix demonstrating the adversarially trained model's performance against the adversarial examples generated with the initial model (Figure 10-3):

Figure 10-3. Code output

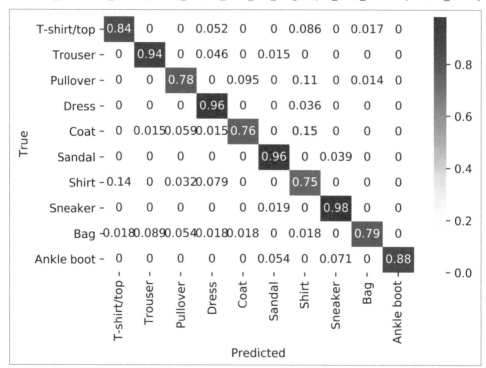

This looks really good—the majority of the adversarial test data has been correctly classified by the model.

Unfortunately, this is a poor evaluation. First, we've only tested the model's robustness to a specific attack (see the following note). Second, for a proper evaluation, we need to assume that the attacker has complete knowledge of the model and its defenses. An attacker with complete knowledge is able to generate adversarial data directly against the adversarially trained model, so this is the scenario that needs to be evaluated.

Testing the Adversarially Trained Model Using Different Attacks

Using the Jupyter notebook, you can further experiment with adversarial training using different attacks to generate training data.

You can also check the generated model against test data created using a different attack. Unless the test attack is similar in approach to the one used to train the model, the resulting confusion matrix is unlikely to classify the resulting data as effectively as that shown in Figure 10-3.

The first step is to regenerate the test data using the adversarially trained model. We'll call this x_test_adv_images2:

```
fmodel_adv = foolbox.models.TensorFlowModel.from_keras(model_adv,
                          bounds=(0, 1)) ❶
attack_fn = foolbox.attacks.GradientSignAttack(fmodel_adv,
                          criterion=attack_criterion,
                          distance=foolbox.distances.Linfinity)

(x_test_adv_images2, x_test_adv_perturbs2, x_test_labels2) =
                    generate_adversarial_data(original_images = x_images,
                          predictions = model_adv.predict(x_images), ❶
                          attack_fn = attack_fn)
```

❶ Notice the use of the adversarial model on these two lines.

This output is generated:

```
Warning: Unable to find adversarial example for image at index:  76
```

Figure 10-4 shows the resulting the confusion matrix:

```
show_confusion_matrix(model_adv, x_test_adv_images2, x_test_labels2, class_names)
```

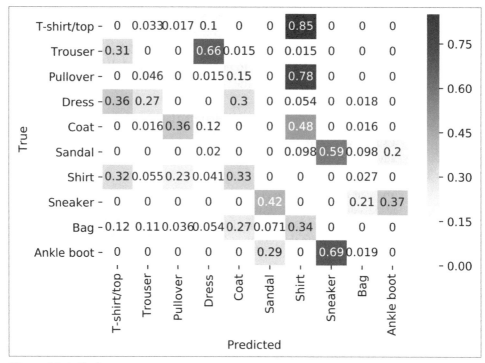

Figure 10-4. Code output

You can see that this time the model has performed far worse and has failed to correctly classify any of the adversarial examples (see the diagonal line of zeros from top left to bottom right). This is no surprise, as the examples in x_test_adv_images2 were all developed to fool this adversarially trained model.

Now let's take a look at whether it's more difficult for the adversary to *create* adversarial examples for the adversarially trained model. We'll plot success rate against required perturbation.

The helper method generate_adversarial_data returns distance measurements for each of the adversarial examples that were found. Assuming the GradientSign method attempts to optimize for the minimum distance, these should indicate the minimum distance required for each adversarial example.

Let's plot the perturbations required to generate adversarial examples against the original model and the adversarially trained model:

```
plt.hist((x_test_adv_perturbs1['foolbox_diff'], ❶
          x_test_adv_perturbs2['foolbox_diff']), ❷
         bins=20, ❸
         cumulative=True, ❹
         label=('Original model','Adversarially trained model'))
```

```
plt.title("Adversarial example success rate")
plt.xlabel("Perturbation")
plt.ylabel("Number of successful adversarial examples")
plt.legend(loc='right')

plt.show()
```

❶ This gives a list of each adversarial example's perturbation measurement (in this case, the L^∞-norm) for the examples generated using the original model.

❷ This gives a list of each adversarial example's perturbation measurement (in this case, the L^∞-norm) for the examples generated using the adversarially trained model.

❸ This defines the number of histogram "bins."

❹ This specifies a cumulative histogram plot.

Figure 10-5 shows the resulting graph.

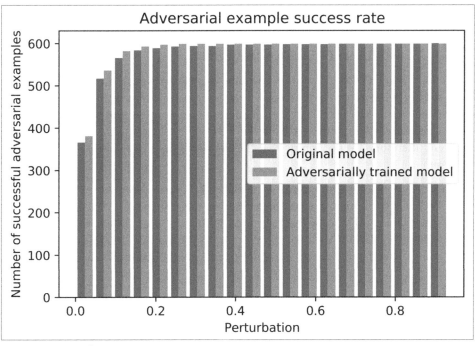

Figure 10-5. Code output

What a disappointment! The graph indicates that the adversarial success rate with respect to perturbation is *no worse* on an adversarially trained network than the original one. The adversarial training hasn't made it any more difficult to create adversarial examples using the same attack method.

To understand why this is the case, once again consider the prediction landscape. There are thousands of directions in which the image might be perturbed to create an adversarial example. The trained network has closed off some of these options, but there are many more still available to the algorithm. With extensive adversarial training we might remove increasing numbers of options, but this is unlikely to cover every possibility open to the adversarial algorithm (although it might take the algorithm longer to locate adversarial input).

If you look carefully at the lower perturbations on the histogram, you'll notice that the success rate is slightly better on the adversarially trained network than the original one. This suggests that the algorithm didn't produce the best results on the original model—in other words, it does not always return an adversarial example with the minimum perturbation possible. This may be because each iteration of the gradient attack is based on the gradients in the prediction landscape at the point of the current image. If those gradients don't reflect those further away from the image, the algorithm may step in directions that don't produce the optimum result.

Out-of-Distribution Confidence Training

As we have seen, DNNs sometimes produce incorrect results with high confidence because they fail to generalize correctly for all the possible inputs. Many of the generalizations that a DNN will struggle with fall into the more general *out-of-distribution* (OoD) category—those inputs that are not within the distribution of the training data, and therefore are not inputs that the network could be expected to safely perform on.

We initially considered OoD inputs in Chapter 5. Figure 10-6 illustrates the concept of OoD data. The input space on the left shows the distribution of training data for three classifications. The fully trained model taking test data shown on the right will work well for test data of a similar distribution to the training data. However, there is no guarantee that it will perform correctly given a point outside this distribution.

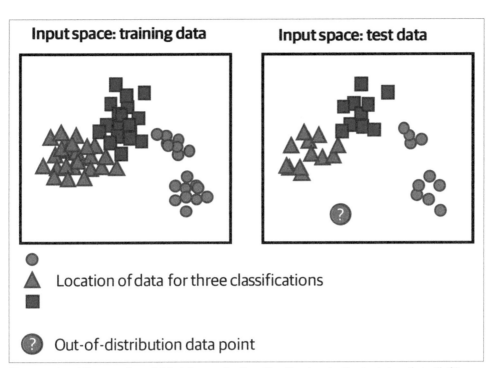

Input space: training data

Input space: test data

●
▲ Location of data for three classifications
■

? Out-of-distribution data point

Figure 10-6. The test data (right) has a similar distribution to the training data (left) except for one OoD point.

OoD input is not necessarily adversarial. It might be simply an edge case that was not represented by the training dataset. Alternatively, it may be an unrealistic or nonsensical image. The problem with OoD input is that the network may still return a confident prediction for this data, but the reliability of this prediction is lower than that of input with similarities to the training dataset.

Chapter 1 illustrated this point with OoD adversarial examples that did not look anything like real-life images but resulted in high-confidence predictions for a particular classification. As a reminder, Figure 10-7 illustrates one of these examples.

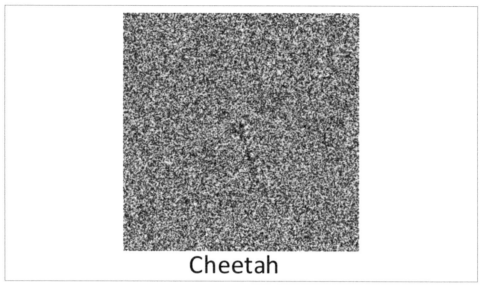

Cheetah

Figure 10-7. A digitally generated adversarial example that is OoD but results in a high-confidence prediction of "cheetah" from an image classifier (image from Nguyen et al. 2015)

So, are all adversarial examples also OoD? Not necessarily. While adversarial examples might lie in areas of the input space that are OoD (like the OoD data point shown in Figure 10-6), they may also exploit points in the input space where the algorithm has failed to generalize properly. These points may still be in the same distribution as the training data. The two cases are shown in Figure 10-8, which depicts the prediction landscapes resulting from a training dataset. Adversarial point 1 is clearly OoD, whereas adversarial point 2 lies comfortably within the training data distribution, but at a point where the algorithm has been unable to generalize correctly.

If we were able to detect OoD input, this would not guarantee detection of all adversarial examples. However, associating some confidence with a model's predictions also has broader benefits. Any method of measuring the distribution of data that the network is most likely to perform well against will be helpful in identifying whether an input falls into the "safe" distribution or not.

There are some methods for checking for realism in images, such as detecting high contrast between neighboring pixels. These methods may be successful in capturing "obvious" OoD data such as the "cheetah" shown in Figure 10-7, but they are less successful at detecting OoD images with clearer shapes and patterns.

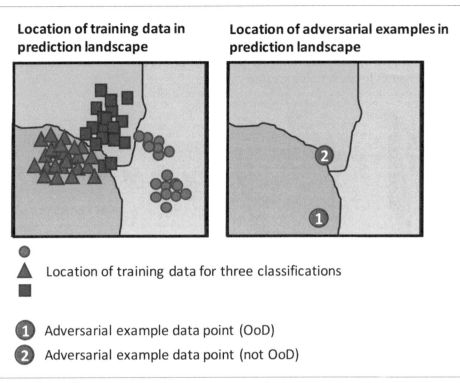

Figure 10-8. Adversarial examples are not necessarily OoD.

Although it's difficult to detect OoD statistically outside the network, other techniques have been proposed using the network itself. A promising approach is for the network to calibrate its score (make it less confident) or flag input when it is classed as OoD. To achieve this we train a DNN to output not only predicted scores but also the *confidence* that the network has in its prediction. For example, the way that this approach would fit into the DNN architecture introduced in "DNNs for Image Processing" on page 52 is illustrated in Figure 10-9.[5]

During training, the network learns to estimate confidence in its predictions as it also learns to make the predictions itself.

The training cost function introduced back in Chapter 3 can be rearticulated to optimize the accuracy of its confidence as well as the accuracy of the actual predictions. So, if the training network is making bad predictions for a training example, it should return a low confidence score. In this case, the network would be penalized during

5 Terrance De Vries and Graham W. Taylor, "Learning Confidence for Out-of-Distribution Detection in Neural Networks" (2018), *http://bit.ly/2XZHpH1*.

training (the cost would increase) if it returned a high confidence score. Similarly, the modified cost function ensures that a low confidence score returned for an incorrect prediction is also penalized. The network is trained well when it has not only learned to generate predictions close to the target labels, but can also generate accurate confidence measures for each training value.

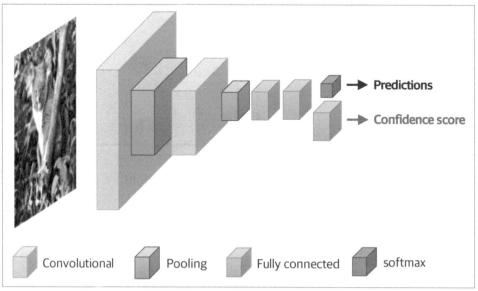

Figure 10-9. Extending a CNN architecture to calculate confidence scores for predictions

This additional feedback from the network indicates whether the input lies in the distribution of data on which it is safely trained to perform. For example, the cheetah probability score for the image in Figure 10-7 might be high, but if the network works correctly, its confidence in that score will be low. At the time of writing, this is nascent research, but it's showing promising results.

Randomized Dropout Uncertainty Measurements

There is a group of techniques collectively known as *regularization* used during neural network training to reduce the possibility of the network overfitting to the training data. These techniques reduce the complexity of the neural network, forcing it to generalize more and therefore work over a wider variety of data. *Dropout* is one of these regularization techniques—it randomly "removes" neurons so that they do not contribute to training iterations, and reinstates them for subsequent iterations. This may seem counterintuitive; surely that makes it more difficult for the network to learn? Yes, it does, but that is the whole point of the technique; it prevents the network from relying too heavily on specific units in the network when making a decision, and thus ensures that the network generalizes better.

Dropout is not only useful to prevent the model overfitting during training time, it can also be used when the model goes live, forcing the model to rely on different units each time it is queried. This introduces some uncertainty to the network, so the predictions for a particular input are not deterministic. Repeated queries to the network using the same input will return different results, and the variance of these results provides a measure of uncertainty of the network for a particular instance.

In their research, Feinman et al.[6] propose a method of adversarial detection called *Bayesian neural network uncertainty* whereby adversarial examples are detected because the randomized network is less certain of them than their natural counterparts. This defense relies on the premise that the predictions for a nonadversarial input will be more consistent than those for an adversarial one. So, if the same input were presented to a network incorporating randomized dropout multiple times, its predictions would vary more if that input were adversarial. When the variance metric for a specific input is over a defined threshold, the input is classified as adversarial. This approach has shown promising results in detecting adversarial inputs even when the attacker is assumed to have knowledge of the defense.[7]

Code Example: Dropout for Adversarial Detection

The code snippets in this section are from the Jupyter notebook chapter10/fashionMNIST_dropout_for_detection.ipynb (*http://bit.ly/2XZw7T8*) in the book's GitHub repository.

You can use this notebook to further experiment with randomized dropout, such as by changing the dropout parameters or altering the attack methods.

We'll use the Keras "functional" API here rather than the "sequential" API used up to now in this book, as it enables us to create a network that incorporates randomized dropout after it has been trained.[8]

Here is the code to create the same Fashion-MNIST classifier as previously, but with dropout enabled on one of the hidden layers:

```
from tensorflow.keras.layers import Input, Dense, Flatten, Dropout
from tensorflow.keras.models import Model
```

---

6 Reuben Feinman et al., "Detecting Adversarial Samples from Artifacts" (2017), *http://bit.ly/2XpavTe*.

7 Nicolas Carlini and David Wagner, "Adversarial Examples Are Not Easily Detected: Bypassing Ten Detection Methods" (2017), *http://bit.ly/2WTMhBe*.

8 For details of the two different programming approaches, refer to the Keras documentation for the Sequential model (*http://bit.ly/2FZbUrq*) and the functional API guide (*https://keras.io/getting-started/functional-api-guide/*).

```
inputs = Input(shape=(28,28))
x = Flatten()(inputs)
x = Dense(56, activation='relu')(x)
x = Dropout(0.2)(x, training=True) ❶
x = Dense(56, activation='relu')(x)
predictions = Dense(10, activation='softmax')(x)

model = Model(inputs=inputs, outputs=predictions)

model.compile(optimizer=tf.train.AdamOptimizer(),
              loss='sparse_categorical_crossentropy',
              metrics=['accuracy'])
model.summary()
```

❶ This line adds the dropout. The `training=True` parameter indicates (un-intuitively) that dropout should be applied *post*-training as well as during train-ing. This will add uncertainty to the network's predictions. The proportion of uncertainty is determined by the parameter passed to the `Dropout` function. You can experiment with this level of uncertainty in the notebook to see its effect.

This generates the following output:

Layer (type)	Output Shape	Param #
input_5 (InputLayer)	(None, 28, 28)	0
flatten_4 (Flatten)	(None, 784)	0
dense_12 (Dense)	(None, 56)	43960
dropout_4 (Dropout)	(None, 56)	0 ❶
dense_13 (Dense)	(None, 56)	3192
dense_14 (Dense)	(None, 10)	570

```
Total params: 47,722
Trainable params: 47,722
Non-trainable params: 0
```

❶ Here's the additional dropout layer.

Next, we train the model and take a look at its accuracy against the test data in the Fashion-MNIST dataset:

```
model.fit(train_images, train_labels, epochs=12) ❶
```

❶ A model incorporating dropout during training requires more epochs to establish the same accuracy. Hence the `epochs` parameter is set higher than in the previous examples.

This produces the following output:

```
Epoch 1/12
60000/60000 [================] - 4s 63us/sample - loss: 0.3243 - acc: 0.8777
Epoch 2/12
60000/60000 [================] - 4s 63us/sample - loss: 0.3174 - acc: 0.8812
Epoch 3/12
60000/60000 [================] - 4s 61us/sample - loss: 0.3119 - acc: 0.8834
Epoch 4/12
60000/60000 [================] - 4s 61us/sample - loss: 0.3114 - acc: 0.8845
Epoch 5/12
60000/60000 [================] - 4s 63us/sample - loss: 0.3042 - acc: 0.8854
Epoch 6/12
60000/60000 [================] - 4s 61us/sample - loss: 0.2987 - acc: 0.8882
Epoch 7/12
60000/60000 [================] - 4s 61us/sample - loss: 0.2982 - acc: 0.8870
Epoch 8/12
60000/60000 [================] - 3s 53us/sample - loss: 0.2959 - acc: 0.8889
Epoch 9/12
60000/60000 [================] - 4s 61us/sample - loss: 0.2931 - acc: 0.8902
Epoch 10/12
60000/60000 [================] - 4s 63us/sample - loss: 0.2894 - acc: 0.8909
Epoch 11/12
60000/60000 [================] - 3s 53us/sample - loss: 0.2859 - acc: 0.8919
Epoch 12/12
60000/60000 [================] - 4s 66us/sample - loss: 0.2831 - acc: 0.8927
Out[11]:
<tensorflow.python.keras.callbacks.History at 0x156074c26d8>
```

Let's check the network's accuracy:

```
test_loss, test_acc = model.evaluate(test_images, test_labels)
print('Model accuracy based on test data:', test_acc)
```

Which we see in the following output:

```
10000/10000 [================] - 0s 40us/sample - loss: 0.3827 - acc: 0.8689
Model accuracy based on test data: 0.8689
```

If you rerun this cell in the Jupyter notebook, the accuracy will keep changing due to the uncertainty of the network.

Now we require a batch of nonadversarial images and a batch of adversarial ones. We'll use the test data supplied with Fashion-MNIST and some adversarial images that have been generated previously. For this example, we'll use the images generated using the `FastGradient` Foolbox attack against the original model:

```
import numpy as np
```

```
num_images = 1000
x_images = test_images[:num_images]
x_images_adv = .... ❶
```

❶ To generate the adversarial images, use the `generate_adversarial_data` helper utility that we used previously. For conciseness, this code is not included here.

We repeatedly generate predictions using the dropout model for both batches of data. The number of times each image will be submitted to the model is defined by L:

```
L = 100
num_classes = 10

predictions_matrix = np.zeros((L, num_images, num_classes))  ❶
predictions_matrix_adv = np.zeros((L, num_images, num_classes)) ❷

for i in range(L):
    predictions = model.predict(x_images)
    predictions_adv = model.predict(x_images_adv)
    predictions_matrix[i] = predictions
    predictions_matrix_adv[i] = predictions_adv
```

❶ `predictions_matrix` is a matrix representing the predictions for all the non-adversarial images over L submissions.

❷ `predictions_matrix_adv` is a matrix representing the predictions for all the adversarial images over L submissions.

Next we calculate a single value of uncertainty for each image that represents the amount of variation over all the image's predictions. Here's the function for determining the uncertainty of a set of predictions for a single image:

```
def uncertainty(predictions):
    return(np.sum(np.square(predictions))/predictions.shape[0]
        - np.sum(np.square(np.mean(predictions, axis=0)))) ❶

uncertainty_results = np.zeros((num_images))
uncertainty_results_adv = np.zeros((num_images))

for i in range(num_images): ❷
    uncertainty_results[i] = uncertainty(predictions_matrix[:,i])
    uncertainty_results_adv[i] = uncertainty(predictions_matrix_adv[:,i])
```

❶ This is an implementation of the following calculation defined in Carlini and Wagner 2017: $U(x) = \left(\frac{1}{L}\Sigma_{i=1} \parallel F_r(x) \parallel\right) - \parallel \frac{1}{L}\Sigma_{i=1}F_r(x) \parallel$, where $\parallel y \parallel$ is taken to be the square of the L^2-norm. It's simply a way of calculating a measure of variance for a set of predictions.

❷ Calculate the uncertainty measure for each image to generate two lists—one for the uncertainties associated with each of the nonadversarial images and one for the uncertainties associated with the adversarial ones.

Finally, let's plot the results:

```
import matplotlib.pyplot as plt

plt.hist((uncertainty_results, uncertainty_results_adv),
         bins=50,
         label=('Nonadversarial','Adversarial'))

plt.title("Model prediction uncertainty")
plt.xlabel("Uncertainty per image")
plt.ylabel("Number of images")
plt.legend(loc='right')

plt.show()
```

Figure 10-10 shows the resulting graph.

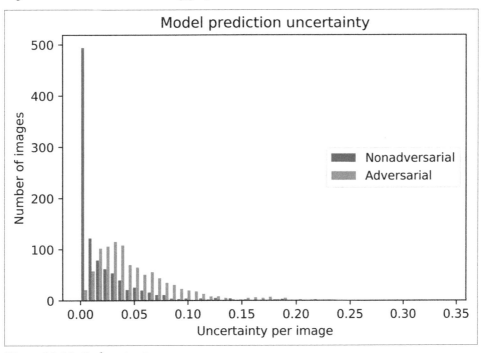

Figure 10-10. Code output

You can see that the predictions returned from the model tend to have greater uncertainty for adversarial images, so this is a good result. In this case, the threshold at which we would classify data as "adversarial" or "normal" is not clear-cut.[9] The threshold might be established by using an ROC curve, as described in the following note.

ROC Curves

An important tool in machine learning is the *receiver operating characteristic* (ROC) curve, often used to address the problem of setting a prediction threshold at which a binary decision is made. The ROC curve plots the true positive rate against the false positive rate in the *ROC space*. This plot can be used to establish a threshold by comparing the true positives (the benefit) against the false positives (the cost).

In the case of an adversarial defense, the binary threshold might be the threshold at which the probability of an input being "adversarial" means that it is treated as such. If the defense identifies adversarial inputs when it's 50% certain, for example, what is the false positive rate? That is, how many nonadversarial inputs are misclassified as adversarial with this threshold? The acceptable threshold of false positives versus false negatives will depend on the scenario; is it more important to catch adversarial input at the cost of reducing the accuracy across nonadversarial data, or is it better to ensure that nonadversarial data is not misclassified? A ROC curve can be used to articulate this as part of the evaluation, allowing the thresholds to be established for specific scenarios.

Using the Jupyter notebook, you could also experiment with other attacks, or with adversarial data generated on the dropout model itself (with dropout enabled during training only). If you try to generate the adversarial examples using a model that has dropout enabled after training, it may give interesting results; it's difficult for attacks to work with a continually shifting prediction landscape.

A model using dropout to detect adversarial input might be used alongside a non-dropout operational model to ensure that the functional behavior of the system is deterministic.

Data Preprocessing

Now let's take a different approach and consider whether we can remove adversarial data in the broader processing chain *prior* to it being submitted to the DNN.

We'll focus on two areas:

---

9 The researchers achieved better results than this, with a clearer distinction between normal and adversarial. This may be due to use of more accurate models than our very simple classifier.

Preprocessing in the broader processing chain

We'll first look at the effects preprocessing in the broader processing chain might inadvertently have on adversarial input.

Intelligent removal of adversarial content

Next we'll consider whether there are any proven statistical methods to deliberately remove adversarial content before it reaches the DNN. This could be detecting the adversarial input itself or removing aspects from all data that are likely to cause the model to return a result that is incorrect.

Preprocessing in the Broader Processing Chain

In real-world applications, DNNs do not exist in isolation. The efficacy of an adversarial example depends on many more factors when tested outside the laboratory environment as a result of the broader processing chain. Our adversary cannot be confident that their beautifully crafted adversarial examples will not be rendered benign (either deliberately or unintentionally) or detected by the target system's processing.

As part of the wider processing chain, network and computer security solutions provide protection against threats by automatically detecting data likely to contain malicious content. Most commonly, this is achieved through firewalls and antivirus software that assess risk based on either the provenance of the data (whether or not it is acquired from a trustworthy source) or the data itself (whether it contains content indicative of malware).

Unfortunately, because DNNs processing image, audio, and video often take data generated directly from the physical world (e.g., by cameras) or from untrusted digital sources (such as web uploads), adversarial examples cannot be detected according to trustworthiness. Similarly, detection based on content is challenging because adversarial examples appear benign to the target system.

Once the data has passed any firewall or other security boundaries, it is subject to organizational processing. It's helpful to consider a couple of different example scenarios:

Example: Social network image upload filtering

A processing chain for uploading images or video to a social networking site might involve images undergoing various preprocessing steps prior to vectorization and ingest to the neural network. This might include potential transformations, such as compression, normalization, smoothing, and resizing.

Example: Digital assistant

In this scenario, the input is also subject to limitations or preprocessing at the input sensor (in this case, the microphone) that may introduce noise to the signal or filter the data being captured.[10] It then undergoes further processing, such as Fourier transformation, before reaching the DNN.

Often, it is precision of the data that is being exploited to make input adversarial, so a transformation that ultimately removes some of the precision from the data may render an input nonadversarial.

Consider the impact a reduction in image precision might have on adversarial examples. In Chapter 4 the precision of an image was defined as its spatial resolution and pixel density. An adversarial example dependent on a few pixels (perhaps generated by minimizing the L^0-norm measurement) may be more likely impacted by reduced spatial resolution because the changed pixels may be lost when pixel density is reduced. Conversely, an adversarial example with minuscule changes to pixels across the whole image (possibly by minimizing the L^∞-norm) may be less robust to reduced color resolution where those subtle variations in color are lost. Adversarial input that unwittingly exploits characteristics that are lost or approximated during the processing chain may therefore be rendered less robust.

There are several reasons for data reduction during preprocessing, including:

Normalization and compression

The processing chain may perform normalization steps (for example, converting data to a consistent format or resizing images prior to submitting them to the DNN). If this normalization step results in a reduction of information contained in the data, it may remove the information that makes the input adversarial.

Compression is also an important aspect of the digital encoding step, and this may be relevant to adversarial input if it results in a reduction in precision (see the following note).

The precision of any digital information is constrained to the lowest precision of its previous processing. An image stored as 640 x 480 pixels, suitable for photographic display, will always retain that resolution; displaying it on an HD television screen will not increase the spatial detail, nor will storing it in a file format with higher resolution.[11]

Removal of noise and extraneous data

The processing chain will remove noise or extraneous data from the source if it is likely to aid the processing of that data or improve it for human perception.

---

10 Other challenges imposed by the physical environment were discussed in Chapter 8.

11 There are processing techniques that increase the resolution of image and audio through inference of missing data, but these techniques would not reinstate adversarial perturbations previously lost during data compression and normalization.

Noise refers to distortion in the data, often introduced during the data capture step. Visual distortion in images might show as pixels that do not represent the scene accurately. Speckles, for example, might appear in an image taken in a low-light situation. Audio noise might manifest itself as crackles or interference introduced by the microphone sensor or audio equipment, reverberation, echo, and background noise.

Gaussian blur is a blurring method commonly used to remove noise from images. This could be performed in the broader system preprocessing unrelated to the DNN to clean up images. Any adversarial perturbation or patch that might be categorized as "noise" or not relevant by the processing chain is subject to removal.

Other extraneous data might also be removed during preprocessing. For example, speech processing systems might exploit specific audio processing techniques to extract the most relevant aspects of the sound—those that correspond to the human vocal tract—using MFC (as introduced in "Audio" on page 58).

Lossless and Lossy Data Compression

Digital, audio, and video formats are often compressed to save space. When compression is simply a shorthand way of storing the same data using fewer bytes, it is known as *lossless*.

In contrast, *lossy* compression uses intelligent algorithms to also remove data that is likely to be superfluous. This has the advantage that the image, audio, or video takes up less space without incurring any noticeable reduction in quality. Any data lost during lossy compression will be lost forever; it is not reinstated when the image, audio, or video is uncompressed.

For example, the MP3 format compresses audio data using intelligent (lossy) compression that bases the bit rate on the audio's complexity; less complex aspects may be stored at a lower bit rate.[12] JPEGs also use lossy compression to reduce image size by removing information that is nonessential and unlikely to be missed by humans.

Data preprocessing may thwart simple attacks where the adversary is not aware of the transformation steps.[13] It may also make attacks more difficult by placing additional

---

12 The Fourier transform is also used in MP3 compression.

13 See for example, Xin Li and Fuxin Li, "Adversarial Examples Detection in Deep Networks with Convolutional Filter Statistics," *International Conference on Computer Vision* (2017), *http://bit.ly/2FjDIVu*. The authors prove that passing a filter over an image could be successful in removing the adversariality from examples that had been generated by simple techniques such as FGSM.

constraints on the attack. However, data preprocessing should not be relied upon for effective defense.

Intelligently Removing Adversarial Content

For now, there are no statistical methods that can test for adversarial examples prior to submission to the DNN (see the following note for a discussion).

Statistical Methods for Detecting Adversarial Examples

A few methods have been proposed for the statistical detection of adversarial examples.

For example, Grosse et al.[14] use data distribution methods to ascertain whether adversarial input can be distinguished using a technique called *Maximum Mean Discrepancy*, and Feinman et al.[15] propose analyzing the distribution of the final hidden layer neural network outputs to detect adversarial input, rather than the raw input. The output of this hidden layer represents the extracted higher-level features of the input, so this approach considers the distribution of semantic information, rather than raw pixel data.

Unfortunately, these approaches have not yet proven to be effective defenses.[16]

As an alternative approach, it might be easier to apply an intelligent transformation that will not affect the classification of nonadversarial input, but will alter adversarial input so that the characteristics that make it adversarial are removed. This doesn't require detecting input that is adversarial, just removing aspects of the input that are likely to be exploited for "adversariality" during a preprocessing step before the data is passed to the DNN.

For example, it may be that some pixels in an image are not very important in determining the image's classification for nonadversarial data, but are exploited by adversarial examples to force the DNN to create an incorrect result. Removing these pixels from the data might remove "adversariality" while not adversely affecting the predictions for "good" data. Similarly, removal of audio frequencies outside speech thresholds removes the potential for creating adversarial input outside the vocal range without affecting the effectiveness of a speech recognition system.

---

14 Kathrin Grosse et al., "On the (Statistical) Detection of Adversarial Examples" (2017), *http://bit.ly/2IszblI*.

15 Reuben Feinman et al., "Detecting Adversarial Samples from Artifacts" (2017), *http://bit.ly/2XpavTe*.

16 See Carlini and Wagner, "Adversarial Examples Are Not Easily Detected: Bypassing Ten Detection Methods."

One approach that has been explored is the use of *principle component analysis* (PCA), a mathematical technique to identify the characteristics of data that are most influential in a decision. PCA has been tested as a method to establish which parts of data are exploited by adversarial examples that do not influence the decisions for good data. Unfortunately, it turns out that there aren't any obvious characteristics that influence "adversariality," so once again, this is not yet an effective defense.[17]

Concealing the Target

An important aspect of target concealment is that the target is not just the DNN; it's the complete processing system, including the defense mechanisms in place.

Chapter 7 explored the challenges of generating robust adversarial content in the real world. Lack of knowledge of the DNN or an inability to query the target greatly impacts the ease with which adversarial input can be created. Conversely, knowledge of the DNN enables the attacker to create a replica to develop and sharpen adversarial input prior to launching it on the target system. The ability to test an attack on the target system is also a valuable aid in either verifying adversarial input or developing an attack using black box methods (the latter usually requiring many queries to the target).

If your organization is using a pretrained, openly or commercially available model, it will be fairly easy for the adversary to generate a replica DNN to develop accurate adversarial examples. As seen in Chapter 7, even access to the training data provides the adversary with sufficient information to generate a model substitute close enough to the original for adversarial examples to successfully transfer. However, while basing a DNN algorithm on a commercially sourced or openly available model may not be ideal, it may be the only practical option given the quantities of labeled data typically required to train a network.

Knowledge of the complete processing chain includes knowledge of preprocessing steps that might transform adversarial input to nonadversarial and the treatment of the output from the neural network. This includes prediction thresholds for making decisions and, the organizational response to such predictions.

Knowledge of any active defenses in place includes the knowledge of methods to identify or remove adversarial input. Knowledge of such defenses might also be established through testing—querying the system and checking the broader organizational response to adversarial input. For example, if the attacker is aware that, on identifying an adversarial patch, you will then use that patch to search for other

---

17 In Carlini and Wagner, "Adversarial Examples Are Not Easily Detected."

adversarial images, they may know not to reuse the patch, or might even exploit it to generate false positives.

There are practical measures that can be put in place to limit an adversary's access to the target and, therefore, their ability to generate adversarial input. These include:

Throttling queries
A black box direct attack requiring high volumes of queries might be made more difficult by hindering the speed at which queries can be made. However, throttling based on client identification may have little effect, as a determined attacker will then simply issue queries using a variety of the identifiers that you are exploiting—a variety of IP addresses or accounts, for example.

Detecting based on query patterns
Alternatively, the target system could detect an attempted black box direct attack by testing for large quantities of very similar but nonidentical inputs, because such an attack would also require many similar queries, each an iterative tweak to the previous input. For example, input similarity might be detected quickly though *image hashing*. Image hashing assigns a "hash" value to an image, where similar images are assigned hash values that are close to each other.[18] There is, of course, the risk that a high volume of similar queries are not necessarily adversarial, so the relevance of this defense depends on the scenario.

Minimizing feedback
An adversary can exploit responses from queries to the target system to generate robust adversarial examples. These responses might be used to develop the adversarial input itself, or to test the adversarial input after it has been initially crafted on a substitute model. Reducing the amount of useful information returned from a query will increase the difficulty of generating adversarial input. This includes ensuring that model scores are not released and error messages do not reveal unnecessary information.

Providing nondeterministic responses
A nondeterministic response is an extremely powerful defense if it prevents the attacker from establishing the detailed workings of your system. "Randomized Dropout Uncertainty Measurements" on page 196 presents an example of such an approach, but nondeterminism could also be introduced in the broader processing chain if it was acceptable to the operational scenario.

---

18 Not to be confused with a cryptographic hash, where the hash value does not indicate similarity of the input.

Building Strong Defenses Against Adversarial Input

This chapter has introduced a combination of approaches for detecting or removing adversarial input.

As the robustness of neural networks increases, so will the sophistication of the attacks. This continual process—an "arms race" between attacker and defender—is similar to the evolution of malware detection or spam email filtering, and the adversarial example landscape will similarly change along with the available defenses.

Open Projects

While currently there are no sure defenses, several current initiatives seek to bring the exploration of adversarial attacks and defenses into the public domain and to help improve the robustness of DNN algorithms by pitting attacks against defense mechanisms. Some of these were mentioned previously, in Chapter 6. Good places to start include:

CleverHans
> CleverHans (*http://bit.ly/2WNNs0c*) is an open source library and code repository for the development of attacks and associated defenses with the aim of benchmarking machine learning system vulnerability to adversarial examples.[19]

Foolbox
> Foolbox is a toolbox for creating adversarial examples to enable testing of defenses.[20] Start by reviewing the documentation (*http://bit.ly/2FmRpmx*).

IBM's Adversarial Robustness Toolbox
> This library's code repository (*http://bit.ly/2XZ7EgW*) includes adversarial attacks, defenses, and detection methods. It also supports robustness metrics.

Robust ML
> Robust ML (*https://www.robust-ml.org/*) aims to provide a central website for learning about defenses and their analyses and evaluations.

Robust Vision Benchmark
> Robust Vision Benchmark (*http://bit.ly/2L9A3gT*) provides a platform for testing the effectiveness of attacks and the robustness of models.

---

19 Nicolas Papernot et al., "Technical Report on the CleverHans v2.1.0 Adversarial Examples Library" (2017), *http://bit.ly/2Xnwav0*.

20 Jonas Rauber et al., "Foolbox: A Python Toolbox to Benchmark the Robustness of Machine Learning Models" (2018), *http://bit.ly/2WYFgPL*.

Competitions

Several competitions have encouraged participation in the generation of adversarial attacks and defenses, including some organized by Google.[21]

In addition, see the Unrestricted Adversarial Examples Challenge (*http://bit.ly/2L0setv*) and Kaggle (*https://www.kaggle.com*).[22]

Taking a Holistic View

Defense depends on the context in which the DNN is deployed and the risks that adversarial examples could potentially pose to your organization. If you have complete control over and trust in the data that the AI is processing, there may be no risk of attack from adversarial input.

Developing end-to-end solutions that are robust to adversarial examples requires a multipronged approach. It is important to consider the *complete system* and not just the model (or models) used by your organization in isolation. The risk of some threats can be reduced through simple process or processing chain changes.

For example, you may not be able to remove capabilities (resources and skills) from an adversary, but you can increase the difficulty of an attack by reducing the attacker's ability to affect the input or removing access to target information. This could be achieved by preventing inadvertent and unnecessary information leakage in responses. Where there is risk of a physical-world attack, simple nontechnical measures such as monitoring of physical areas where an adversarial attack could take place may be sufficient to remove the threat.

In practice, many applications already have additional Information Assurance (IA) protecting the AI components; for example, digital assistants provide additional levels of security to prevent inadvertent commands, such as requiring authentication to perform impactful actions like money transfers and providing audio responses to voice commands. You may also be able to reduce the risk by establishing the veracity of the model's output through information acquired from other data sources. An example of this is an autonomous vehicle that might augment its knowledge with camera data, but does not wholly rely on this image information.

Defenses should be evaluated assuming that the attacker has complete knowledge. So, you should evaluate the the robustness of a system to attack with full knowledge of the model, the processing chain, and all defenses. You should also use the strongest attacks available to perform any evaluation. This requires remaining informed of the

---

21 Alexey Kurakin et al., "Adversarial Attacks and Defences Competition" (2018), organized as part of the Neural Information Processing Systems (NIPS) conference 2017, *http://bit.ly/2WYGzy9*.

22 Several competitions as part of NIPS 2017.

latest developments in attacks and defenses. The evaluation is not a static one-time process, but is ongoing as better attacks and defenses are developed. Evaluation should be a combination of formal assessments and cybersecurity testing of the complete system, so that adversarial examples are incorporated into any "red-blue" team approach to testing.

A holistic view is not only about defenses in place in the technical solution, but also understanding the broader impact that such attacks have on the organization and how to prevent inappropriate responses. For example, having a human in the loop to check alerts from surveillance cameras prior to acting on them may be appropriate to prevent a DoS attack. The AI processing is then performing a triage of the surveillance data, and leaving the ultimate decision to a human.

If you are able to detect adversarial attacks, consider your response. It may be appropriate to ignore and log the attempted attacks, similar to dealing with spam email. Alternatively, in some scenarios, it may be appropriate to respond more actively. Repeated detected adversarial input could be grounds to (for example) limit subsequent access of a user to a social media platform. If you are explicitly detecting adversarial input, ensure that your organization does not respond in a way that would leave it open to a DoS attack if it was flooded with adversarial examples.

Finally, detecting and dealing with adversarial input is only part of the assurance of machine learned models. Assurance also involves ensuring that a model is able to operate safely over the inputs it could receive, whether they are adversarial or not. In addition, there are other adversarial threats to machine learning that should be considered as part of information assurance, such as poisoning of training data impacting the integrity of the model, and model "reverse engineering" to extract confidential training data.

## CHAPTER 11

Future Trends: Toward Robust AI

This book has been about techniques for fooling AI that would not fool a human being. We should not forget, however, that we are susceptible to optical and audio illusions. Interestingly, research has shown that some adversarial examples can also fool time-limited humans.[1] Conversely, some optical illusions can also trick neural networks.[2]

These cases suggest that there may be some similarities between biological and artificial perception, but adversarial inputs exploit the fundamental principle that deep learning models process data differently than their biological counterparts. While deep learning may create models that match or exceed human capability in processing sensory input, these models are likely to be a long way from how humans actually learn and perceive visual and auditory information.

There are fascinating areas of investigation opening up in the field of deep learning that are likely to bring about greater convergence between artificial and biological perception. Such research may result in AI that has greater resilience to adversarial examples. Here is a selection.

Increasing Robustness Through Outline Recognition

Neuroscientists and psychologists have known for many years that our understanding of the world around us is built through movement and physical exploration. A baby views items from different angles by moving, or because the items themselves move.

---

1 Gamaleldin F. Elsayed et al., "Adversarial Examples that Fool both Computer Vision and Time-Limited Humans" (2018), *http://bit.ly/2RtU032*.

2 Watanabe Eiji et al., "Illusory Motion Reproduced by Deep Neural Networks Trained for Prediction," *Frontiers of Psychology* (March 2018), *http://bit.ly/2FkVxmZ*.

We know that visual perception is very dependent on movement and viewing angles, allowing us to learn about objects and their boundaries. If DNNs placed greater emphasis on object outlines, a perturbation attack would not be feasible. A similar principle applies to audio, where certain broad temporal patterns and relative pitches determine understanding. The salient features that we extract from sensory data to understand the world are clearly very different from those extracted by a DNN.

Researchers Geirhos et al.[3] argue that CNNs trained on ImageNet data (such as ResNet50) place greater emphasis on textures in images than on object outlines. In contrast, humans place greater emphasis on object shape in making a decision. The researchers tested this with images generated from ImageNet that had conflicting shape and texture information. For example, Figure 11-1 from the paper illustrates how ResNet50 makes a classification biased toward texture when presented with an image where the texture and shape conflict.

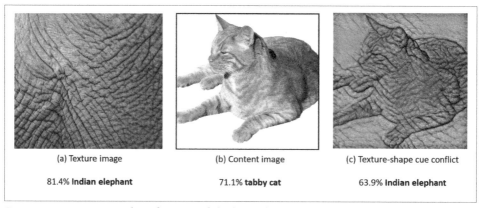

(a) Texture image   (b) Content image   (c) Texture-shape cue conflict

81.4% **Indian elephant**   71.1% **tabby cat**   63.9% **Indian elephant**

Figure 11-1. ResNet50 classification of elephant skin (a), a cat (b), and a cat with elephant skin texture cues (c) (from Geirhos et al. 2019)

By generating a new training dataset comprised of "stylized" images with training labels that corresponded to the shape of the object rather than the texture, the researchers were able to retrain CNNs to reduce their bias toward texture and make them more reliant on outlines in the image. This approach has the benefit that the classifiers were more robust to distortion in an images because such distortions tend to affect texture, whereas the object outline stays relatively stable.

From the perspective of creating neural networks robust to adversarial examples, this research is promising. If the CNN places greater emphasis on outlines to make its

---

3 Robert Geirhos et al., "ImageNet-Trained CNNs Are Biased Towards Texture; Increasing Shape Bias Improves Accuracy and Robustness" (2019), *http://bit.ly/2N0FuB2*.

decision, the decision is less likely to be affected by adversarial perturbation that spans the image.

Multisensory Input

There are other fascinating new ideas originating from theoretical neuroscience on how the brain might work. These ideas may provide new approaches to building AI that more accurately mimics human perception.

For example, the human brain successfully combines multiple sensory inputs (such as sight, hearing, touch, temperature sensitivity) in order to establish an understanding of the world. Multiple sensory inputs provide constant validation of data around us (though sometimes we can get it wrong, as described in the following note).

The McGurk Effect

The McGurk effect is an auditory illusion that illustrates the brain's perception of speech based on both visual and audio information.

When presented with an audio stimulus (such as someone making the sound "bah") paired with conflicting visual information (such as video showing someone making the sound "fah"), our brains override the audio with the visual stimulus and "hear" the sound "fah."

Watch the BBC Two video *Try The McGurk Effect!—Horizon: Is Seeing Believing?* (*http://bit.ly/2ISlb3v*) and try it for yourself.

As AI systems evolve, they will increasingly fuse data from disparate sources—both sensor data and nonsensor data—to verify their understanding of the world. If we can understand nature's approach to this problem, we may be able to create AI systems that work to higher levels of accuracy when fusing unstructured data such as audio and images.

In their research, Hawkins et al.[4] present the "Thousand Brains Model of Intelligence." They theorize that the neocortex comprises many mini-brains called "cortical columns" all working in parallel to process sensory information. Each of these cortical columns has a complete understanding of objects in the world. They each ingress specific sensory input—say from a small area of the visual field or from the touch of a finger—and use this data to establish the object that the sensory input is from (for example, a cup or hat) along with the location of the input relative to the rest of the object.

---

4 Jeff Hawkins et al., "A Framework for Intelligence and Cortical Function Based on Grid Cells in the Neocortex," *Frontiers in Neural Circuits* 12, 121 (2018), *http://bit.ly/2ZtvEJk*.

The researchers give the example of cortical columns simultaneously receiving sensory input from a mug that someone is looking at and touching with one finger. One column might receive "touch" data originating from the finger that is touching the mug, while other columns receive data from the visual cortex that represents different visual parts of the mug. Based on the learned model of the world that each cortical column holds, each column will make an educated guess as to what object it is sensing and the location of the sensed data on the object. The resulting information is collated from all the columns to determine what the object is, with some kind of "voting mechanism" in the case of disputes.

The idea that thousands of models of a single object are being generated by the brain simultaneously is very different from the strict hierarchical approach of a DNN, where one object is understood by gradually extracting higher-level features. This parallelism also merges multiple inputs from different senses, enabling greater resilience to error, and perhaps goes some way to explaining the McGurk effect.

Object Composition and Hierarchy

The Thousand Brains theory also proposes a mechanism for how the brain processes composition of objects within other objects. The researchers posit that, along with location information, the cortical columns also understand displacement and therefore the relationship between one object and another.

Other researchers recommend alternative approaches to rethinking the CNNs that have become the staple approach for image processing. The convolutional layers extract features from across the image but do not incorporate learning based on the relative position of those features within an image. For example, a CNN might recognize a face based on the existence of features such as eyes, nose, and mouth, but the relative position of those features is unimportant.

Geoffrey Hinton and his team propose *capsule networks*[5] to better formulate hierarchical representations and relationships of objects in the world. Making these relationships core to the capsule network's calculations means that these networks incorporate an understanding of the relationships between the parts that make up objects, enabling them to better understand objects in images, regardless of viewing angle. Capsule networks have been shown to display greater resilience to adversarial attacks due to their better contextual understanding of images.

---

5 Sara Sabour et al., "Dynamic Routing Between Capsules" (2017), *http://bit.ly/2FiVAjm*.

Finally...

There is increasing interest in the reconvergence of the neuroscience and AI disciplines. Better understanding of how the brain works and the application of these new ideas to AI methodologies is likely to result in better imitations of human learning. This, however, implies that our AI algorithms will be susceptible to the same foibles as our brains are, unless we program deliberate strategies to prevent this. From a neuroscience perspective, AI provides a way to test hypotheses regarding the workings of the brain. Researching how and when data is interpreted incorrectly by humans and AI will aid this convergence.

As AI moves closer to biological intelligence, we might remove any discrepancy between how humans and machines are fooled. Perhaps, as the neural networks evolve to better mimic human perception, image and audio adversarial examples will become a thing of the past.

Mathematics Terminology Reference

To serve as either a refresher or an introduction, Table A-1 summarizes the key mathematical terminology in the context in which it is used in this book.

Table A-1. Mathematics terminology summary

Terminology	Description
x	A nonbold variable refers to a scalar.
$\mathbf{x}$	A variable in bold refers to a vector.
$y = f(\mathbf{x}; \theta)$	The result of function f on the vector input $\mathbf{x}$, where f is dependent on the parameters θ. In the context of this book, this represents the output of a DNN model for a particular input: f represents the DNN model algorithm, θ represents its parameters determined during training, and $\mathbf{x}$ is the input to the model.
$C(f(\mathbf{x}; \theta), \mathbf{y})$	The result of function C given $f(\mathbf{x}; \theta)$ and the vector $\mathbf{y}$. In the context of this book, this represents the cost (or loss) of the DNN model for a particular input with respect to the required output $\mathbf{y}$.
x_i	The element i of vector $\mathbf{x}$.
$\dfrac{dy}{dx}$	The derivative of y with respect to x.
$\dfrac{\partial y}{\partial x}$	The *partial* derivative of y with respect to x, wh - ere x is one of the variables that affects y.
$\nabla_x f$	The *nabla* (upside-down Greek *delta*) symbol means "gradient." $\nabla_x f$ refers to the vector of partial derivatives of the function f for the vector $\mathbf{x}$. Put more simply, this means the effect that a very small change to the value of $\mathbf{x}$ has on the function f.
$\{1, 2, \ldots L\}$	The set of numbers from 1 to L.
$\mathbb{R}$	The set of real numbers.
$\{x : P(x)\}$	The set of all values of x for which $P(x)$ is true, where $P(x)$ is a boolean statement.
$\underset{x}{\arg\min} \{f(x) : P(x)\}$	Returns x at which $f(x)$ is minimized such that $P(x)$ is true.
$x \in \mathbb{R}$	Indicates that x belongs to the set of real numbers.
$\|\mathbf{x}\|_p$	The L^p-norm of the vector $\mathbf{x}$. L^p-norms are explained in "A Mathematical Approach to Measuring Perturbation" on page 90.

Terminology	Description
$\sum x$	The sum of all the possible values of x.
$\sum_{x \neq t} x$	The sum of all the possible values of x where $x \neq t$.
ε	The Greek letter ε (epsilon) is used to indicate an extremely small (infinitesimal) quantity.

Index

A

absolute threshold of sensation, 94
activation function, 36
activity recognition with video, 66
adversarial attacks
    methods of (see attack patterns)
    targeted, 76, 168
    untargeted, 76
adversarial confidence, increasing, 119-121
adversarial examples
    defined, 7
    in physical world, 12-14
    in theoretical environment vs. real world,
      145
    mathematics of, 95-97
adversarial input, 6-16, 75-97
    adversarial perturbation, 8-9
      (see also perturbation attack)
    and adversarial machine learning, 14
    and adversarial patches, 11-12, 89-90
    and attack constraints, 148
    and environmental conditions, 148
    capturing in digital form, 148
    creation of, 148
    defined, 6-8
    DNN thinking with, 83-87
    implications of, 15-16
    in physical world, 12-14
    input space, 76-83
    measuring detectability with, 90-95
    motivations for creating (see attack motiva-
      tions)
    perturbation attack, 87-88
    positioning and proximity of, 148

unnatural, 9-10
adversarial machine learning, 14
adversarial objects in physical world, 148-155
    fabrication and camera capabilities, 149-150
    printing, 150
    viewing angles and environment, 151-155
adversarial patches, 11-12, 75, 89-90
adversarial perturbation, 8-9
    defined, 75
    generating, 99-129
    limited black box methods, 100, 121-127
    score-based black box methods, 100,
      127-129
    white box methods, 100, 102-121
adversarial saliency, 113-119
adversarial sound in physical world attacks,
    155-159
    audio positioning and environment,
      157-159
    audio reproduction and microphone capa-
      bilities, 156-157
adversarial subspaces, 139
adversarial training, 181, 183-192
AIS (Automatic Identification System), 22
algorithms, genetic, 128
amplitude, 58
angles, viewing, 151-155
ANNs (see artificial neural networks)
artificial intelligence (AI) (generally)
    and adversarial input (see adversarial input)
    and DNNs, 1
    emitting incorrect images, 5-6
    future trends in (see future trends)
artificial neural networks (ANNs), 28

M

machine learning (ML)
  adversarial, 14
  and DNNs, 25-27
  and reverse engineering, 15
malware, 7
map, feature, 55
maps, saliency, 84
mathematical functions
  DNN representing, 3
  DNNs as, 30-33, 38
  for C&W attacks, 120, 168
  for FGSM, 108
  for JSMA, 114
  for measuring detectability, 90-93
  in adversarial examples, 95-97
  saliency, 83
  terminology for, 219
McGurk effect, 215
mean squared error (MSE), 41
mel-frequency cepstrum (MFC), 61
metrics parameter, 45
metrics, robustness, 172-176
MFC (mel-frequency cepstrum), 61
microphone capabilities, 156-157, 157
minus in FGSM, 105
ML (see machine learning)
ML model reverse engineering, 15
model
  evaluation of (see model evaluation)
  exploiting linearity of, 105-113
  improving for defense (see improving
    model for defense)
  learned algorithm as, 1
  robustness (see model robustness, evaluat-
    ing)
model architecture, defined, 67
model evaluation, 171-178
  empirically derived metrics, 172-177
  importance of, 163-165
  theoretically derived metrics, 176-177
model parameters, defined, 67
model robustness, evaluating, 163-178
  about, 163-164
  and threat model, 165-171
  through model evaluation, 171-178
motivations, attack (see attack motivations)
MSE (mean squared error), 41
multilayer perceptron, 28

multisensory input, 215-216

N

neurons, 29, 33, 34
nondeterministic responses, 208
normalization, 70, 204

O

object composition, human perception of, 216
objects
  detection of, 52
  fabrication in physical world attacks,
    149-150
  localization of, 52
off-board data, 22
onboard sensor data, 22
online reputation, 19-20
OoD data (see out-of-distribution data)
open projects, 99, 178, 209-210
optimizer parameter, 45
out-of-distribution (OoD) data, 81
  and input space, 82-83
  confidence training with, 192-196
  detection, 181
outline recognition, increasing robustness
  through, 213-215
output layer, 28
overfitting, 47

P

patches
  adversarial (see adversarial patches)
  reusable, 141-144
PCA (principle component analysis), 207
perceptibility (see human perception; perturbation limit)
personal privacy, 21
perturbation
  adversarial (see adversarial perturbation)
  reusable, 141-144
perturbation attacks, 13
  (see also adversarial perturbation)
  and adversarial input, 87-88
  defined, 8
  in real world settings, 13
  input space through many, 104
perturbation limit, 166
physical world attacks

goals, 165-169
perturbation limit, 166
specificity, 165
success rate, 166
target access and knowledge, 171
3D printing, 150
throttling queries, 208
training data, 79-81
training=True parameter, 198
transfer attack, 102, 134, 137-140
translation, 152
2D printing, 150

U

ultrasounds, 94
universal transfer attack, 134, 140-141
unnatural adversarial input, 9-10
unsupervised learning, 3, 26
untargeted attacks, 76

V

VGG, 57
video
circumventing classification of, 141
digital representation of, 65
DNN processing for, 65-66

DNNs for, 65-66
uploading on social media, 203
voice controlled devices, 23-24, 159

W

web crawlers, 19
web filters, circumventing, 18-19
weights of neural network, 35
white box attack methods, 100, 102-121
adversarial saliency, 113-119
Carlini and Wagner (C&W) attacks, 119,
168
exploiting model linearity, 105-113
Fast Gradient Sign Method (FGSM), 105
finding input space, 102-105
increasing adversarial confidence, 119-121
Jacobian Saliency Map Approach (JSMA),
113
Limited-memory Broyden-Fletcher-
Goldfarb-Shanno (L-BFGS) algorithm,
104
variations on, 121

Z

zoom, 152

About the Author

Katy Warr gained her degree in AI and computer science from the University of Edinburgh at a time when there was insufficient compute power and data available for deep learning to be much more than a theoretical pursuit. Following many years developing enterprise software, she now specializes in AI and considers herself fortunate to be part of this exciting field as it becomes an integral part of everyday life.

Colophon

The animal on the cover of *Strengthening Deep Neural Networks* is a "Slim Aesop" nudibranch (*Facelina auriculata*), which is found along the seashores of northwestern Europe and south into the Mediterranean Sea.

Nudibranchs (pronounced "noo-di-branks"; the name means "naked gills") are small, soft-bodied molluscs that live in oceans and seas around the world and are known for their colorful and fantastic appearance, despite their usually tiny size. Though often called "sea slugs," these creatures are a unique group of molluscs (a large family that includes snails, clams, and octopuses) which shed their shells early in their growth. Most nudibranchs crawl across reefs and the ocean floor hunting for sea anemones, hydroids, and other small creatures, ingesting their food using a radula, a toothed organ something like a tongue. *Facelina auriculata* lives in shallow coastal waters but may also be found at low tide under rocks onshore.

These small (up to 1.5 inches long) creatures search for their prey by smell and taste, doing so using rhinophores (branch-like sensory appendages) to sense chemicals in the seawater. Nudibranchs are hermaphrodites; mating entails an exchange of materials between animals. Eggs are then laid in a ribbon-like case.

The nudibranch's attention-getting coloring is believed to be aposematic; this type of coloring warns predators that this animal is either toxic or bad-tasting. Because *Facelina auriculata* is partly translucent, at times it takes on the tint of the prey it's consumed. Many nudibranchs also have appendages called cerata; the stinging tissue contained in these finger-like growths is ingested from the nudibranch's prey (such as anemones), which the animal then uses for its own defense.

Many of the animals on O'Reilly covers are endangered; all of them are important to the world.

Color illustration by Karen Montgomery, based on a line drawing in *The Genera of Recent Mollusca* (1858), by Henry Adams and Arthur Adams. The cover fonts are Gilroy Semibold and Guardian Sans. The text font is Adobe Minion Pro; the heading font is Adobe Myriad Condensed; and the code font is Dalton Maag's Ubuntu Mono.